SECOND EDITION

Writing for Psychology

Mark L. Mitchell and **Janina M. Jolley**
Clarion University of Pennsylvania

Robert P. O'Shea
University of Otago, Dunedin, Otago, New Zealand

THOMSON
™
WADSWORTH

Australia • Brazil • Canada • Mexico • Singapore • Spain
United Kingdom • United States

Publisher: *Vicki Knight*
Assistant Editor: *Sheila Walsh*
Editorial Assistant: *Juliet Case*
Technology Project Manager: *Adrian Paz*
Director of Marketing: *Caroline Croley*
Marketing Assistant: *Natasha Coats*
Senior Marketing Communications Manager:
  Kelley McAllister
Content Project Manager: *Megan Hansen*
Creative Director: *Rob Hugel*
Senior Art Director: *Vernon Boes*

Senior Print Buyer: *Judy Inouye*
Permissions Editor: *Roberta Broyer*
Production Service: *Interactive Composition
  Corporation/Scratchgravel Publishing Services*
Copy Editor: *Mary Anne Shahidi*
Illustrator: *Scratchgravel Publishing Services*
Cover Designer: *Larry Didona*
Cover Image: *Still life of monitor and keyboard on
  desk by large window.* © *Jupiter Images/Thinkstock.*
Compositor: *Interactive Composition Corporation*
Printer: *Thomson West*

Thomson Higher Education
10 Davis Drive
Belmont, CA 94002-3098
USA

For more information about our products, contact us at:
Thomson Learning Academic Resource Center
1-800-423-0563
For permission to use material from this text or product,
submit a request online at
http://www.thomsonrights.com.
Any additional questions about permissions can be
submitted by e-mail to thomsonrights@thomson.com.

Printed in the United States of America
1 2 3 4 5 6 7 10 09 08 07 06

Library of Congress Control Number: 2006904377

ISBN 0-495-09206-1

CONTENTS

CHAPTER **1**

What Every Student Should Know About Writing Psychology Papers   1

CHAPTER **2**

Writing Term Papers   25

CHAPTER **3**

Writing Research Reports and Proposals   53

CHAPTER **4**

Finding, Reading, Citing, and Referencing Sources   101

CHAPTER **5**

Making Your Case: A Guide to Skeptical Reading and Logical Writing 145

CHAPTER **6**

Writing the Wrongs: How to Avoid Gruesome Grammar, Putrid Punctuation, and Saggy Style   163

CHAPTER **7**

Preparing the Final Draft   195

TO THE STUDENT

Your professor has asked you to use this book to guide you in writing a paper. In response, you may be asking yourself three questions:

1. Why is my professor asking me to write a paper?
2. Why is it important to write a good paper?
3. How can this book help me?

In the next few sections, we will answer these questions.

Why Teachers Assign Papers

Your term papers and research reports show that you can find out things on your own. Ideally, your papers will show that you have learned enough from your teacher that you can now become your own teacher. Specifically, you can do the following:

- find relevant material in journals
- read and understand complex material
- evaluate what you read
- organize both your notes and your thinking about what you read
- create new knowledge by pulling together information from several different sources and critically analyzing that information

Your papers also show that you are capable of completing complex assignments. A good paper shows that you can do the following:

- make a case using evidence
- express ideas clearly
- complete tasks on time
- balance independence with following directions
- produce a professional looking product
- please your teacher, supervisor, or client

Finally, a good paper reflects well on your fairness, honesty, and intellectual integrity. You display fairness, honesty, and intellectual integrity by doing the following:

- including evidence that goes against your position
- giving proper credit to others for their ideas
- giving proper credit to others for their words
- giving proper credit to others for their help

Why You Should Write a Good Paper

Writing a good paper will help you impress teachers and employers with your integrity, independence, and competence. Writing will also help you achieve the goals that make psychology appealing: describing, explaining, and controlling thoughts and behavior. As a writer, you are trying to describe, explain, and control your own thoughts. By writing well, not only will you discover your own thoughts (as E. M. Forster said, "How can I know what I think until I see what I say?"), but you will also learn to evaluate your own thinking. You will see where your thinking is logical, where it is biased, where it is based more on faith than on evidence, and where it is slightly disorganized—and you will use those insights to improve your thinking.

Successful writing also requires that you understand and control the mind of the reader. Indeed, King (2000) argues that writing is almost like telepathy—your vision is sent into a reader's mind. At a more practical level, you want to control the behavior of the reader. For example, you want the reader (your professor) to give you a good grade.

How This Book Can Help You

This book is full of tips, checklists, and practical advice to improve your writing. You will gain so much insight into how professors look at papers that you will be able to grade—and correct—your paper before it reaches your professor.

- Chapter 1 helps you understand what teachers look for in papers so that you can avoid the most common errors that students make, regardless of what kind of paper you are writing.

- Chapter 2 helps you write better term papers by telling you the secrets of writing a good term paper, showing you an example of a model paper, and giving you a checklist that helps you evaluate and improve your own paper.

- Chapter 3 helps you write better research reports by giving you useful tips, a sample research report, and a research report checklist.

- Chapter 4 helps you find the references you need and shows you how to make sense of them after you have found them. Then, it helps you avoid two common student mistakes: (a) not citing sources correctly and (b) not referencing sources correctly.

- Chapter 5 helps you understand what professors mean by critical thinking. After reading Chapter 5, (a) you will be more likely to find flaws that others made in their research and in their arguments, and (b) you will be less likely to make those mistakes in your research and in your arguments.

- Chapter 6 contains a review of basic grammar as well as some tips on how to write well. You will probably consult this section when you are editing the next-to-final draft of your paper. You may also find the definitions of grammatical terms helpful in trying to decipher the American Psychological Association (APA) *Publication Manual.*

- Chapter 7 will be useful as you prepare to print out the final draft of your paper. Following the formatting tips in that chapter will ensure that your paper makes a good first impression.

■ Appendix A lists the key differences between APA copy style (the format of
an unpublished manuscript submitted to an editor for review) and APA final-
form style (the format of a published article). If your professor asks you to
use APA final-form style, Appendix A will be invaluable. By highlighting the
formatting rules that published articles follow, it will help you use a published
article as a model for your paper. If your professor asks you to use APA copy
style, Appendix A will still be valuable. Specifically, because Appendix A
highlights the differences between published articles and unpublished
manuscripts, it will help you avoid errors caused by modeling the formatting
you see in published articles. For example, you will know that although
published articles are single-spaced, your unpublished manuscript should be
double-spaced.

The website for this book (http://www.writingforpsychology.com) contains many useful resources, including the following:

■ screen shots that show you exactly how to set up your word processor to make it
work for you

■ templates that you can use so that your paper will be correctly formatted

■ practice quizzes that you can take

■ sample papers that you can grade

Formatting Practices We Use That You Should Not

Like many writing guides, we have divided chapters into sections, numbered each section, and put each section's number in the section's heading. Section numbers consist
of two or three digits separated by periods; the first digit specifies the chapter, the others refer to the section within that chapter. When you have a specific question about
how to write your paper, these section numbers will help you quickly find the answer
to your question. However, *you should not use numbers in the headings of your term papers
or research reports*.

We have also used formatting to help you easily spot examples. All examples are in
a "typewriter" font (like this). When we are contrasting examples of correct and
incorrect writing, we include these symbols for quick reference:

✓ a check mark next to good examples

✗ an "x" next to bad examples

Finally, we use two techniques for drawing your attention to particular points:
bullets and footnotes. However, when you write papers for psychology classes, *do not
use bullets and do not use footnotes*.[1]

---

[1]Different fields have different views about footnotes. For example, if you are writing a term paper for a
history class, your teacher will probably require you to use footnotes.

TO THE PROFESSOR

When you ask students to write an APA style paper, many of them are clueless both about why you are forcing them to go through such an odd ritual and about whether you will find their sacrifice (their papers) acceptable. In this book, we help students understand and meet your expectations by (a) explaining the purpose behind papers, (b) helping students understand how to write for an academic audience, (c) giving them strategies for accomplishing the many tasks involved in writing a good paper, (d) tipping them off about how to avoid common mistakes, (e) giving them examples they can model, and (f) giving them checklists so that they can monitor their own performance.

Admittedly, if you had enough time, you could do what this book does. You could give your students lectures on APA style, assign the *APA Publication Manual*, prepare handouts that explain the *Manual*, take students on tours of both the library and the writing center, and teach students about grammar, logic, and plagiarism. However, if you assign this book, you will not need to provide detailed instructions about your assignment, APA style, plagiarism, library searching, citing, or referencing. Instead, the only instructions you will need to give your students are a general description of the project, a due date, and a word limit.

Acknowledgments

The first edition of this book was an adaptation of the fourth edition of Robert O'Shea's *Writing for Psychology: A Guide for Students*. Therefore, we owe a great debt to the individuals whose constructive comments shaped that successful book: Kypros Kypri, Lea McGregor Dawson, Lorelle Burton, Sue Galvin, Jamin Halberstadt, Cindy Hall, Neil McNaughton, Jeff Miller, David O'Hare, Ann Reynolds, Rob Thompson, Diana Rothstein, and 13 anonymous reviewers.

As was true with the first edition, this edition of *Writing for Psychology: A Guide for Students* owes a tremendous debt to English professor Darlynn Fink and Psychology professor Jeanne Slattery for their insights into teaching writing as well as for their editing skills, to History professor Robert Frakes (author of an excellent writing guide for History majors) for his insights into teaching writing, to award-winning journalist K. Lee Howard for his editing skills, to Philosophy professor Todd Lavin for his insights into teaching critical thinking, to Psychology professors Ruth Ault and Eric Landrum for their editing skills as well as for their useful advice on teaching APA style, and to Publisher Vicki Knight for her skillful guidance.

We would also like to thank the following reviewers for their constructive comments: Marie Balaban, Eastern Oregon University; Shannon Edmiston, Clarion

University; Michael Hulsizer, Webster University; Hal Miller, Brigham Young University; Jamie Phillips, Clarion University; Moises Salinas, Central Connecticut State University; Vann B. Scott Jr., Armstrong Atlantic State University; Linda Mezydlo Subich, University of Akron; and Daniel Webster, Georgia Southern University. In addition, we would like to thank the entire team at Thomson Wadsworth, particularly Megan Hansen, Project Manager; Caroline Croley, Director of Marketing; Rob Hugel, Creative Director; and Vernon Boes, Senior Art Director.

CHAPTER

1

What Every Student Should Know About Writing Psychology Papers

1.1 Understanding Your Assignment

To write successfully, you need to write for your audience. Unfortunately, most students do not understand how to write for a psychology professor. Some do not realize how writing for a psychology professor is different from writing an e-mail to a friend, an editorial in the school newspaper, or an essay in an English composition class. Others realize that writing for their psychology professor is different from most other kinds of writing, but they do not know what the differences are. They know only that they are frustrated because they do not know what their professor wants from them. In this chapter, we will help you find out what your professor's expectations are and how you can meet those expectations.

Some professors, aware of the common student complaint, "I have no idea what that professor wants," try to spell out their expectations in writing. However, even if your professor gives you written instructions, you will still need to do some work to make sure that you understand your professor's formatting and content requirements.

Most professors will want you to write your paper using American Psychological Association (APA) copy style, the style used for submitting a manuscript to a journal. APA copy style differs from what the final form of the published work will look like. This book will help you write in APA copy style, a style so prescribed that APA has published a 439-page book to list and explain that style's rules. However, you need to pay attention to your professor's formatting instructions because you cannot assume that your professor wants you to follow APA copy style. For example, instead of requiring APA copy style, your professor may require *APA final-form* style—the reader-friendly format that you would see in a published article (to learn more about final-form style, see Appendix A). Even if your professor wants you to follow APA copy style, you still need to pay attention to your professor's instructions because your professor may impose formatting requirements that are more extensive than APA's. For example, your professor may require a special cover sheet or require that your paper be between 10 and 12 pages long.

Although you should know your professor's formatting requirements, it is more important that you know what type of assignment you have and what goals your professor has for the assignment. You should know whether you are writing a term paper in which you will review the literature (if so, you should consult Chapter 2) or whether you are writing a paper about a study that you either conducted or plan to conduct (if so, you should consult Chapter 3).

Once you know what type of assignment you have, you should try to find out your professor's goals for the paper. For example, if your professor's main goal for a term paper is to show that you can analyze strengths and weaknesses of research studies, you should write a different paper than if your professor's goal was to find and summarize the relevant literature. Similarly, if your professor's main goal is to show that you could synthesize information from many sources to come up with an original conclusion, you should write a different paper than if your professor's goal was for you to show that you could write a paper in APA format.

Even if you understand your professor's main goals, you may still have questions about how to meet those goals. One problem is that if your professor told you exactly how to write the paper, the professor would essentially be writing the paper for you.

A second problem is that there are so many goals to achieve and so many rules to follow that your professor must use shorthand. For example, "appropriately referenced" is shorthand for the rules you will find in Chapter 4; "making a logical argument and informed criticisms" is shorthand for following the rules you will find in Chapter 5; "grammatical and well written" is shorthand for following numerous grammatical rules, the most important of which are explained in Chapter 6; and "conforming to APA format" is shorthand for following the rules we describe in Chapter 7.

A third problem is that, because many of your professor's goals for the paper are the same goals that almost all professors have, your professor may think those goals "go without saying." One reason that almost all professors have similar expectations is that almost all professors share certain underlying values—and those shared values affect what professors expect from a paper. As a result of those shared values, if you write a paper that your professor likes, other professors will probably like it too; and, if you a write a paper that your professor does not like, other professors probably will not like it either. Thus, if you do not understand your professor's expectations for a paper, chances are that the problem is not that you do not understand your professor's specific tastes, but that you do not understand academic values. Therefore, we will devote the next section to helping you understand academic values.

1.2 Understanding Academic Values

As you will see in the next sections, to be consistent with academic values, you should possess the following:

- the curiosity to find out what others have said, done, and thought
- the wisdom to learn from what others have said, done, and thought
- the honesty to give others credit when you use what you have learned from them, such as when you quote, paraphrase, or summarize what others have said
- the originality to come to a conclusion that is not merely a summary of what others have said, but rather is based—at least in part—on your own thinking
- the rationality to support your conclusion with logic and evidence
- the fairness and objectivity (a) to acknowledge evidence that does not fit with your conclusion and (b) to acknowledge alternative explanations for the evidence that you present in support of your conclusion

1.2.1 Be Informed

Professors value knowledge, learning, and tracing the history of an idea. Most professors want you to demonstrate these values by expressing well-supported and well-informed opinions. Therefore, before turning in your paper, find, study, and understand the relevant background material. (In section 4.1, we will show you some strategies for using the library and the Internet to get resources that both you and your professor will find worthy. In section 4.2, we will discuss strategies to help you digest the information you obtain.)

1.2.2 Make a Claim

If you quote or paraphrase what others have written, you show that you have found background material, but you do not show that you understand that material. Therefore, rather than merely regurgitating the information you have found, use that information to support a claim. Ideally, that claim will be an original idea based on thinking about what you have read.

If you are writing a term paper, your claim will be a thesis statement. You must support that thesis statement by interpreting, analyzing, and synthesizing the information you have uncovered.

If you are writing a research paper, your claim will be a hypothesis. You will use the works of others to argue that (a) the hypothesis being tested is reasonable and interesting, (b) the procedure used was a good way to test the hypothesis, and (c) the results have important implications.

1.2.3 Defend Your Claim

Not only must you make a claim, but you must also support it. However, you should not support it by asserting how strongly you feel that it is true. Instead, support your claim with logic and evidence. Although you can get detailed advice about how to use logic and evidence by reading Chapters 4 and 5, note that there are only two basic approaches to using empirical evidence to support a claim.

First, you can cite empirical evidence that others have obtained. For example, suppose you needed to establish that children of high socioeconomic status tend to be more resistant to conformity than children of low socioeconomic status. Empirical support would be that someone has tested children's resistance to conformity and found that children of high socioeconomic status tend to be more resistant to conformity pressure than children of low socioeconomic status. If you find that someone has done such a study, you can present that evidence. Your citation should include a description—in your own words—of the study, along with the last name(s) of the person(s) who conducted it, and the year in which it was published.

```
Brown (1978) tested 40 children in an Asch-type conformity
setting (Asch, 1956) and found that children from high
socioeconomic backgrounds were more resistant to conformity
than children from low socioeconomic backgrounds.
```

A full reference to each citation should appear in the reference list at the end of your paper (see 4.4). The reference list enables the interested reader to find and read the original source. (To learn more about citing material in the body of your paper and referencing it in the References section, see Chapter 4.)

The second way to mount an empirical defense is to present evidence from a study you conducted. We will discuss how to report that evidence in Chapter 3.

Although you should present evidence to support your main point, you should make the case for both sides because (a) your professor will expect you to present both sides, and (b) fairness and honesty demand that you present both sides. In short, to avoid being unfair, identify weaknesses in studies that appear to support your main point and discuss studies that seem to contradict your main point.

1.2.4 Be Honest

Whereas being unfair may hurt your grade, being dishonest may lead to your expulsion from school. The two types of dishonesty that are most likely to lead to a range of penalties including expulsion are (a) falsifying data and (b) plagiarism.

Falsifying data is either altering or inventing data. Most of your professors are deeply committed to seeking truth and see data as a way to truth. Therefore, most of your professors would be outraged at anyone who falsified data. In short, do not falsify data: For most class projects, both the chances and the costs of getting caught are high.

Plagiarism involves passing off someone's words or ideas as your own. In most cases, if you were to plagiarize, the person plagiarized would be either a person you have come into contact with at your school or the author of a work you have read.

Sometimes, you can work on a paper with other students. Even on individual assignments, your professor may encourage you to work with other students to share readings and to review each other's work. On group projects, your professor may require you to work with other students. However, unless your professor clearly says otherwise, when you turn in a paper with your name on it, you are pledging that you wrote that paper and that the content and ideas—except for the ones that you have specifically credited to others—are your own. To reiterate, your instructor will expect any assignment that you turn in to be independent of, and different from, every other student's paper. If the words or ideas of even a small section of your assignment are identical to another student's work, you—or that other student—may be accused of plagiarism.

Plagiarism is not limited to lifting passages or ideas from a classmate's paper. Plagiarism can sometimes result just from not giving people credit for something they said to you. For example, if a professor, study partner, classmate, or roommate gave you an idea that you used in your paper, you should give that person credit (to see how, see 4.3.3). If you do not give the person credit, you are guilty of plagiarism.

Often, when people think of plagiarism, they think of the easiest type of plagiarism to detect: plagiarism of words from a published work. For example, suppose you had the following text (taken from the 1974 *APA Manual*, p. 91).

> Psychologists have developed various approaches to
> therapeutic change, most involving one-to-one relationships
> between practitioner and client. However, for many people
> these therapies are unavailable, undesirable, or too
> expensive. So these people have often turned to popularized
> self-help techniques. (Mikulas, 1974, p. 91)

If you were to use the preceding paragraph in your paper, you would have to make it clear that you were quoting it.[1] Otherwise, you would be guilty of plagiarism. As a general rule, if you take three or more consecutive words from another author, you should place those words in quotation marks, cite the author, and list the page(s) of the quoted words. Thus, if you turned in the following passage, you would be guilty of plagiarism.

> ✗ Mikulas (1974) has stated that various approaches to
> therapeutic change have been developed.

---

[1] If it were a quote shorter than 40 words, you would cite the author, year, and page number, and you would surround the quotation with quotation marks. However, because the quotation is longer than 40 words, you should use the block quote format that APA prescribes for long quotes (see 4.7.2).

You would be guilty of plagiarism because you would be using Mikulas's words without admitting that you were doing it. The five-word phrase "various approaches to therapeutic change" should have been surrounded by quotation marks, and the page number from which those five words were taken should have been cited.

Thus far, we have presented cases of stealing words. To see a case of stealing ideas without stealing words, imagine we wrote the following.

✗ Most people find these therapies too expensive, undesirable
  or unavailable and so have turned to self-help techniques.

Although we paraphrased Mikulas's words, we would still be guilty of plagiarizing Mikulas's ideas. To avoid plagiarizing Mikulas's ideas, we should have made it clear that he—rather than we—originated them. If we did not want to quote Mikulas, an acceptable version of the whole text would be

✔ Mikulas (1974) noted that many people dislike current
  psychotherapies in which a single client is seen by a
  single counselor. He gives their unavailability, expense,
  and lack of appeal as reasons. Mikulas suggests that many
  prospective clients have instead tried self-help
  techniques.

In the previous paragraph, we avoided plagiarism by using two techniques that you should use. First, to avoid plagiarizing words, we used our own words as much as possible. Second, to avoid plagiarism of ideas, we provided a citation for every sentence that was based on our source's ideas (Mikulas's name is in the first and third sentence, and "he" is used in the second).

1.2.5 Use Your Own Words

To make sure you do not plagiarize, you might be tempted to put most of your assignment in quotation marks. Resist that temptation. Your professor is interested in your thoughts about a topic, not in your ability to string others' words together with linking sentences. Indeed, your professor will probably not let you get away with having more than 50 words of quotation for every 1,000 words (four double-spaced pages) of your own.

One reason professors dislike quotation marks is that when you quote, the professor does not know whether you understand what you have quoted. Therefore, always try to paraphrase the author. There are only two conditions under which you should revert to using quotation marks: (a) You fear that your paraphrase is so close to the original passage (e.g., you have merely replaced a couple of words with synonyms) that you could be guilty of plagiarism; or (b) you fear that your paraphrase, because you disagree with the author's position, unfairly represents the position expressed in the original passage.

1.3 Understanding APA Style

As you have seen, your professor expects you to write a paper that does the following:

- draws on the work of others but proposes an original idea
- cites the work of others but describes their work in your own words
- uses logic and evidence to build a case for an idea but addresses contradictory evidence

You may think that meeting those demands would be enough to get a good grade. However, your professor will also require that your paper meet some style and formatting guidelines. A few of these guidelines may be specific to a certain assignment (e.g., a particular word limit). Most, however, will be the same no matter what psychology class you are taking. These style and formatting requirements are set out in the *Publication Manual of the American Psychological Association* (2001). In the next section, we will provide an overview of APA's requirements. (APA style requirements will be discussed in more depth in Chapter 6; APA formatting requirements will be discussed in Chapter 7.)

1.3.1 Ideals

APA style requires that grammar, spelling, and punctuation be perfect. Consequently, your professor will probably penalize you for each grammatical error, each spelling error, and each punctuation error. However, avoiding these errors in mechanics does not mean that you have met APA's standards for good writing. According to APA, good writing[2]

> must be precise in its words, free of ambiguity, orderly in its presentation of ideas, economical in expression, smooth in its flow, and considerate of its readers. A successful writer invites readers to read, encourages them to continue, and makes their task agreeable by leading them from thought to thought in a manner that evolves from clear thinking and logical development. (American Psychological Association, 1974, p. 25)

If you think that meeting APA's requirements is easier said than done, you are right. Although Chapter 6 provides useful writing tips, writing well is a skill that must be attained like any other—through practice.

---

[2]The passage quoted from the *Manual* is longer than 40 words and therefore is not surrounded by quotation marks. Readers know the passage is quoted because it is indented and "blocked." In addition, note that the citation for a quotation contains not just the source and the year but also the page number.

Apart from practice, the next best way to improve your writing is to read good writing. The more you read articles in psychological journals, the more you will be exposed to the works of authors who have met APA's writing standards. We do not mean that all published works are of high quality. Unfortunately, some are poorly written, hard to follow, and boring. Others are a pleasure to read: Imitate those.

1.3.2 Appropriately Personal Prose

One thing you will learn by studying good writers is that you can write in a professional, formal style without writing in a completely impersonal style. For example, although APA style essentially bans the use of the word "you," it does allow you to use the personal pronoun "I." Note, however, that being allowed to use "I" is not a license to write in an extremely personal way. The focus of a paper should be on the ideas and findings of the paper, not on the author. Consequently, most skilled writers never use the phrases "I feel," "I think," or "I believe." Many of them never use the word "I." All of them will check sentences in which they used the word "I" to see whether the sentence would be better without the "I." They will take the "I" out of the sentence if they believe that it is focusing the reader's attention on the writer when the reader's attention belongs elsewhere.

To remove the "I" from a sentence such as "I read the list to participants," an author could write, "The list was read to participants." That is, rather than use the stronger *active voice*, in which the subject actively does something (e.g., "I hypothesized . . ."), writers sometimes use the weaker *passive voice*, in which the subject passively has something done to it (e.g., "It was hypothesized . . ."). In unskilled hands, the passive voice can sound clumsy and wordy (e.g., "It was hypothesized by me . . ."). Even in skilled hands, the passive voice should be used sparingly.

Fortunately, writers can often replace "I" without using the passive voice. Rather than write, "The list was read to the participants," they may write, "The participants listened to the list." Rather than write, "It was hypothesized," they may write, "The hypothesis was. . . ."

However, as we mentioned earlier, writers do not always have to replace the word "I." Skilled writers can use the words "I" or "we" when that is what they mean. In other words, skilled writers do not twist reality or grammar to avoid personal pronouns.

In the real world, people perform actions. For example, researchers make hypotheses, conduct studies, and come to conclusions. Skilled writers respect both (a) the fact that researchers perform actions and (b) the laws of grammar. Therefore, skilled writers may use verbs to describe researchers' actions and make the researcher performing the action the subject of the sentence. Such skilled writers may also occasionally add an adverb (such as "occasionally," "slowly," "interestingly," and "thoroughly") to an action verb to describe how the researcher performed the action (e.g., "The researcher *thoroughly* debriefed the participants.").

Some less skilled writers, on the other hand, attempt to disown their own thoughts and end up violating the laws of grammar. For example, some authors use the adverb "hopefully" when they mean "I hope." They write, "Hopefully, future researchers will use a more representative sample," when they should write, "I hope future researchers will use a more representative sample."[3] The problem is that they are using an adverb ("hopefully"), which is supposed to modify a verb, to do the work of a subject ("I") and a verb ("hope"). Similarly, less skilled writers may use the adverb "interestingly," when they mean, "I find it interesting that."

In the past, writers were encouraged to disown their own thoughts—even if that meant violating the laws of nature. For example, authors routinely pawned off their thoughts to nonliving entities, such as experiments (e.g., "this experiment will test the hypothesis") and papers (e.g., "this paper will argue" or "this paper will examine"). Currently, however, APA's position is that writers should not *anthropomorphize*: give human qualities to nonhumans. To avoid both anthropomorphism and using "I," some authors attribute their actions to a role. For example, they might write, "It will be argued by the present author that" rather than "I will argue that." The price they pay for avoiding "I" is that they write a wordier and clumsier sentence. Other authors get into more serious trouble by attributing their actions to the researcher. For example, instead of writing "I told the participant," an author will write, "The experimenter told the participant," leaving the reader to guess whether the author paid someone else to be the experimenter or whether the author is also the experimenter. Another, even more awkward technique for avoiding "I," is to replace "I" with "we." For example, when the writer of a single-author paper, instead of writing "I hypothesized," writes, "We hypothesized," readers may suspect that the author is either a plagiarist or a member of a royal family.

In short, you should not use "I" frivolously. Furthermore, as you will see later, you should never use "I" in a paper's Abstract (a summary of the paper; see 2.4). However, if using "I" is the only way to meet the APA ideal of saying what you mean as clearly and simply as possible, use "I."

1.3.3 Simple Language

The APA ideal of saying what you mean as clearly and simply as possible applies not only to using simple, active sentences but also to using simple vocabulary. To use vocabulary that complies with the APA ideal, you should obey two rules.

First, do not use fancy words or fancy phrases just to impress your professor. If you do, you will be disappointed. Rather than being impressed with your writing, your professor will probably see it as pretentious, wordy, or unclear.

Second, do not banish technical terms from your paper. Your professor will expect you to show that you understand the field's key terms well enough (a) to use those terms to express your ideas more precisely and concisely than if you had used everyday language and (b) to make distinctions between related concepts. Thus, if you wrote a paper on behavior modification and never used the term "reinforcement," your professor would be disappointed. In such an assignment, your professor would probably

---

[3]Alternatively, as an anonymous reviewer pointed out, they could write, "Future researchers should use a more representative sample."

expect you to use key terms in a way that showed that you understood key distinctions between related concepts, such as the distinction between negative reinforcement and punishment. In such an assignment, your professor would probably also hope that you would use key terms, such as "schedules of reinforcement," in a way that showed that your understanding of the effects of reinforcement was more sophisticated than "giving rewards increases behavior."

1.3.4 Respectful Language

To write in APA style, you must not only use clear language, but you must also use respectful, inclusive language. Do not use language that might suggest that another group is less competent, less important, less moral, or less likely to occupy a certain role (e.g., professor) than your own. If you must differentiate among individuals on bases such as gender, race, disability, or age, then be accurate, specific, cautious, and respectful. To see what you should do, study the following examples of disrespectful language (italicized) and solutions:

✗ *Subjects* were 10 men and 10 *girls*.

✔ Participants ["subjects" is considered disrespectful because it does not acknowledge that individuals voluntarily participated in the study] were 10 men and 10 women [if you use "men" to describe male participants, then use the equivalent, parallel term "women" when describing female participants].

✗ He [the participant] was required to use *his* right index finger to press the response button.

✔ Participants used their [using the plural is often a good way to avoid the problem of using the generic "he," a term that is sexist because it excludes women] right index fingers to press the response button.

✔ Participants used the [when using a pronoun that would be sexist or awkward, see if you can eliminate the pronoun] right index finger to press the response button.

✗ These results have important implications for the development of *man*.

✔ These results have important implications for human development. ["Human" includes both women and men.]

Although you should use gender-inclusive language, you still have a duty to write clearly and smoothly. Thus, you would be penalized for using such clumsy—but nonsexist—phrases as (s)he and he/she. Furthermore, inclusiveness should not come at the expense of accuracy. Thus, if all the participants were boys, you could write

✔ Participants were 10 boys. . . . He was required to use his right index finger to press the response button. . . . These results have important implications for male development.

Now, study an example of disrespectful language involving race (italicized) and a solution:

✗ `Participants were 100 Whites and 100` *`Non-Whites`*`.`

✔ `Participants were 100 Whites, 60 African Americans, and 40 Asian Americans.` [Relative to the term "Non-White," the terms African Americans and Asian Americans are (a) more specific and (b) describe individuals in terms of belonging to—rather than being excluded from—a group.]

Next, examine a case of disrespectful language involving individuals with disabilities (italicized) and a solution:

✗ `Participants were 100` *`normals`* `and 100` *`schizophrenics`*`.` [Labeling the group as schizophrenics depersonalizes them. They are individuals who have a condition, but they are not the condition. Avoid labels that focus on an individual's limitations or problems.]

✔ `Participants were 100 people with no previously diagnosed psychiatric illness and 100 people diagnosed with schizophrenia.`

Finally, consider an example of disrespectful language involving age (italicized) and a solution:

✗ `Participants were 100 adults and 100` *`elderly`*`.` [The term "elderly" is out of favor: "Older adults" is now the preferred term.]

✔ `Participants were divided into two groups based on age: a middle-aged group (ages 45-60) and an older group (ages 70-85).`

1.4 Writing and Revising

1.4.1 Plan to Finish Early

Now that you understand what your professor wants, you need to produce it. Perhaps the greatest obstacle to meeting your professor's expectations is procrastination. Procrastination may prevent you from turning in the paper on time—and that can mean flunking the assignment. Most professors strictly enforce due dates. Few, if any, instructors will accept "pressure of other commitments" as an excuse for an extension.

Most students have other commitments. Most students would do a better job if they were given more time. Therefore, it is unethical for professors to give you more time than other students without penalizing you (Keith-Spiegel, Wittig, Perkins, Balogh, & Whitely, 1993). If you fear you are going to run late, a visit to your professor will help you decide whether you are better off handing in a poorer paper on time or a better paper late.

You might believe that "I had some unexpected problems" is an acceptable excuse. It is not. Your professor expects you to know that Murphy's Laws apply to any major project:

- Anything that goes wrong will have the worst possible outcome.
- Anything that can possibly go wrong will.
- It will go wrong at the worst possible time.

Therefore, do not expect to be exempt from the deadline just because you had some unusual problem at the last minute. Your professor expects you to have everything done at least 48 hours before the due date because, when applied to writing assignments, Murphy's Laws mean that 48 hours before the due date, you can expect the following:

- Your vital piece of equipment (computer, printer, disk, car, bicycle) will break down irreparably.
- Any people vital to the assignment (typist, study companion, person commenting on your drafts, reference librarian, computer repair person, professor, head of department, head of the United Nations) will disappear.
- Anything about you vital to the assignment will cease functioning (your hand will become paralyzed, your memory will go blank, your motivation will evaporate).
- All material vital to the assignment (your notes, photocopies, rough drafts, computer disks, the piece of paper with the assignment details on it, the library itself) will disappear.

Even if you meet the deadline, procrastination can hurt you. Waiting until the last minute can lead to sloppiness. Consider yourself lucky if your sloppiness leads to errors that hurt only your grade: spelling errors, grammatical errors, punctuation errors, and formatting errors. Sloppiness can lead to plagiarism—which can lead to expulsion.

Often, students do not realize how much their procrastination has hurt them. They do not know about the sources they could have obtained through interlibrary loan. They are too tired and too rushed to evaluate their paper before they give it to the professor. They do not study the professor's comments on their paper when they get it back, and they do not know how much better they would have done had they spent more time revising, editing, and proofing.

To avoid the many problems that procrastination can cause, start work on any major paper at least 3 weeks before the due date.[4] Draw up a schedule (e.g., days 1 to 3

---

[4]Five weeks would be better, especially if getting materials through interlibrary loan at your school takes three weeks.

for reading, days 4 to 6 for producing a first draft, days 7 to 10 for showing the assignment to others, days 11 to 14 for producing the final draft, days 15 to 18 for emergencies). Then, stick to your schedule.

1.4.2 Think, Search, Read, and Get Organized

Sticking to your schedule will not be easy. Even before you start to write, you may start to procrastinate. The problem is that getting started means doing five tasks that you may be uncomfortable doing:

1. choosing a topic
2. developing a question or thesis statement that will guide you in searching, reading, summarizing, and evaluating articles
3. finding relevant articles (for tips on using the library and computers to find relevant literature, see 4.1)
4. reading and critiquing those articles (see 4.2)
5. taking, retaining, and organizing your notes on those articles

Once you have accomplished these five tasks, you are almost ready to write the first draft. However, before you do so, you should organize your thoughts.

One way to organize your thoughts is to use an outline. You may find it useful to outline your paper on the computer. Fortunately, almost all word-processing programs have tools that can help you outline your paper.

Another way to organize your thoughts is to make a diagram of your ideas.[5] (Your English teacher might call such diagramming "clustering," "concept-mapping," or "mapping.") You can use concept-mapping software such as Inspiration[6] to help you visualize how your ideas fit together.

Yet another way to organize your thoughts is to make a table. For example, you could make a two-column table in which the left column lists evidence for a certain idea and the right column lists evidence against that idea.

Finally, you could just jot down a list of points you want to include in your rough draft. Once you have listed your key points, rearrange your list until those points are in a logical order.

1.4.3 Write Your First Draft

After you have organized your thoughts, start writing. Resist the biggest stumbling block in sticking to your schedule: talking yourself out of writing your first draft. Realize that almost any reason you give yourself for not writing is an excuse. If you are

---

[5]For more information on how to diagram ideas, see our website (http://www.writingforpsychology.com).

[6]Information on how to order Inspiration, as well as additional information on concept-mapping, is available from our website (http://www.writingforpsychology.com).

waiting for inspiration, realize that almost all good writers let a schedule—not a muse—dictate when they write. If you are waiting for your thoughts on the topic to be clearer and more coherent, realize that writing will often help your thoughts become clearer. As Howard and Barton (1986) put it, writing is "thinking on paper" (p. 1).

In your first draft, just get your ideas on paper. Do not worry about wording. As the saying goes, "Don't get it right; get it written." Think of your rough draft as just a starting point for your paper. It will help you understand your own thinking on the topic, and it will help you remember the points you wanted to make (Howard & Barton, 1986).

If you need some help getting started on your rough draft, engage in *free-writing*. To free-write, just write continuously (no pausing or editing allowed) for 3 minutes. Try to get down as many words as you can in those 3 minutes.

You may wish to free-write using the computer for any of the following reasons:

- You can type faster and longer than you can write things out by hand.
- You have voice recognition software on the computer that allows you to talk to the computer rather than type.
- You like having the computer correct many of your spelling and grammatical mistakes.
- You like being able to make corrections and minor changes on screen.
- You like how the computer makes it easy to move sentences and paragraphs.
- You find you can edit your free-writing better when the computer speaks it aloud to you.
- You find that you can edit your free-writing more easily when looking at a nicely printed, double-spaced copy of your writing rather than when looking at your messy handwriting.
- You can move directly from your edited free-write version to a revised draft.

1.4.4 Revise Your First Draft: Reorganize, Rethink, Reread, and Rewrite

As we have stated, your first draft is a rough draft. It is only the first of many steps in the writing process. In a way, writing is like going on a geological dig to produce a mineral exhibit for a museum.

When you start writing, you are digging around in your mind, hoping to find something useful. Much of what you dig out is stuff that you cannot use. Some of it is, like dirt, clearly worthless. Some of it seems valuable, but on further examination, is really fool's gold. Some of it is valuable, but it is not suitable for the particular collection you have been asked to create. As you dig, you will find that some veins are dead ends and should be abandoned; whereas other veins, although promising, need to be dug into more deeply before they yield valuable material.

Once you find the right material, you still have work to do. You must lay out the individual pieces, categorize them, and figure out how to organize them into a suitable collection. As you try different configurations, you may realize that (a) you must cut some pieces from the collection because they are redundant, distracting, or do not fit, and (b) you must acquire additional pieces to fill in the gaps in your collection.

Once you have a collection of pieces that you are excited about, you still need to do some work before viewers will share your excitement. You will have to clean up, cut, and polish each individual piece. You will have to add labels and text to help viewers appreciate what each piece is and how the pieces fit together. Finally, you will have to display the collection in a professional format so that viewers can fully appreciate the collection's beauty.

If the whole writing project is like the mineral collection project we just described, the rough draft corresponds to the early phase of the project: the "digging around" phase. That is, by using writing to talk to yourself, you have dug up some of your thoughts. When reading over the draft, you can extend this conversation with yourself (Howard & Barton, 1986)—and thus dig deeper—by saying things such as, "Yes, and it is also true that . . ." and "What I really mean to say here is. . . ."

Once you have unearthed your thoughts, the next step is to organize them. To organize your thoughts, ask two questions of each paragraph. First, "What do I want this paragraph to do?" Second, "If I want the paragraph to accomplish that goal, is the paragraph in the right place?" As a result of asking these two questions, you may eliminate some paragraphs and move others.

Once you have moved and deleted material, you should outline your revised paper again. Even a glance at the outline may help you see the following:

- You are not pleased with the order in which the ideas are presented.
- You have included some ideas that do not relate to your main point.
- You have either not included or not emphasized some ideas you think are important.
- You have made some assertions that you have not supported with either logic or evidence.
- You have discussed one idea or topic much more thoroughly than you have discussed an equally important topic.
- You have failed to make connections between related ideas.

As you struggle to rectify the problems in your thinking that were apparent by looking at the outline, you will refine your thinking.

- You will put your ideas in a more logical order.
- You will ignore ideas and evidence that could distract you from your main point.
- You will distinguish between important ideas and less important ideas.
- You will develop support for unsupported assertions.
- You will see connections among concepts that you had not previously recognized.

Like re-outlining, rereading will help you refine your thinking—if you ask questions as you read (Howard & Barton, 1986). At the very least, ask the following two questions: "Does this make sense?" and "Do I have adequate support for this idea?"

Like re-outlining and rereading, rewriting also helps you refine your thinking. With each rewrite, you will find that you have more arguments, more support for those arguments, and that your paper is becoming more organized, more insightful, and more original. Thus, as you rewrite, you will probably find that (a) passages you quoted in your rough draft now make enough sense to you that you can put them into your own words; and that (b) the outline of your revised draft is more organized and more detailed.

In short, as a result of "talking to yourself," outlining what you have said, and questioning yourself, you should have a fair, focused, and properly sequenced set of arguments in support of your main point. At this stage, it is time to stop writing to yourself and start writing for the people who will read your paper.

1.4.5 Help the Reader Navigate Through Your Paper

Once you are satisfied that your own thinking on the topic is clear, you can devote your next few drafts to making your thinking clear to your audience. Although the audience of your paper may number in the thousands, we will call your audience "the reader" for two reasons. First, it is more useful to picture a particular individual, such as a friend, another psychology major, or your professor, reading your work and anticipating how that person will react than it is to picture an anonymous audience reading your work. Second, your audience may be a single reader—your professor.

A first step to making your thinking clear to the reader is to make the organization of your paper clear to the reader. You can do this by (a) adding short subheadings (often taken from the major headings of your outline) so that the reader does not read more than two pages without encountering a subheading, (b) adding topic sentences (often taken from your outline) to each paragraph, and (c) adding transitions between paragraphs (some of these transitions may be entire paragraphs that preview what the next few paragraphs are going to do). After you have tried to make the organization of your paper clear to the reader, you are ready for the real test: See if a friend can re-create your outline from reading your paper.

Once you are sure that a reader could follow the general outline of your paper, it is time to help the reader understand the individual paragraphs. Thus, in the next few drafts, you may work on refining your topic sentences. If the topic sentence is the paragraph's first sentence, ask, "Does the topic sentence provide a preview of the paragraph?" If the topic sentence is the paragraph's last sentence, ask, "Does the topic sentence provide a summary of the paragraph?"

Once you have good topic sentences, you have done much of the work of organizing your paragraphs. However, there are still four things you should do to improve the organization within each paragraph. First, you should split long paragraphs into two: No paragraph should be longer than a page. Second, if a sentence is not tied to the topic sentence, you should remove it from that paragraph. Third, if a sentence reiterates what another sentence in the same paragraph said, delete one of those sentences. Fourth, if it is not clear how two adjoining sentences relate to each other, you should consider using transition words (such as "consequently," "therefore," "however," and "although") to connect the sentences inside a paragraph with each other.

Once you have taken steps to prevent readers from getting lost between paragraphs and from getting lost between sentences, you should take at least three steps to prevent readers from getting lost within your sentences. First, see if you can eliminate, reword, or move tangential remarks. Often, you can eliminate tangential remarks that are set off from the rest of the sentence by parentheses, a pair of commas, or a dash. Second, shorten sentences that are longer than 40 words. Usually, you can split these longer sentences into two shorter sentences. Third, go back and look at pronouns such as "it," "they," "those," "these," and "this" that you are using to refer back to another word or idea. If your pronouns do not clearly point back to their nouns, see 6.3.5.

Although you want to make each paragraph and sentence clear to the reader, there are at least two reasons you may fail to revise an unclear section. First, you know what you are trying to say, so you may not recognize when a section is confusing. Second, you may be too attached to what you have written to delete irrelevant sentences, phrases, and words.

You can overcome both of these self-imposed obstacles to revising an unclear section by using the following four tactics. First, put the draft aside for a few days. By the time you reread it, you may forget what you meant to say and be more able to focus on what you actually wrote. In addition, you may be less infatuated with passages that you should cut. Second, pretend that someone else has written the draft and that your task is to improve it. Third, read your paper aloud—or have the computer read it aloud to you. Fourth, have a friend read your paper and make comments. If you show your friend how to use the computer's voice annotation feature,[7] you can click on sections in the paper to hear your friend's comments ("I'm confused about this point because . . .").

1.4.6 Address Readers' Objections

Some of your friend's comments may deal with objections to your argument. Even if your friend does not introduce objections, realize that other readers might. You want to address possible objections so that your reader does not say, "But the writer did not consider. . . ."

In addressing potential objections, be firm but fair. If you can successfully fend off an objection, explain why the objection is not serious. If the objection is serious, admit it. Modify your argument or qualify your conclusions to take the objection into account.

1.4.7 Polish Your Writing

Now that you have polished your ideas, you can start polishing your writing. One way to do this is to vary the words you use. Here, a thesaurus can help. Use a thesaurus to find a synonym and then consult a dictionary to make sure that your synonym means

---

[7]For instructions on how to use this feature, go to our website (http://www.writingforpsychology.com).

what you want it to mean.[8] (Note that, because most word-processing software contains both a thesaurus and a dictionary, finding a synonym and then finding its definition often involves little more than a few clicks of a mouse.)

In addition to varying the words you use, vary your sentences. For example, if almost all of your sentences are short (fewer than 10 words), combine some of your sentences so that you can show how your ideas are connected, and so your writing style is more interesting. To appreciate how overusing short sentences can lead to writing that is disconnected, repetitious, and boring, imagine reading a 2,000-word paper composed of sentences like the following: "See Spot. See Spot run. See Jane. See Jane run." You would not know whether Spot caused Jane to run, and, after reading several hundred words written in such a tiresome, repetitious, and "choppy" style, you would not care about Spot, Jane, or their relationship.

Although we will discuss more tips on improving your writing in section 6.4, we will give you one tip now. You can usually improve your style by deleting words: When it comes to writing, less is more. To have a more compact and powerful style, go through your paper and see what words you can eliminate. Your computer's grammar checker, because it points out wordy phrases and sentences, can be a powerful tool for helping you purge unnecessary words. For example, your grammar checker might highlight the following:

- a clumsy phrase ("at this point in time") that you could replace with a single word ("now")
- a wordy, passive sentence ("It was written by me.") that you could replace with a shorter active sentence ("I wrote it.")
- an unusually long sentence that you could split into two

1.4.8 Check Language, Grammar, Spelling, Usage, and Punctuation

As we have pointed out, your grammar checker can help you cut "dead words" that make your writing less lively. In addition, grammar checkers and related tools can alert you to some of the following writing errors: improper language, improper grammar, improper usage, and improper punctuation.

Your grammar checker can be a valuable tool for catching inappropriate language that might otherwise slip into your paper. By alerting you to any contractions, clichés, and slang terms that it finds in your paper, it can help you rid your paper of inappropriately informal language. By alerting you to words in your paper that are either noninclusive ("chairman") or offensive, it can help you rid your paper of biased language. However, you cannot rely on a grammar checker to catch all instances of offensive language for at least two reasons. First, terms that were not offensive when the grammar-checking program was first released may now be considered offensive.

---

[8]If the synonym does not really reflect what the original word meant, you can have problems. One of the authors received a paper in which a student wrote, "We must defecate prejudice." Apparently, the student, tiring of using the word "eliminate," used the thesaurus to find an alternative.

Second, what is offensive may depend on context rather than on a specific word or phrase.

In addition to checking for inappropriate language, grammar checkers can help check your paper's grammar. However, do not delegate the entire job of grammar checking to software. If you do, you will run into two problems. First, the grammar checker will fail to tell you that some ungrammatical passages are ungrammatical. Second, the grammar checker will tell you that some grammatical passages are ungrammatical. Therefore, to check the grammar of your work, you need to have a clear understanding of grammar (see Chapter 6).

Although you may not be able to rid your paper of all grammatical errors, you should at least focus on the ones that are most likely to irritate your professor. Those errors probably include the following:

- subject-verb disagreement (the subject of a sentence is plural, but the verb used is appropriate only for singular noun ["They is," "Data is"]—or vice versa ["It are," "Datum are"])

- pronoun-noun disagreement (the noun is plural, but the pronoun referring to it is singular ["The male experimenter received their training"]—or vice versa ["The male experimenters received his training"])

- disagreements between verbs (one verb in the sentence is in one tense, but the other is in a different tense ["The results supported dissonance theory but do not support self-perception theory."])

- "paragraphs" that are only one sentence long

- "sentences" that are really sentence fragments (they are incomplete sentences because they do not contain a complete thought ["To deal effectively."])

- any other grammatical error that your professor mentions

Although your professor may not expect your paper to be completely free of grammatical errors, your professor probably will expect your paper to be completely free of spelling errors. As was the case with grammatical errors, software can help you, but it will not do all the work for you. Although your spell-checking software will correctly catch some errors, it will make mistakes. Spell-checking software will report many correctly spelled words as errors (e.g., names and psychological terms) and will not report cases in which you typed "there" for "their," "to" for "two," "then" for "than," "right" for "write," "filed" for "field," "casual" for "causal," or any other case in which you have "the wrong word spelled right" (Barkas, 1985, p. 75).

Using the wrong word is not always the result of a finger slipping on the keyboard. Sometimes, you may think you know what a word means, but you do not. By taking advantage of both our table of commonly misused words (see our "problem pairs" table in Chapter 6) and your computer's dictionary, you can avoid common but costly mistakes such as using "imply" when you mean "infer." If you learn that you have consistently misused a word, term, or phrase, use your word processor's "find and replace" feature to replace all instances of that wrong word with the correct word.

You have checked your paper for inappropriate language, grammar, spelling, and usage. Now, read your paper aloud to (a) recheck it for inappropriate language, grammar, spelling, and usage, and to (b) check punctuation. If you are like most students, you will tend to have the most punctuation problems with the comma. Remember that when dependent clauses such as "If the hypothesis is correct," "Although support for the hypothesis is weak," or "When researchers have tested the hypothesis" start a sentence, you need to insert a comma at the end of that clause. Remember that you do not need to put a comma before every "and." For example, you should not use a comma when "and" is connecting two verbs belonging to the same subject (e.g., "The participant ran and hid."). Remember that you should put commas inside, rather than outside, of quotation marks. If you need to learn or review how to use commas, see 6.2.2. (If you need a more complete review of punctuation, read 6.2.)

1.4.9 Final Formatting

Once you have proofed your paper for writing errors, you should proofread it for formatting errors. For example, make sure that your entire paper is double-spaced. Fortunately, if you use word-processing software, you do not have to worry about memorizing many formatting rules because your word-processing software's normal formatting is usually the correct formatting. For example, APA has set the following formatting rules to be the same as most word-processing software's normal settings: how many spaces to indent a paragraph (five), how many spaces to leave after most punctuation marks (one), and what margins to leave (1 inch). Whereas people using a typewriter might have to make sure they pressed the space bar five times to indent each paragraph and worry about whether their margins were correct, you have no such worries. Instead, for much of the paper, your main formatting worry may just be making sure that you turned on the "double-spacing" option.

You have even fewer worries if you use APA's Style Helper software (for ordering information see http://www.writingforpsychology.com). Style Helper works with your word-processing software to make sure that headings, margins, and typefaces are consistent with APA style. If you do not have Style Helper, you can still set up your word-processing software to format your headings, margins, and typeface (to see how, consult http://www.writingforpsychology.com). Regardless of how you compose your paper, you should check your paper against our format checklist (see 7.4).

1.4.10 Five Final Checks

You are almost finished. Still, potential disasters lurk, so take five steps to avoid them. First, make sure that you have not plagiarized by checking your paper against your original sources and against the checklist at the end of this chapter (1.6). Second, make sure your citations follow APA format (see 4.3) and that they match your reference list. Third, make sure that your References section is in APA format (see 4.9). Fourth, make sure that your title page is in APA format (see 7.4.6). Fifth, make sure that your paper conforms to any additional requirements (e.g., word and page limits) that your professor has imposed.

Note that computer software can help you with the last four steps. The APA Style Helper program, for example, can work with your word-processing software to ensure that your citations follow APA format, that your citations match your reference list, that your individual references are in the proper format, that your reference list is in alphabetical order, and that your title page conforms to APA format. Even without Style Helper, your word-processing program can count the number of words in your paper to make sure you have not exceeded the word limit.

1.5 Submitting the Finished Product

You have properly formatted your paper. As a result, it looks good on your computer screen. To make sure it looks good when it reaches your professor's hands, you should (a) put plain, clean, white, sturdy (20-pound), bond paper into a printer that produces dark, clear, clean print; and then (b) staple it together using one or two staples in the top left-hand corner.

1.6　Avoiding Common Problems: A Checklist

___ I started my paper early enough that I could find important sources, carefully read those sources, write a rough draft, and then revise, edit, proof, and polish subsequent drafts.

___ I did not plagiarize.

　　___ When I borrowed a person's words, it was clear that I was quoting that person.

　　___ I double-checked my sources to make sure that I had neither inadvertently quoted someone nor paraphrased someone too closely.

　　___ When I borrowed someone's ideas without quoting them, it was clear that I was using their ideas.

___ I made an honest, original, fair, and evidence-based argument.

　　___ I supported my argument with logic (see Chapter 5) and with evidence from high quality sources (see 4.1).

　　___ I reported evidence that ran counter to my argument.

　　___ I quoted fewer than 50 words for every 1,000 (four pages) of my own.

　　___ If I was unsure about my criticisms of the literature or the quality of the reasons for my position, I consulted Chapter 5.

___ My argument was easy to follow because my paper was well organized.

　　___ I wrote several drafts of my paper.

___ I outlined each draft and used that outline to improve the organization of subsequent drafts.

___ I revised any paragraphs longer than a page.

___ I made sure that every paragraph had a topic sentence that summarized my goal for that paragraph.

___ I checked to make sure my paper did not contain offensive language (see 1.3.4) or irritating grammatical errors (see Chapter 6).

    ___ I checked my paper against all examples, instructions, and warnings my professor gave the class.

    ___ I read my paper aloud.

    ___ I used computerized proofing tools, such as a spell checker and a grammar checker.

    ___ If I was unsure about the grammar or writing style of my paper, I consulted Chapter 6.

___ I checked to make sure that my sources were correctly cited in the body of my paper.

    ___ Every reference in my References section is cited in the body of my paper.

    ___ When I cited a source, I mentioned only the authors' last names and the year the source was published. I did not mention the authors' first names, university affiliations, degrees, or professional titles.

    ___ When I cited, I did not mention the title of the source—unless the source had no accredited author.

    ___ When I was unsure about how to cite a source in text, I consulted Chapter 4 or the *APA Publication Manual*.

___ I properly formatted quotes (see 4.7).

___ I made sure my reference section was properly formatted (see 4.9 and 4.10.4).

    ___ Except for any "personal communication" citations (see 4.3.3) and any citations to classical works (e.g., the Bible), every citation in text is cited in the reference page.

    ___ I started the first line of each reference flush against the left margin.

    ___ I indented subsequent lines of each reference five spaces.

    ___ If I was unsure about how to format a reference or how to format the reference section, I consulted Chapter 4.

___ I ensured that my paper looked professional and conformed to APA style.

    ___ I correctly formatted my title page (see model in 2.11, checklist in 7.4.6).

    ___ I double-spaced everything.

    ___ I used white, nonerasable, 8.5 × 11 in. (22 × 28 cm), 20-pound bond paper.

___ I used clear, dark, and black type.

___ I used an APA approved typeface such as 12-point Times Roman or 12-point Courier.

___ If I had any doubts about the format of my paper, I consulted Chapter 7 or the *Publication Manual.*

1.7 Summary

1. Writing well means knowing your audience. The audience for a scholarly paper will be members of the academic community. This audience shares certain values. For example, the academic community finds plagiarism and falsification of data completely unacceptable.

2. Plagiarism involves using other people's words or ideas without giving them credit.

3. The academic community values making a fair, logical argument based on careful consideration of the evidence.

4. To make your paper consistent with APA style, you must do more than follow APA rules on how to format your paper. For example, to make your paper consistent with APA style, you must use simple, clear language; you must use respectful, inclusive language; and you must use the active voice much more than you use the passive voice.

5. In your first draft, the goal is to get your ideas on paper. Remember, your first draft is just a starting point.

6. In your second draft, revise the paper to make sure your ideas are well supported and well organized. Outlining your paper can help you revise it.

7. After you have revised the paper so that it makes sense to you, you need to start editing it so that it will make sense to other people. Rework your paper (a) to address objections that a skeptical reader might have and (b) to make it easier for the reader to follow your argument. To help readers follow your thinking, you may want to add subheadings, strengthen topic sentences, cut out unnecessary words, divide long paragraphs, and divide long sentences.

8. After you have edited your paper, you should proofread it. Check your paper to make sure that it is consistent with the APA style that your professor requires, as well as with any other requirements your professor has specified. In addition, make sure that it does not contain grammatical, spelling, or usage errors.

9. Procrastination is one of the biggest obstacles to producing a good paper. Procrastination may prevent you from (a) obtaining valuable sources from interlibrary loan, (b) carefully evaluating your sources, (c) properly citing and referencing your sources, (d) revising, editing, and proofing your paper, and (e) turning in your paper on time.

CHAPTER

2

Writing Term Papers

In the research proposals and research reports we discuss in Chapter 3, your task is to discuss a study that either you conducted or that you plan to conduct that addresses a research question. In a term paper, on the other hand, your task is to discuss other people's studies and come to a conclusion. More specifically, you should collect information from multiple sources, summarize and evaluate that information, come to a conclusion, state your conclusion as a thesis, and defend that thesis in a professional and objective manner. Thus, writing a good term paper will help prepare you to write the professional reports that you will probably write as part of your postcollege job.

2.1 Thesis Statement

One key to a good term paper is choosing a manageable topic. Usually, the topic you start out with will be too broad, and you will have to narrow it down to a subtopic that can be treated within the limits of a term paper. For example, suppose your initial topic was aggression. You could not possibly learn everything there is to know about aggression in the next few weeks, much less fit that information into a 15-page term paper. Therefore, you need to choose a narrower topic.

One way to narrow your topic is to go to the library and look up "aggression" in the *Psychological Thesaurus* (look for it near the hardbound volumes of the *Psychological Abstracts*) to discover narrower terms for aggression.[1] As a result of consulting the *Thesaurus*, you may decide that you want to look at a specific type of aggression, such as instrumental aggression. Even a casual literature search, however, will probably reveal that you need to narrow your topic further. To do so, look at how another variable influences or is influenced by instrumental aggression. Thus, you might do a literature search on the effects of television violence on instrumental aggression. Based on your search, you may decide to limit your topic further by looking at a specific type of televised violence (e.g., cartoon) on a specific group (e.g., boys). After selecting a narrow topic, you are ready to write a *working thesis statement*.

Your working thesis statement should be a concise description of what you think your paper will show to be true. Rather than present a glib generalization, it should specify under what conditions a certain relationship will hold (see also 5.1). If your topic is aggression, your working thesis statement might be "Viewing cartoon violence on television leads to aggression in boys."

Even if your working thesis statement turns out to be incorrect, it will still be useful. It will help you ask relevant questions, find relevant articles, and take relevant notes.

After you have read several articles (if you are having trouble finding enough articles, consult 4.1.1 and 4.1.2), you may realize that your working thesis is wrong. If so, modify it into a thesis statement that is consistent with the literature. Depending on what you find out, your thesis statement might be one of the following:

- Viewing cartoon violence on television does not lead to aggression in boys.
- Viewing cartoon violence on television leads to aggression in introverted boys.
- Viewing cartoon violence on television leads to tolerance of aggression in boys.
- It is unknown whether viewing cartoon violence on television leads to aggression in boys.

You would choose one of these thesis statements, or one that we did not list, after extensive reading on the topic convinced you of its truth.

---

[1] In the *Thesaurus* entry for your term, the narrower term will be to be the right of a capital "N" ("N" stands for "narrow").

Your thesis statement will guide you in writing three important parts of your term paper: Introduction, Body, and Conclusion. In the first section of your paper (Introduction), you will present your thesis statement and outline how you plan to defend it. In the second section (Body), you will review evidence and theories in favor of your thesis statement and show how evidence and theories that seem to conflict with your thesis statement can be made consistent with it (see 5.9). In the third section of your paper (Conclusion), you will summarize your defense of your thesis statement and then reiterate your thesis statement.

2.2 Basic Sections, Headings

There are seven parts of a term paper: Title (page), Abstract, Introduction, Body, Conclusion, References, and Author Note. As you can see from Figure 2.1, most of these parts begin on the top of a page with a centered heading.

FIGURE **2.1**   Headings (Centered) and Other Subdivisions (in Parentheses) for a Term Paper

2.3 Title Page

As you can see from Figure 2.1, page 1 of your paper should be the title page. The title page has five components: the page header, the running head, the title itself, your name, and the name of your institution.

The page header consists of the "short title" (the first two or three words of the title) and the page number. To type your page header, you could put the short title (e.g., "Intellectual Declines"), followed by five spaces, and "1" (for page 1) in the top right-hand corner of the title page.[2] Thus, if your title was "Intellectual Declines in Old Age: Fact or Artifact?" the top right corner of your page might look like this:

```
                                    Intellectual Declines       1
```

One double-spaced line below the page header, but starting in the left-hand margin, type the phrase: "Running head:" and a two- to six-word description of your paper. For example, you might type the following line:

```
Running head: INTELLECTUAL DECLINES IN OLD AGE
```

Note that your running head should follow this format:

- be in all capital letters
- be fewer than 51 characters
- usually include the names of the two main variables you discussed (typically joined by the word "AND") or the name of your general topic area
- ideally be either a shortened form of the title (e.g., if the title was "The Evidence Suggests That the Overjustification Effect Is Not Robust," the running head could be "OVERJUSTIFICATION EFFECT") or, if the title is short enough, the title itself.

Center the remaining three components (the title, your name, and your institution's name) on the page, being sure to start each component on a new line and being sure to capitalize the first letter of each major word.[3] Start by putting the title about halfway down the page. Then, on the next line, put your name—including your middle initial. On the following line, put your school's name. Thus, the middle of your title page might look like this:

```
      Intellectual Declines in Old Age: Fact or Artifact?
                      Anne A. Student
                    Clarion University
```

---

[2]If you are using a word processor, type the short title and the page number into the header. If you do not know how to use the header, you can find instructions at our website (http://www. writingforpsychology.com).

[3]Major words are (a) all words longer than three letters and (b) all adjectives, adverbs, nouns, pronouns, and verbs. Thus, the articles "a," "an," and "the"; prepositions such as "on"; and conjunctions such as "and," "but," and "or" would not be capitalized.

To verify that you have formatted your title page correctly, do two things. First, compare your title page to the sample paper's title page (2.11). Second, compare your title page to our title page checklist (7.4.6).

Although the format of your title page is important, so is its content: the title. The title is your first chance to impress your professor. Write it last to ensure that it reflects the main point of your paper. Keep the title focused on your topic and short, fewer than 15 words. For example, if you have written a term paper about the influence of psychoanalysis on modern counseling practice, a catchy and informative (eight-word) title might be "Modern Counseling: Freudian Theory With a New Face."

2.4 Abstract

If your professor requires an Abstract, you must write a one-paragraph summary of your paper. In this paragraph, devote a sentence each to (a) the general topic area, (b) your thesis statement, and (c) how you showed that your thesis statement is probably true. Do not exceed 120 words.

Wait to write this one-paragraph summary until after you have written the rest of your paper because you will find it easier to write a summary once you have written what it is you are going to summarize. Indeed, you may be able to use an outline of your final draft to guide you in writing your summary.

The Abstract is formatted as follows:

- It begins on page 2.
- It is announced by the centered title "Abstract."
- It is one paragraph long.
- It is free of personal pronouns such as "I," "we," and "mine."
- It is, except for any cases in which a number begins a sentence, free of spelled-out numbers (all numbers, except those that begin a sentence, are expressed using numerals).
- It is not indented.

For an example, see 2.11.

2.5 Introduction

The Introduction should be the first paragraph of your paper following the Abstract. Its heading is not "Introduction." Instead, its centered heading is the title of your paper. Like the Abstract, the Introduction should be short. Like the Abstract, the Introduction should be self-contained: People reading your Introduction should understand it even if they have not read any other part of your paper. Despite the similarities between the Abstract and the Introduction, they have different goals: The goal of the Abstract is to summarize the paper; the goal of the Introduction is to foreshadow the rest of the paper.

2.5.1 Introduce Generally and Gently

Begin foreshadowing the rest of the paper by introducing your paper's general topic. Your first two sentences should engage the reader. You hope that the reader will be saying, "That is interesting," "That is an important topic," or "I know something about that, and I would like to know more."

After you make the reader receptive to your topic, your next step is to make the reader receptive to your thesis. You hope the reader will be saying, "That sounds reasonable," or "I never thought about it like that, but that does make sense."

2.5.2 Introduce Key Issues

The way to make readers receptive to your argument is to outline the empirical and theoretical issues that set up your thesis. A popular and efficient way of outlining those issues is to trace, concisely, the history of thought on the particular topic. Be sure to use citations to document this brief history.

Although you will have citations in the Introduction, do not use those citations to introduce specific findings. Instead, use citations only to introduce issues, themes, and alternative approaches to a particular topic. At this point in your Introduction, do not go into specific details about a particular study.

2.5.3 Introduce Key Definitions

Although you should not go into detail about data, you should provide detailed and clear definitions of terms crucial to understanding your thesis. However, do not define so many terms that your Introduction looks like a page from a dictionary. Instead, define a term only (a) if the definition of the term is an issue of debate, (b) if there are multiple accepted uses of the term, or (c) if your paper uses a specific definition of a more general term.

2.5.4 Introduce and Present Your Thesis Statement

Once you have defined key issues and key terms, introduce and present your thesis statement. Often, you can introduce and present your thesis statement by outlining the plan of your paper (e.g., "I will review [this side of the question], then I will review [the other side of the question], to show that [my way of reconciling or combining these two sides—my thesis statement—is the best answer to the question, given the available evidence]").

No matter how you introduce your thesis statement, make sure you put your thesis statement in your introduction. As a last resort, write, "In this paper, I will show that [my thesis statement] provides the best explanation of the available evidence" at the end of the last paragraph of your Introduction. If you include such a sentence, you will not get any style points for how smoothly you introduced your thesis statement, you will at least get points for putting your thesis statement in your Introduction.

2.5.5 Invite Inquiry

State your thesis, but be sure to state your thesis in a way that arouses the reader's curiosity. To stimulate the reader to think about your thesis, avoid the common error of stating your thesis as an established fact. For example, in a paper on the origins of handedness, do not state, "It has been established that handedness is caused by genetic factors (Annett, 1972)." If the reader believes you, the reader should not be interested in reading the rest of your paper. Not only are you saying that the answer to your paper's question is not a subject for debate, but you are also saying that the answer to your paper's question is in Annett (1972). Therefore, if the reader wants to know more, rather than reading the rest of your paper, the reader should read the definitive source—Annett (1972).

Thus, if you had drafted such a thesis statement, you should rewrite it. You might write, "Annett (1972) has argued that handedness is caused by genetic factors; others, however, have suggested the importance of the environment (e.g., Collins, 1975)." Alternatively, you might write, "In this paper, I will argue that handedness is caused by genetic factors." Notice the differences in the three versions of the thesis statement. In the first, the relationship between handedness and genes was described as "established." In the better versions, the relationship was "argued" or other factors were "suggested." The tentative forms allow further discussion; the definite form does not.

2.6 Body

In the Body of your paper, fulfill the promises you made in the Introduction. Introduce theories, data, procedures, and criticisms. However, your goal is not merely to introduce information. Instead, your goal is to develop your thesis and work systematically toward a conclusion.

2.6.1 Integrate Material

Working systematically toward a conclusion means that you cannot merely summarize one study after another. It means that instead of transcribing your notes into a disorganized and purposeless set of article summaries, you must organize the body of your paper around ideas. If you are not sure how to do this, use one of the following five tried-and-true ways to integrate a term paper:

1. Trace the development of ideas on the topic (i.e., an historical approach).
2. List the similarities and differences between two major theories (i.e., a comparative approach).
3. If the topic is posed as a problem, set out possible solutions, and then evaluate each (i.e., a problem-solution approach).
4. Present current opinions on a topic, then evaluate those opinions in light of scientific evidence and theory (i.e., an opinions-reasons approach).
5. Concentrate on the procedures of different studies to find out why seemingly similar ones produced conflicting results (i.e., a methodological approach).

Once you decide on an approach to organizing your paper, organize your notes so that they are consistent with that approach. For example, suppose you have decided to use the methodological approach. Put your notes on studies with results that support your thesis in one pile, put your notes on studies that neither support nor refute your thesis in another pile, and put your notes on studies that appear to refute your thesis in another pile. To help organize the studies, you might try constructing a table. Your first draft of the table might be little more than two lists: (a) a list of studies that obtained results consistent with your thesis, and (b) a list of studies that obtained results that are not consistent with your thesis. Your second draft will usually be a more complex table, in which you evaluate the studies according to common criteria and list the similarities and differences among them (to see an example, see Exhibit 4.2 in Chapter 4). Your table may enable you to see that the studies that support your thesis are more methodologically sound than those that do not support your thesis.

2.6.2 Be Both Concise and Precise

When you describe studies that support your thesis, you must be both concise and precise. You must be concise because you cannot describe every aspect of every study. Instead, most of the time, you can highlight only what happened in the study, what was found, and what was concluded. You must be precise because you need to show the reader how each study supports your point—and sometimes you can do that only by producing relevant details. Without those relevant details, you can tell the reader only that the study supports your point. Telling ("Trust me: I am right") is not nearly as convincing as showing ("See for yourself that I am right").

Showing, rather than telling, is especially important when describing a study that, on the surface, appears to contradict your thesis. The results of such a study can usually be interpreted in many different ways, some of which will be consistent with your thesis. Therefore, you may be able to show that the study, if interpreted properly, does not contradict your thesis. To do so, you need to present enough relevant details so that you can show your readers that your interpretation makes sense.

2.7 Conclusion

2.7.1 Conclude

The Conclusion is usually your last paragraph. In it, you summarize the main points you made ("tell them that you told them"), show how you have ruled out possible criticisms of your thesis, and restate your thesis. In your concluding paragraph, you should be able to make a statement that essentially says: "I have shown that [my thesis statement] is probably true."

2.7.2 Follow the Body's Logic to Your Conclusion

Anything you say in the Conclusion must follow logically from the Body of the paper. Therefore, if, as you are writing the Conclusion, you realize that you have left out some important citations or reasons that support your thesis, do not sneak that support into the Conclusion. Instead, go back and insert that support in the Body of your paper. Similarly, if, as you are writing your ending paragraph, you have an insight that leads to a new generalization, you cannot stick that generalization into the Conclusion without rewriting the Body of your paper. Specifically, you will have to insert the citations and reasons that set up your new generalization into the Body of your paper.

To reiterate, the concluding paragraph is not the place for introducing new data, introducing new interpretations of previously discussed data, or in any other way surprising your reader. Surprise endings are allowed in some mystery stories, but not in a term paper.

2.8 References

Start the reference list on a new page with the centered heading: References. All the sources cited in your term paper should appear on this list, with three exceptions. First, do not reference the source if it is a "personal communication" (see 4.3.3) because your reader will not be able to retrieve a conversation you had, a lecture you heard, a letter or e-mail you read, or an Internet site that you can no longer retrieve. Second, do not reference the original work if you know about it only through a secondary source. Instead, reference only the source you read. For example, suppose the citation in your paper was "Original's study (as cited in Interpreter, 2002)." In that case, you would not put "Original" in your reference list. Instead, you would provide a reference only to "Interpreter"—the source you did read (see 4.3.2). Third, do not reference classic (usually over 1,000 years old), well-known philosophical or religious texts (e.g., Aristotle's works, the Bible).

Realize that aside from the three exceptions we just mentioned, the reference list is a "works cited" list. It is not a bibliography. It is not a list of suggested readings. Therefore, when writing your reference list, include only those sources that you cited in your paper.

Formatting each reference is tricky. To see examples of acceptable formats for the major reference types and to learn the logic behind formatting references, see 4.9. For an example of how to format your references, see the sample term paper's references (2.11). Once you have each reference properly formatted, you need to make sure each reference is in the right place in your reference list. Looking only at the first author's last name, arrange your references in alphabetical order. Thus, "Alpha, R. T., & Omega, J. B. (2006)" would come before "Omega, J. B., & Alpha, R. T. (2006)." If you need more information on how to put your references in the right order, see 4.9.3.

2.9 Author Note

If your professor wants an Author Note (a note that contains your name and affiliation, acknowledgments, and information about how to contact you), start the Author Note on the last page of your paper using the centered heading: Author Note. For your paper, the most important aspects of the Author Note are making disclosures about (a) who, if anyone, helped you with your paper and (b) what part of your paper, if any, was used in another class. To write an Author Note, follow the example in the sample paper (2.11).

2.10 Tense

Most of the time, use the past tense (for more information on tense, see 6.1.3). Use the past tense for anything that has a definite date in the past. Thus, when you cite a work published on a given year, you will use the past tense (e.g., "In 2005, Sanders studied"). Use the present perfect tense (e.g., "For many years, researchers have studied") if the activity happened in the past but either (a) cannot be tied to a specific year or (b) is still ongoing. Use the present tense for (a) stating conclusions and (b) anything current, including material in your paper, that you are inviting the reader to consider. Use the future tense when introducing your thesis (e.g., "I will argue that").

2.11 Sample Term Paper

On the next few pages, you will find a sample term paper. There are only three aspects of the sample paper that you should not imitate. First, we have used footnotes to make comments so that you can appreciate particular points. In your own term paper, do not use footnotes. Second, we have used only old references so that no one could use this paper in a real class. In your own paper, do not use many old references. Instead, make sure that most of your citations are to articles published within the last 3 years. Third, we have not double-spaced and not used 12-point font so that the book will cost less. In your own reports, double-space everything and use a 12-point font.

To appreciate this particular term paper, imagine that you had been asked to write a term paper in an adult development and aging course. You narrowed your topic to "Intellectual declines in old age." Your working thesis statement was that "Intellectual abilities decline in old age." You found sources by using *PsycINFO, Current Contents,* and *Social Science Citation Index* (see 4.1). After reading those sources, you decided your working thesis was wrong. Instead, you now believe that (a) methodological errors may have misled early researchers and (b) old age does not necessarily lead to declines in intellectual ability. You write the Body of your paper, then the Introduction and Conclusion, then the Abstract, title page, and reference page(s). You use a computer to write your first draft and then print out some copies, which you give to your friends to get their comments. You write the draft early, so you have some free time before you have to revise, rewrite, edit, polish, proof your rough drafts, and print out your final version. As a result, when you revisit the draft, you can take a fresh look at it and spot some of the problems a person reading it for the first time might have. You are not under extreme time pressure and so you are calm enough to take your friends' suggestions as helpful advice rather than as hurtful attacks. You use a spelling checker and a grammar checker before printing out the next-to-final version, which you read aloud and proof carefully. You then check your paper against our checklist (2.12), print out a final version, and hand it in on time. You are happy with your paper. When you get it back, you see that your professor is also happy with your paper.

Intellectual Declines   1

Running[4] head: INTELLECTUAL DECLINES IN OLD AGE[5]

Intellectual Declines in Old Age: Fact or Artifact?[6]

Ann A. Student[7]

Alpha University

---

[4]Ann is using APA copy style (also called "APA manuscript format"). If your instructor wants you to use published (also called "APA final-form format"), see Appendix A. If your instructor asks you to also add a cover sheet, do what your professor asks.

[5]Ann was able to verify that her running head was short enough (had fewer than 51 characters, including spacing) by using the "Word count" feature of her word-processing software. Note that the running head is in all capital letters and appears only on this page.

[6]The first two words of the title became the short title. The short title appears on the top right-hand corner of each page (five spaces to the left of the page number). (On our website, http://www.writingforpsychology.com, you can find directions for using Microsoft Word to insert the short title and page number on each page.) Also, note that prepositions such as "in" and conjunctions such as "or" that have fewer than four letters are not capitalized.

[7]Include your middle initial. Do not include the word "by."

Abstract[8]

Researchers[9] using cross-sectional designs found evidence that IQ scores decline with age. Researchers using longitudinal designs, on the other hand, showed that, for healthy participants taking nonspeeded tests, IQ scores do not decline with age. Although both cross-sectional and longitudinal designs have methodological deficiencies, their good points can be combined in a cross-sequential design. An analysis of research using the cross-sequential design confirms that intelligence does not necessarily decline in old age.[10]

---

[8]The Abstract starts on page 2 and is announced by the centered heading "Abstract."

[9]Unlike other paragraphs, the Abstract is not indented (2.4). Like the rest of the manuscript, the Abstract is double-spaced (7.1.1).

[10]In 72 words, Ann has introduced the topic, the argument, the evidence, and the conclusion.

Intellectual Declines in Old Age: Fact or Artifact?[11]

Growing old involves a decrement in most biological processes (Botwinick, 1973). Some researchers have assumed that growing old also involves a decrement in intellectual function (e.g., Chown, 1972). Research using cross-sectional designs supports this assumption (e.g., Jones & Conrad, 1933). Specifically, Wechsler (1939) thought that intelligence "declines progressively after reaching a peak somewhere between the ages of 18 and 25" (p. 135).[12] Yet studies using longitudinal designs showed a less pronounced rate of decline (e.g., Owens, 1953). I will argue[13] that the two designs' different methodological weaknesses account for why the designs produce different results. Then, I will describe Baltes and Schaie's (1974) technique for combining the two designs into a cross-sequential design that avoids the problems of both the longitudinal and cross-sectional designs (Schaie, 1974). Finally, I will show that the results from studies using the less flawed cross-sequential designs, as well as the results from more flawed designs, are consistent with the view that intelligence does not substantially decline with age.[14]

---

[11]The Introduction begins on a new page. Its "heading" is the paper's title. Like all of your paper, it should be double-spaced.

[12]Note the skilled use of quotation to summarize an idea that the writer is going to attack.

[13]Use future tense for introducing your argument (2.10).

[14]In the opening paragraph, the author has introduced the topic and described what the author plans to prove. The paragraph ends with the author's thesis statement.

Cross-Sectional Research

In the simplest case, cross-sectional researchers compare a group of people of one age (e.g., 45-year-olds) with a group of people of a different age (e.g., 75-year-olds). Researchers using cross-sectional designs have consistently found that the older adult groups score lower on IQ tests than younger adult groups (e.g., Jones & Conrad, 1933).

Interpreting the older adult group's lower IQ scores, however, is difficult because of a serious weakness in cross-sectional designs. The weakness, as Botwinick (1967) pointed out,[15] is that the older group is not merely older than the younger group, but also belongs to a different cohort[16] from the younger group. Consequently, with cross-sectional designs, it is hard to separate the effects of age from the effects of generation. In the case of cross-sectional research on IQ, the older group's lower IQ scores are not necessarily due to biological aging. Instead, the older group may score lower because their cohort was less prepared to take IQ tests than the younger cohort was. For example, Botwinick (1967) pointed out that IQ scores are positively correlated with amount of education and that younger cohorts receive more education than older cohorts.

---

[15]Note that Ann used the past tense ("pointed out") rather than the present perfect tense ("has pointed out") because the activity can be tied to a date (1967).

[16]You might wonder why Ann did not use a nontechnical term such as "generation" instead of "cohort" (a term used by developmental psychologists to refer to a group born in a certain year). Ann used "cohort" to demonstrate that she knows an important technical term that her professor would expect her to know.

Longitudinal Research

Unlike cross-sectional researchers, longitudinal researchers study a single group as it ages. Researchers using longitudinal designs have found[17] little evidence of decline in IQ with age (Bayley & Oden, 1955; Owens, 1953).[18]

Although longitudinal designs avoid confounding age with cohort, they have two methodological problems. First, participants with the lowest scores may either die early or refuse to cooperate on subsequent retestings (Riegel, Riegel, & Meyer, 1967). As a result, longitudinal studies may fail to detect age-related declines in IQ. Second, changes observed during the study may be the result of environmental events rather than the result of aging. For example, if the same group of participants performs better on an IQ subtest at 70 years than at 65 years of age, this improvement[19] might be due to aging, but it might be due to new medications, improved nutrition, a new government program, or some other environmental change.

---

[17]Note the use of present perfect tense ("have found") because the research referred to is continuing.

[18]When you have more than one citation within parentheses, put the citations in alphabetical order and use semicolons to separate citations relating to different authors.

[19]Ann added "improvement" after "this" so that readers would know that "this" referred to improvement.

Cross-Sequential Designs[20]

To overcome the shortcomings of both cross-sectional and longitudinal designs, Baltes and Schaie (1974) advanced the cross-sequential design. The cross-sequential design starts as a cross-sectional design. Then, researchers add a longitudinal aspect to the study by returning in a few years to retest the groups.

Cross-sequential designs allow the researcher to avoid mistaking either environmental effects or cohort effects for age effects (Mitchell & Jolley, 1988). To illustrate, suppose that both the cross-sectional and the longitudinal parts of a cross-sequential design revealed consistent age-related differences. The longitudinal aspect of the design, in which the researcher compares the same cohort with itself over time, allows the researcher to rule out the possibility that the age-related difference is a cohort effect. The cross-sectional aspect of the design, by allowing the researcher to test the age groups at the same time, permits the researcher to rule out the possibility that the age-related difference is due to recent environmental events. Using the cross-sequential method, Baltes and Schaie[21] (1974) and Schaie and

---

[20]Note that (a) subheadings help readers see how the paper is organized and that (b) the heading "Cross-Sequential Designs" is a second-level heading. You can tell it is a second-level heading from its formatting: It is italicized, capitalized, and flush against the left margin. To learn more about how to format headings, see 7.2.3.

[21]Note that because the citation is not in parentheses, the two authors' names are joined by "and" rather than by "&."

Labouvie-Vief (1974) found virtually no decline in overall intellectual performance with age. Declines were usually limited to tests and subtests in which speed was important.

Reinterpreting Past Research

At first glance, the conclusion that intellectual performance does not decline with age seems to be at odds with previous research. However, one can reconcile this conclusion with past research by considering problems in the following three areas: (a) cross-sectional designs, (b) IQ measurement, and (c) speed tests.[22]

Problems with cross-sectional research.[23] Most evidence for the idea that IQ declines with age comes from the results of cross-sectional studies. However, the results of cross-sectional studies misrepresent the degree to which IQ declines with age because the results of cross-sectional studies are unduly influenced by (a) the low IQ scores of a few individuals suffering from chronic diseases and (b) cohort effects.[24]

Cross-sectional studies provide information about the average IQ of one age group relative to the average IQ of another age group. However, the average IQ of the older age group could be unduly influenced by a sharp decline in the

---

[22]This paragraph previews and outlines the next sections. Using the term "speed tests" is an example of the appropriate use of terminology: By using that term, Ann is able to be both concise and precise.

[23]The heading "Problems with cross-sectional research" is a third-level heading. As such, it is italicized and indented, ends with a period, and is not capitalized. To learn more about formatting headings, see 7.2.3.

[24]Note how the paragraph introduces the next two paragraphs.

performance of a few adults. Riegel and Riegel (1972) made
the case that a few individuals in the older age group do
suffer such sharp declines and that those individuals'
scores mask the fact that most healthy adults do not suffer
intellectual declines in old age. Specifically, Riegel and
Riegel[25] found that people who die of old age exhibit a
complex array of intellectual losses. They named this
complex pattern of decline "terminal drop" (p. 306)[26] and
detected it up to a year before death (Riegel et al.,
1967).[27] They pointed out that if people with terminal drop
are included within the older group in a cross-sectional
study, those people's low scores would reduce the average
IQ of the entire group.

Even if a cross-sectional study includes only
individuals whose scores are not declining with age, the
older age group may score lower than the younger group
because their cohort is, relative to the younger cohort, at
a disadvantage on IQ tests. For example, younger people are
more likely to have taken an IQ test than older people

---

[25]Ann could have followed this reference with the year. However, she did not have to because (a) she has already provided the year in the earlier reference and (b) she has only one Riegel and Riegel reference so the reader does not need the year to find the reference in her reference section.

[26]"Terminal drop" is a short quotation, so it is surrounded by quotation marks and followed by the page reference. If Ann had been using "terminal drop" as a technical term rather than as a quote, she should have italicized it.

[27]Note the use of "et al." Ann can use et al. because this is the second time she has mentioned this study and the study had three authors. Note how tricky the punctuation is (no comma between "Riegel" and "et," no period after "et," but a period and a comma after "al.").

(Botwinick, 1967). Furthermore, as Schaie (1974)[28] noted, modern education relies more on problem-solving skills (a major component of intelligence tests) than memory skills, which characterized earlier educational methods.

Problems in measuring intelligence. Another problem that may lead both cross-sectional and longitudinal researchers to overestimate intellectual declines in old age is that IQ tests may not be appropriate for testing older adults. Historically, the function of IQ tests was to predict school performance (Binet & Simon, 1908, cited in Wechsler, 1939),[29] not to test older adults. Test items involve situations that have little meaning for older adults. According to Schaie (1974), younger people are less fearful of IQ tests and are more highly motivated to do well on IQ tests than older people. These differences in attitudes and motivation—differences that have nothing to do with intellectual ability—may cause older adults to score lower on IQ tests than younger adults (Schaie, 1974).

Problems with speed tests. Older adults are especially likely to score lower than younger adults on IQ tests and subtests in which speed is important. However, there are two problems with interpreting decreased performance on timed tests as declines in intelligence. First, as

[28]Note how each major statement of fact is defended with a parenthetical citation (4.3.1). The citations not only give credit where credit belongs (thus avoiding plagiarism) but also make Ann's case stronger.
[29]Note use of a secondary citation (4.3.2). Ann shows integrity by admitting she did not read Binet and Simon. Note that Binet and Simon will not appear in the reference list.

Botwinick (1971) pointed out, poor performance on a timed
test by older people may represent slowed physical
movements and greater susceptibility to fatigue rather than
any intellectual decline. Second, mental speed may not be
the same thing as intelligence.

Researchers have recognized the problem of what
constitutes intelligence. Cattell (1963) differentiated two
major kinds: (a) crystallized abilities that are maintained
with age and are culturally determined and (b) fluid
abilities that are innate and subject to the same decrement
as other biological processes.[30] Schaie and Labouvie-Vief
(1974) showed that crystallized abilities, such as
vocabulary and other abilities shaped largely by formal
education, increase throughout adulthood but that fluid
abilities, such as speed and fluency, decline throughout
adulthood.

---

[30]Note how Ann shows that (a) she understands the field's terminology and that (b) she has used that understanding to make a critical distinction that qualifies her argument. This paragraph will impress her professor. In fact, this paragraph may boost her paper grade by an entire letter grade.

Conclusion

When researchers compare intellectual performance of widely different age groups, results from traditional cross-sectional studies show older adults to be intellectually inferior to younger adults. When researchers examine age-related changes using the more appropriate cross-sequential design, they find no decisive intellectual decrements over most of the adult life span (Schaie, 1974). I have shown that although older adults might have lower scores on IQ tests than younger adults, their lower scores are primarily due (a) to cohort effects rather than to the effects of age, (b) to attitudinal differences rather than to ability differences, and (c) to items reflecting fluid, rather than crystallized, intelligence.[31]

---

[31]The Conclusion restates the argument, making appropriate qualifications.

References[32]

Baltes,[33] P. B., & Schaie, K. W. (1974, July[34]). Aging and
   IQ: The myth of the twilight years. *Psychology Today,*[35]
   10, 35-40.

Bayley, N.,[36] & Oden, M. H. (1955).[37] The maintenance of
   intellectual ability in gifted adults. *Journal of*
   Gerontology, 10, 91-107.

Botwinick, J. (1967). *Cognitive process in maturity and old*
   age.[38] New York: Springer.

Botwinick, J. (1971).[39] Sensory-set factors in age
   differences in reaction time.[40] *Journal of Genetic*
   Psychology,[41] *119,* 241-249.

---

[32]Start the reference list on a new page (4.9.1) and center the heading ("References").

[33]In the reference section, the indenting style is the opposite of the indenting for the rest of your paper. Specifically, APA advocates "hanging indent style" in which the first line of a reference is not indented, but additional lines are indented five spaces. To see how to program your word processor to make hanging indents, see our website.

[34]For a magazine article, put the year, then a comma, and then either the month of publication (for magazines that are published once a month) or the month and day (for magazines that are published more than once a month).

[35]*Psychology Today* is a magazine, not a journal. Your professor will probably require that most of your articles be from journals rather than magazines (see 4.1.3).

[36]Always use a comma between authors' names—even when you have only two authors.

[37]You would not be able to use this term paper in any class because there are no recent references.

[38]Usually, only the first letter of the first word of a book title is capitalized. The entire title is always italicized.

[39]Although references are in alphabetical order, in the case of a tie, older references come first.

[40]Usually, only the first letter of the first word of the title of an article is capitalized.

[41]All major words in a journal name are capitalized.

Intellectual Declines 13

Botwinick, J. (1973). *Aging and behavior.* New York: Springer.

Cattell, R. B. (1963). Theory of fluid and crystallized
intelligence: A[42] critical experiment. *Journal of
Educational Psychology, 54,* 1-22.

Chown, S. M. (1972). The effect of flexibility-rigidity and
age on adaptability in job performance. *Industrial
Gerontology,[43] 13,* 105-121.

Jones, H. E., & Conrad, H. S. (1933). The growth and
decline of intelligence: A study of a homogeneous group
between the ages of ten and sixty. *Genetic Psychology
Monographs, 13,* 223-298.

Mitchell, M. L., & Jolley, J. M. (1988). *Research design
explained* (1st ed.).[44] New York: Holt, Rinehart and
Winston.

Owens, W. A., Jr. (1953). Age and mental abilities: A
longitudinal study. *Genetic Psychology Monographs, 48,*
3-54.

Riegel, K. F., & Riegel, R. M. (1972). Development, drop,
and death. *Developmental Psychology, 6,* 306-319.

Riegel, K. F., Riegel, R. M., & Meyer, G. (1967).[45] A study
of the drop-out rates in longitudinal research on aging

---

[42]"A" is capitalized because it comes right after a colon and begins the subtitle.

[43]Note the difference in the rules in capitalization for titles of articles versus the titles of journals, books, or other publications.

[44]The title is italicized, but not the edition.

[45]The fact that this reference occurs after the Riegel and Riegel reference illustrates one rule of alphabetizing: All other things being equal, the entry with fewer authors goes first.

and the prediction of death. *Journal of Personality and Social Psychology, 5,* 342-348.

Schaie, K. W. (1974). Transitions in gerontology—from lab to life: Intellectual functioning. *American Psychologist,*[46] *29,* 802-807.

Schaie, K. W., & Labouvie-Vief, G. (1974). Generational versus ontogenetic components of change in adult cognitive behavior: A fourteen-year cross-sequential study. *Developmental Psychology, 10,* 305-320.

Wechsler, D. (1939). *The measurement of adult intelligence.* Baltimore:[47] Williams & Wilkins.

---

[46]The *American Psychologist* is a fine journal meant for a broad audience. It summarizes current thinking and research on a topic. Reading an article from the *American Psychologist* can help you in at least two ways: (a) The article can help you understand a certain theory or issue, and (b) the article's reference list can help you identify important articles that you should read. However, your professor may not want you to use the *American Psychologist* because (a) using an article from it may prevent you from doing your own thinking on the topic and (b) reading an article from it, like reading a textbook account, does not allow you to develop skills in understanding and criticizing empirical research. In short, do not base your paper primarily on article(s) from the *American Psychologist* without checking with your professor.

[47]Baltimore is one of the few cities that can be listed without a state abbreviation. For a complete list of those selected cities, see page 217 of the *Publication Manual.*

Author Note[48]

Ann A. Student, an undergraduate student at the Alpha University.[49]

I[50] thank M. Y. Tutor for guiding my thinking on this topic and I. M. Good for commenting on previous drafts.

Correspondence concerning this article should be addressed to M. Y. Professor, Department of Psychology, Alpha University, Alpha, CA 97804. E-mail: myprof@alpha.edu

---

[48]The Author Note will often be the last page of your paper.

[49]We know that this is not a grammatical sentence. However, we are following the format specified by the *Publication Manual*.

[50]Thank anyone who gives you general or editorial help.

2.12   Checklist for Evaluating Your Term Paper

___ My thesis statement is an argument about under what conditions a certain relationship holds (see 2.1 and 5.1).

___ My paper is well organized.
    ___ My paper focuses on the thesis statement.
    ___ My paper has a beginning, a middle, and an end.
    ___ The beginning includes my thesis statement and explains how I will make a case for my thesis statement.
    ___ The middle (Body) portion defends the thesis.
    ___ The end concludes by summarizing the case for the thesis statement.

___ I revised all three sections of my paper.
    ___ For the beginning section, I focused on cutting sentences and paragraphs that were not relevant to the main point of my paper.
    ___ For the middle, I emphasized organization: I outlined my paper, reorganized my paper, and re-outlined my paper until I was happy with how the paper was organized. Then, I added subheads and transitions to help readers see how the paper was organized.
    ___ For the end, I worked on (a) making sure that I had not added material that was not set up earlier (sometimes, I cut material from the ending; other times, I added material to the middle section) and (b) cutting material that was distracting, meandering, and rambling.
    ___ I reread my paper making sure that I could answer, for each paragraph, the question, "What is this paragraph doing?"
    ___ I made sure there were transitions between each paragraph so that my readers will not say, "What is this paragraph doing here?" and that each paragraph has a clear topic sentence so my readers will not say, "What is the point of this paragraph?"

___ I found many recent journal articles that were (a) empirical (articles in which authors reported their own research) and (b) related to my topic.

___ I presented evidence that supported my thesis statement by paraphrasing, summarizing, critiquing, and synthesizing journal articles (see Chapter 4).

___ I addressed evidence that seemed to counter my position (see Chapter 5).

___ I proofed my paper for errors in grammar, spelling, punctuation, and usage (see Chapter 6), as well as for inappropriate and biased language (see Chapter 1).

___ I ensured that my paper adheres to APA format (see checklist in 7.4).

___ I cited and referenced my sources according to APA style (for citations, see 4.3–4.5; for references, see 4.9).

___ My title page adheres to APA format (see 2.11 for model and see 7.4 for checklist).

___ I adhered to the standards of academic honesty (see Chapter 1).

2.13 Summary

1. Usually, the first step in writing a term paper is to choose a narrow topic.

2. After selecting a narrow topic, you should write a *working thesis statement:* a brief, clear statement of what you think your paper will show to be true.

3. In the first section of your paper (Introduction), you will present your thesis statement and outline how you plan to defend it. In the second section of your paper (Body), you will defend your thesis statement. In the third section of your paper (Conclusion), you will summarize your defense of your thesis and then restate your thesis statement.

4. If your professor requires an Abstract, you must write a one-paragraph summary of your paper (see 2.4).

5. The Introduction should foreshadow the rest of the paper.

6. The main challenge many students face when writing the Body of the paper is organizing and integrating the material they have read. If you are having trouble organizing the Body of your paper, see 2.6.1.

7. Anything you say in the Conclusion must follow logically from the Body of the term paper.

8. All the sources in your reference list should be cited in your paper. To see an example of how to format your References, see the sample term paper's References (2.11). To learn more about formatting your reference page, see 4.9.

9. If your professor wants an Author Note, start the Author Note on the last page of your paper using the centered heading: Author Note.

CHAPTER

3

Writing Research Reports and Proposals

3.1 Basic Sections, Headings

Your research report may contain up to 12 major sections: Title, Abstract, Introduction, Method, Results, Discussion, References, Appendixes (optional), Author Note, Tables (optional), Figure Captions (optional), and Figures (optional). As you can see from Figure 3.1 (on page 54), each of these major sections begins with a centered heading. As you can also see from Figure 3.1, the first three sections—Title, Abstract, and Introduction—each begin on a new page, as do all the sections that follow the

F I G U R E **3.1**   Main Section Headings (Centered) and Subsection Headings
(Flush Left, Italicized) for a Research Paper

Discussion: the References, Appendixes, Author Note, Table, Figure Caption, and Figure sections. Finally, note that when a section is broken down into subsections (e.g., the Method section is usually broken down into at least two subsections: Participants and Procedure), these subsections have italicized subheadings that begin at the left margin.

We will discuss each of these sections in the order that they should appear in your report. Although you should present the sections in this order in your report, you may find it useful to write the sections in a different order. For example, suppose you are writing a report on a study you did as part of an in-class exercise. In that case, you may find it easiest to start with the Method section because (a) all you have to do is describe what was done in the study, and (b) you can write it while the details of what you did are still fresh in your mind. Next, you may want to write the Introduction section, a section that should set up both the Method and Discussion sections. Then, you may want to write the Results section. In the Results, you should focus on reporting on whether the hypothesis was supported. Having written the Introduction and Results sections, you should have a relatively easy time writing the Discussion, in which you discuss implications of the results. Once you have written the Body of your paper, write the Abstract, which summarizes the paper. Then, write the title, which summarizes the Abstract. Add the References, Appendixes (if you have any), and the Author Note, and you have completed your rough draft.

If, on the other hand, you are writing a research proposal, you should write the paper in a different order than the one we just described. If you are writing a research proposal, write the Introduction first: Once you have described what you want to accomplish, the rest of the paper should be easier to write.

Regardless of the order in which you write the paper, you should understand the structure of a research paper (see Figure 3.2 on page 56). The Introduction is designed like a funnel. The wide mouth of this funnel represents the beginning of the Introduction. In this beginning section, rather than introducing your narrow topic, you attract the reader by highlighting interesting aspects of the broader area within which your topic is set. In highlighting the broader topic, you do not critique studies or theory. Instead, you do little more than cite important research and theory related to that general topic. You quickly move from a general overview to a detailed analysis of the particular, narrow aspect of theory that relates to your research study. This detailed analysis will usually include analysis of the strengths and weaknesses of research findings related to that particular aspect of theory.

At the end of the Introduction, the bottom and narrowest part of the funnel, you state the specific hypothesis you will test.[1] In the Method and Results, you focus narrowly on the specifics of how you tested your hypothesis. The Discussion is like an inverted funnel: You start by considering what your results mean for your hypothesis but then broaden your scope by considering how the results of your study challenge, extend, or support both (a) published research and (b) published theory.

---

[1]In some cases, rather than concluding your Introduction by stating your hypothesis, you might merely state a research question.

FIGURE **3.2**   The Basic Structure of a Research Paper

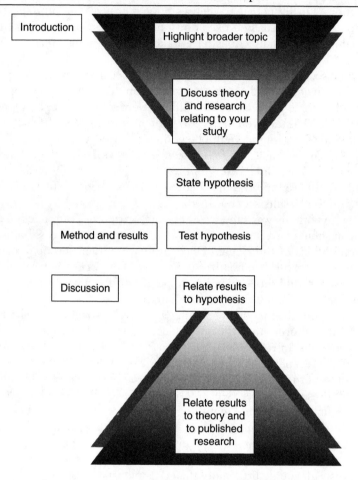

To see how you would write a research report, imagine that you and your class-mates participate in a class exercise in which you are asked to rate how much you like a person described by a list of adjectives. You and your classmates are randomly assigned to one of two groups. One group of your classmates gets the list in this order: humorous, cold, intelligent, polite. The other group gets the list in a different order: cold, intelligent, polite, humorous. Both groups rate their liking of the person. After the students have completed their ratings, the professor leads a discussion about the study. As a result of this discussion, you realize that (a) the independent (manipulated) variable is the position of "humorous" in the list (first vs. last); (b) the dependent (measured) variable is the liking ratings of the person; and (c) the hypothesis is that a person will be liked more when a favorable adjective describing the person comes first in a list than when the same adjective comes last in a list. In the next few sections, we will look at how you would write a report on such a study.

3.2 Title Page

As you can see from Figure 3.1, page 1 of your paper should be the title page. The title page has five components: the page header, the running head, the title itself, your name, and the name of your institution.

Put the page header in the top, right-hand corner. Type the first two or three words of the title, skip five spaces, and then type the page number (e.g., "1").[2] Thus, if your title was "The Primacy Effect in Impression Formation," the top right corner of your page might look like this:

`The Primacy Effect      1`

Put the running head at the top of the page (about one double-spaced line below the page header), flush left. Start by typing the words "Running head" followed by a colon. Then, in all capital letters, type a two- to six-word version of the title. Thus, you might type the following line.

`Running head: DESCRIPTOR ORDER ON LIKING`

The remaining components are all centered on the page. The title itself is about halfway down the page. Capitalize the first letter of each major word of the title. Your name—including your middle initial—appears on the next line. Your institution appears on the following line. Thus, the middle of your title page might look like this:

`The Primacy Effect in Impression Formation`

`Anne A. Student`

`Clarion University`

To verify that you have formatted your title page correctly, do two things. First, compare your title page to the sample paper's title page (3.12). Second, compare your title page to our title page checklist (7.4.6).

Although the format of your title page is important, so is its content: the title. The title should be tantalizing enough to lead the reader on to the next, more substantial morsel: the Abstract. To keep the reader's attention, the title should be both short—no longer than 15 words—and informative: It should summarize the main point of the report and identify the crucial variables or issues.

---

[2]Often, you will want to go to the "View" menu of your word processor, select "Header and Footer," choose "Align right," and then type in the first two or three words of title, skip five spaces, and then select the "insert page number" command. That way, the header will be automatically inserted on all your pages, not just the title page.

Identifying the crucial variables and issues is vital for three reasons. First, potential readers interested in certain variables or issues may search for articles by looking for titles of articles that contain those variables or issues. Second, the first two or three words of the title become the short title (which appears at the top of every page of your paper). Third, a shortened form of the title should become your running head. (If your manuscript becomes a published article, the running head will appear on the top of every other page of that article.)

To practice judging titles, suppose you had written the following four titles for our example experiment:

✘ An Investigation of a Psychological Phenomenon

✘ Influences on Liking Ratings

✔ Effects of Descriptor Order on How Much a Person Is Liked

✔ Favorable First Descriptors Produce Favorable Impressions

Which title did you prefer? The last title is perhaps the best of the four because it communicates the most about the results of the experiment. The third title, however, is the most common sort of title, and its small mystery (what was the effect?) may make it more tantalizing.

3.3 Abstract

As you can see from the sample paper, page 2 of your paper should contain the Abstract. Begin the Abstract with the centered heading "Abstract" and follow that heading with an unindented paragraph. Without exceeding 120 words, and without using any first person pronouns (e.g., "I," "my," or "we"), provide a complete, self-contained summary of the report.

Start the Abstract by stating the research question. Then, describe the method, the number, gender composition, and age of the participants or subjects tested, the main results of your statistical tests, and the main conclusion. Some writers, in trying to meet the word limit, omit some of required information, as in the following case:

✘ Based on the primacy effect in serial recall, it was hypothesized that a target person would be better liked when positive information was presented first rather than last. This hypothesis was tested in a simple experiment in which half the participants were exposed to a description of a person that began with an extremely positive adjective whereas the other half received the identical description except that the positive adjective ended the description. Consistent with the hypothesis, participants whose descriptions began with a highly favorable adjective rated the described person as more likeable than participants who

learned the favorable adjective last. The results are
discussed in terms of whether the primacy effect reflects
assumptions made by participants about how people order
descriptive information.

Although the previous example is consistent with what you will find in journals as well as with the sample Abstract in the *Publication Manual*, it is not consistent with the guidelines for abstracts set out on page 14 of the *Publication Manual*. Specifically, it does not contain detailed numerical information about the number, gender composition, and age of the sample, and it does not contain details about the results of statistical tests. The advantage of omitting specific numerical information from the Abstract is that it allows room to provide a broad overview of the study. However, as you can see from the 108-word sample Abstract that follows, if you are summarizing a single study, you can provide your readers with a general overview of the study, supplement that overview with the specific details necessary to meet the *Publication Manual*'s guidelines, and still stay within the 120-word limit.

✔ Does the order of adjectives describing a person affect how
much raters like that person? To answer this question, 24
introductory psychology students (14 women and 10 men, mean
age = 19.7 years) read a list of adjectives and then rated
how much they liked the described person. Participants were
randomly assigned to two groups. Those receiving "humorous"
as the first adjective in a 4-item list rated the person as
more likeable than those receiving the identical list except
with "humorous" last, $t(22) = 5.62$, $p < .05$. The results
are discussed in terms of whether the primacy effect reflects
assumptions made by participants about how people order
descriptive information.

For more information about how to format the Abstract, see 2.4. In addition, consult the model in 3.12 and the checklist in 3.13.

3.4 Introduction

The Introduction begins on page 3. Its centered heading is the title of the paper, rather than the word "Introduction." In the Introduction, you must introduce both the general research area and your specific hypothesis. As readers scan the first paragraph, they should be thinking, "Yes, that is an interesting and important research area." As they move through the rest of the Introduction, they should be thinking, "That hypothesis makes sense. It really should be tested. I wish I had thought of that hypothesis." In addition, you are also setting up readers for the Method section, so that when they read the Method section, they think, "Yes, that is a good way to test the hypothesis."

3.4.1 Introduce the Broader Issue

Start the text of the Introduction with a sentence that introduces the general topic or problem of which a specific aspect is tested in your study (for more details, see 2.5.1). Use the rest of the first paragraph to convince the reader that the topic is important. If you are having trouble writing that paragraph, try to start it with a sentence resembling one of the following.

- _____ is a major problem in the United States.
- In everyday life, _____ often has an effect on people.
- For centuries, people have contemplated _____.
- _____ is a core assumption of the theory of _____.
- More than 100 studies have examined _____.

Follow with a brief summary of the major research bearing on the general issue. Use citations to introduce these data (for information on how to cite, see 4.3). To show that you know the relevant background material and to put your study in context, you should cite several studies in this section. Therefore, look for studies related to your topic (for tips on how to find such studies, see 4.1), but if no studies specifically relate to your topic, review studies that are somewhat related. In reviewing previous research, (a) discuss the relationship between what was found and what relevant theories would have predicted and (b) show how your study fills a gap in the literature. In this summary, you might have a topic sentence that resembles one of the following:

- Existing research has not looked at whether _____ moderates the effect.
- Existing research has not tested the theory's assumption that _____ is true.
- Despite growing research in _____, all researchers implicitly assume that _____.
- Almost all previous research has assumed a linear relationship between _____ and _____.
- However, systematic research on _____ is lacking.
- With one notable exception, there have been no studies of _____.
- Little research has been done on _____.
- Although there is much research on _____, there is very little research on _____.
- Existing research has failed to distinguish between several possible explanations for these results.
- An often overlooked explanation for these findings is ...
- Existing research has not studied _____ population.

- However, _____ study did not allow a direct test of this hypothesis because ...
- Note that the studies that find _____ are flawed because ...
- The findings with respect to _____ have been inconsistent. The inconsistencies may be due to methodological problems with the studies that find ...
- To date, existing research has been correlational. Thus, it has not been possible to determine whether _____ and _____ are causally related.
- _____ and _____ have been studied separately, but previous research has never examined how they operate together to affect _____.
- What is striking, however, is the extent to which data revealing _____ differences derives almost exclusively from _____ (a single research paradigm, a limited sample of participants, etc.).
- If theory _____ is true, one can predict ...

Your summary should be logically interconnected, and it should go from general, theoretical considerations to the specific background of your hypothesis. As your professor reads your paper, you want your professor to be thinking the following:

"This student has read the recent research."

"This student is critiquing research studies."

"The research cited in the literature review clearly relates to the student's hypothesis."

"I see why this hypothesis is worth testing."

3.4.2 Introduce the Hypothesis

Make sure that the rest of the Introduction clearly and logically leads up to the end of the Introduction: the stating of your hypothesis. Thus, even before you state the hypothesis, the reader should not only know what the hypothesis is but also (a) how your hypothesis follows logically from theory and research, and (b) why it is important to test the hypothesis.

To introduce the hypothesis, use words such as, "In view of [the logic I spelled out earlier], I predicted that [my hypothesis]," or "If [the logic I spelled out earlier] is the case, then it should follow that [my hypothesis]." If the reader leaves your Introduction asking any of these questions, you are in trouble:

1. What was the hypothesis?
2. Why would anyone think that the hypothesis would be supported?

3. Does this study have anything to do with previous research or theory?
4. Why is this study being done?

3.5 Method

Whereas you use the Introduction to explain why you conducted your study, you use the Method section to describe how you conducted your study. In this "how to" section, do not describe everything you did. Instead, describe your procedures in just enough detail that an experienced researcher could replicate your study.

Start the Method section one double-spaced line below the Introduction (unlike the Abstract and Introduction, it does not start on a new page). Label it with the centered heading: Method. Divide the Method section into its appropriate subsections, such as a subsection describing participants and a subsection describing procedures.

Each subsection should start with a label (e.g., "*Participants*") that begins in the far left margin and is italicized. If these subsections are, in turn, subdivided into smaller subsections, label these subsections with italicized, indented paragraph headers (see 7.2.3).

Make sure to use complete sentences. One mistake that beginning writers often make is treating a section's heading as if it were the beginning of the first sentence of that section. As a result, the first line of their "Participants" section might be the incomplete sentence "were 20 students." To avoid making that mistake, write complete sentences that repeat the information contained in the headings. For example, follow the heading "*Participants*" with the complete sentence: "The participants were 20 students."

3.5.1 Participants or Subjects

Usually, you should devote the first subsection of your Method section to describing your sample. Specifically, you should describe (a) the general characteristics (e.g., how many women, how many men, average age) of the individuals you studied, (b) how you recruited and selected those individuals, and, if applicable, (c) how you assigned those individuals to different conditions. In this first subsection, you are providing information that will help (a) researchers who want to replicate your study, (b) reviewers who want to be sure your study was conducted ethically, and (c) readers who want to evaluate how representative your sample was. The way you write and label this section depends on whether you studied a sample of humans or a sample of nonhuman animals.

If you studied humans, label this section "Participants" and refer to the individuals you studied as "participants." Never refer to them as "subjects." Tell how many participants you studied, how many were women, and how many were men. State the average age of the participants, as well as either the age range or standard deviation. You may need to provide additional background information about the participants (e.g., race/ethnicity, religion, political affiliation, socioeconomic status, visual acuity) if (a) you are doing an analysis using one of those background variables or (b) that information is necessary for assessing the generalizability of your results.

To give the reader the ability to evaluate the representativeness of your sample and the ability to replicate your study with an equivalent sample, you must do more than describe the characteristics of your sample: You must also tell how you selected your sample (e.g., "were a random sample of university students" or, more commonly, "were students in an introductory psychology class"), as well as what incentives you used to encourage those selected to participate (e.g., participants received money, received extra credit, received no compensation). In addition, either here or in the Results, you must state (a) the number of participants who dropped out, (b) the number of participants whose data were excluded from analysis, and (c) the reasons for these dropouts and exclusions.

Finally, if you arranged for different participants to receive different treatments, describe how you made these assignments. In an experiment, you would probably use random assignment. For correlational studies, you might assign participants to condition based on their scores on a certain test.

If, rather than studying humans, you studied nonhuman animals, do not use "Participants" as your heading because you did not have any *participants:* individuals who volunteered to participate in your study. Instead, use "Subjects" as the heading for this section. Provide the species name, strains and supplier, ages, sexes, and weights of your subjects. Describe how you treated these subjects: how much they were handled, their feeding schedules, the temperature they were kept at, and the lighting conditions. In addition, be sure to provide any other information about how your subjects were treated that would be necessary to replicate the study.

For both nonhuman and human animals, provide assurances that the study was conducted ethically. If the experiment involved individuals from whom informed consent is difficult or impossible to obtain (such as children or animals), you should state the ethical standards under which the study was conducted. For example, if you had read APA's ethical principles, you might include the following statement: Animals were treated in accordance with the "Ethical Principles of Psychologists and Code of Conduct" (American Psychological Association, 2002). Often, authors suggest that participants were treated ethically by stating that participants were volunteers. However, according to the *Publication Manual,* authors should state, rather than merely suggest, that participants were treated ethically. Thus, for our example study, a Participants section might look like the following:

Participants

    Participants were 24 (14 women and 10 men) students enrolled in an introductory psychology class at Clarion University who volunteered as part of a class exercise. Their ages ranged from 18 to 25 with a mean of 19.25. All participants were treated in accordance with the "Ethical Principles of Psychologists and Code of Conduct" (American Psychological Association, 2002).[3]

---

[3]Include this citation only if you read the *Principles.*

3.5.2 Apparatus

If you used equipment to present or record information (e.g., computers, slide projectors, or stop watches), describe that equipment briefly in a subsection called "Apparatus." Provide brand names and numbers for complicated equipment (e.g., computers, skin-fold calipers) but not for simple, standard equipment (e.g., stopwatches, rulers). If you also used pencil-and-paper tests, you can describe those tests here. Describe your materials well enough so that other researchers can obtain or replicate your stimuli (e.g., "Memory lists were printed on standard-sized (22 × 28 cm) sheets of white, bond paper in 12-point Times font. Distractor material was printed on every alternate line in a 10-point Times font.").

3.5.3 Materials

If you used only pencil-and-paper tests, instead of an Apparatus subsection, use a subsection entitled "Materials." If pencil-and-paper tests are well known, just name, abbreviate, and cite them—for example, "Beck Depression Inventory (BDI; Beck, Ward, Mendelssohn, Mock, & Erlbaugh, 1961)"; if they are not well known, name, cite, and briefly describe the test(s). If you created a test for the research study, put a copy of that test in an appendix (see 3.9). If you borrowed questions from other measures, note that fact and cite those other measures—otherwise you are committing plagiarism. In our example study, a Materials section might look like the following:

```
Materials
     Each participant received a single sheet of white,
8.5 × 11 in. (22 × 28 cm) bond paper with these words
printed on it:

     Imagine you are about to meet a person for the first
     time. You know nothing about the person, except that
     this person's friends describe her as humorous, cold,
     intelligent, polite [or cold, intelligent, polite,
     humorous]. How much do you think you would like this
     person? Rate your answer on a 7-point scale where 1
     means that you would dislike this person a lot, 4 means
     that you would neither dislike nor like this person,
     and 7 means that you would like this person a lot.
```

3.5.4 Design and Other Optional Subsections

If your design is too complicated to describe in a single paragraph, put information about the design in a separate subsection called "Design." Consider setting off any aspect of your Method section that requires more than a paragraph to describe (e.g., your manipulation checks, your coding scheme) in a separate subsection (e.g., "Coding," "Manipulation checks"). In addition, if your procedure is complex enough or long enough that the reader might get overwhelmed, consider beginning the Method section with a general "Overview" subsection.

3.5.5 Procedure

Whereas the decision to use an Overview or Design subsection is usually optional, the decision to use a Procedure subsection is not because it is essential for allowing others to repeat your study. The Procedure is a step-by-step account of what happened to the participants during the study. The section should so clearly focus on participants that readers should be able to imagine themselves as participants in your study. To focus on participants, consider making participants the subject of most sentences. For instance, rather than writing, "I read the stimulus words," you might write, "Participants heard the stimulus words." The following example illustrates how to keep the focus on the participants:

> Procedure
>
>   Participants received a randomly distributed response
>   sheet. They had 2 min to read it and write their responses
>   on it.

In addition to helping readers visualize what it would be like to be a participant in your study, you need to include information that will help readers replicate your study. Specifically, you need to include information about instructions and methodological wrinkles.

Include information about instructions, especially about how these instructions are different for your different groups. However, rather than stating your instructions word-for-word, you can usually summarize them (e.g., "Participants read standard instructions that can be found in Appendix B.").

Include any methodological wrinkles that boost the study's validity. Thus, if you used a double-blind procedure, be sure to mention that you did. If you used a sophisticated procedure to control for order effects, describe that procedure (e.g., "Order and serial position of the six conditions were counterbalanced using Latin squares."). If you have not already described the design (e.g., in a separate "Design" subsection or in a "Participants and Design" subsection), describe the design of the study, including the manipulated and measured variables. For our example experiment, you might end your procedure section with the following paragraph:

>   The study was a two-level, between-participant
>   experiment with sequence of information ("humorous" first vs.
>   last) as the independent variable. The dependent variable
>   was the liking ratings.

3.6 Results

The Results section starts one double-spaced line after the end of the Method section with the centered heading: Results. Start the text of this section by telling the reader exactly which data you analyzed—if those data differ from the measured variable you described in the Method section. For example, you would need to say whether you had transformed data in any way (e.g., percentage correct in a memory test rather than number of items recalled), and if any data were omitted (e.g., data from practice trials).

Once the reader knows what data you are analyzing, you can describe how you analyzed those data. If you did any significance tests, tell the reader the following:

- why you did the test (e.g., "To test the hypothesis that the sequence of presenting the information had an effect on likeability, I . . .").

- what the test was (e.g., "performed an independent-groups t test . . .").

- what your two-tailed significance (alpha) level was (e.g., "using an alpha level of .05" or "The probability of a Type I error was .05 [or whatever level you used] for all analyses.")—unless you are using a one-tailed test. If you are using a one-tailed test, tell the reader (e.g., "Using a one-tailed test and an alpha level of .05, . . .").

- what the result of the test was, both in terms of whether the results were statistically significant and in terms of the reason you did the test. Typically, the reason you did the statistical test was to test a hypothesis (e.g., "As hypothesized, participants who received 'humorous' first rated the person as significantly more likeable than those who received 'humorous' last, $t(22) = 3.46, p < .01$.").

- what the relevant summary statistics (averages and measures of spread) are for the important conditions. These descriptive statistics may help readers see the pattern in your data. For example, you might write, "Specifically, the mean rating from those receiving 'humorous' first was 5.75 ($SD = 1.06$), whereas the mean rating from those receiving 'humorous' last was 4.5 ($SD = 0.67$)."

If you include the previously listed information and present it skillfully, you will give (a) the casual reader a clear understanding of whether the results support the hypothesis, (b) the skeptical reader evidence that your results support your claims, and (c) the reader doing a meta-analysis the information necessary to combine your results with those of related studies. To present the information skillfully, you need to organize the information so it tells a story. For example, you might organize the information like this:

> To test the hypothesis that participants receiving "humorous" first would rate the person as more likeable than participants receiving "humorous" last, I used a between-subjects t test on the likeability ratings. As hypothesized, participants who received "humorous" first rated the person as more likeable ($M = 5.75, SD = 1.06$) than those who received "humorous" last ($M = 4.5, SD = 0.67$), $t(22) = 3.46, p < .05$.

Alternatively, you might find it useful, at least in your first draft, to state the conclusion (the implication of the results for your hypothesis) first. Then, you can use the rest of the paragraph to provide support for that conclusion, as we did in the following paragraph:

> As hypothesized, participants who received "humorous" first rated the person as more likeable than those who

```
received "humorous" last. The mean rating from those
receiving "humorous" first was 5.75 (SD = 1.06), whereas the
mean rating from those receiving "humorous" last was 4.5
(SD = 0.67). Using a between-subjects t test, this
difference was significant, t(22) = 3.46, p < .05.
```

3.6.1 Statistical Significance

If, as in the previous case, your results are statistically significant, the editors of the *Publication Manual* encourage you to supplement significant tests with both (a) effect size estimates and (b) confidence intervals. Check to see whether your professor wants you to provide those additional statistics.

If, on the other hand, your results are not statistically significant, the editors of the *Publication Manual* encourage you to report your study's power. That is, tell the reader that if the variable had an effect of a certain size, what the chances of your study finding that effect statistically significant would be. Check to see whether your professor wants you to do a power analysis and, if so, what form that power analysis should take.

Note that, in the traditional approach to significance testing, results are either statistically significant or they are not statistically significant: There is no middle ground. Thus, according to the traditional view, it would be considered misleading to refer to results that were not significant as either "kind of significant" or as "marginally significant."[4]

Note also that you should use the adjective "significant" only when you mean that the null hypothesis has been rejected. You should not use "significant" as a synonym for "important" or for "large." Therefore, do not use the phrase "significant result" when you mean "important result," and do not use the phrase "significant effect" when you mean "substantial effect."

Finally, note that you can use "insignificant" only when you mean unimportant. You cannot use "insignificant" as a synonym for the statistical term "not significant." Therefore, if you mean that the results fail to disprove the null hypothesis, do not refer to the results as "insignificant results." Instead, refer to results either as "not significant" or as "nonsignificant."

3.6.2 Formatting Statistical Information

As you saw from the examples of result sections in 3.6, formatting statistical information is different from formatting regular text. Some letters are italicized, some numbers below 1 are expressed with a leading zero in front of the decimal point (e.g., 0.20), some numbers below 1 are expressed without a leading zero (e.g., .20), some material

---

[4]If your professor is one of the many professors who are dissatisfied with the traditional approach to significance testing, your professor may allow you to use the term "marginally significant." However, unless you are sure your professor approves of the concept of marginally significant, avoid that term.

is in parentheses, and some commas are used in unusual ways. Fortunately, there are rules:

- Italicize all statistical symbols that are standard alphabetic letters (e.g., t, p, F, df, M, SD).
- Do not italicize any Greek letters (e.g., Σ, β, μ).
- For any inferential statistical test, give its name, the degrees of freedom in parentheses, an equals sign, the statistic's value, and the probability level. For chi-square, give the sample size as well (use N for the whole sample, n for a subsample).
- Separate inferential statistical information from the sentence with a comma.
- State percentage and integer data as whole numbers. For any other numbers, go to two decimal places, except for probability values. With probability values, you can go to as many decimal places as necessary.
- Do not put zeros in front of the decimal point for either (a) probabilities ("p" values) or (b) correlation coefficients.

To see these rules in practice, study the following three examples:

✔ The increase in mean confidence ratings was significantly greater in the experimental condition ($M = 5.01$, $SD = 3.52$) than in the control condition ($M = 3.84$, $SD = 3.02$), $t(26) = 2.66$, $p < .01$.

✔ There was a significant interaction, $F(1, 34) = 123.07$, $p < .001$, plotted in Figure 4.

✔ The distribution of preferences shown in Table 6 was not significantly different among the four categories, $\chi^2 (3, N = 300) = 6.00$, $p > .05$.

3.6.3 Deciding Whether You Need Either a Figure or a Table

If you are going to compare only two means, you do not need either a figure or a table—unless your professor requires one. (Your professor may require figures or tables so you can learn how to format them.) If a table or figure is merely going to duplicate what you have already said in text, omit that figure or table.

3.6.4 When to Use Tables

Sometimes, you must include many numbers in your Results section. However, if you include all those numbers in text, you may overwhelm and confuse your reader. In such a case, you should use either a table or a figure. If your goal is to show that the data fit a pattern (e.g., to show that performance increases over time, to illustrate that there is a linear relationship between two variables, or to show that an interaction is X-shaped), you may wish to use a figure to paint that general picture. If, on the other hand, the exact numbers are important, you will probably want to use a table. Usually, you should use a table if you are presenting the following:

- between 4 and 10 means (and their standard deviations)
- more than four correlation coefficients
- the results of an analysis of variance (ANOVA)
- a list of factor loadings
- the results of a multistage regression analysis

3.6.5 Creating Tables

Your goal in using a table should be to summarize information for your reader. For your table to accomplish that goal, your reader should be able to understand your table without reading the accompanying text. However, the table is not supposed to stand by itself, waiting for the interested reader to absorb it. Indeed, if you cannot refer to the table, it is unnecessary, and you should delete it. When referring to the table, identify it by its number and highlight the table's most relevant numbers or patterns of numbers (e.g., "As can be seen in Table 2, the treatment group scored higher than the control group on every dependent measure.").

One reason it is important to refer to the table by number is that the tables in a manuscript submitted for publication do not appear right next to the text that refers to them. Instead, tables must be placed, one per page, after the References. (You may wish to ask your professor if you can deviate from APA manuscript style and put the table in the text near where it is discussed.)

All tables consist of three parts: (a) a caption appearing above the rest of the table, which includes a table number and title; (b) headings for the table's columns and headings for the table's rows; and (c) the table's data. In addition, some tables contain a fourth part: explanatory notes. We will now discuss each of these four parts. To follow our discussion, you may find it useful to refer to Exhibit 3.1 (on page 70).[5]

The first part of the table caption is the table number. Use Arabic numbers (e.g. "2") and number the tables according to the order in which you refer to them in text. Thus, the second table you refer to will be "Table 2."

The second part of the table caption is the table title. It should be a brief, telegraphic, but meaningful description of the relationship between (a) the data in the table and (b) the variables or statistics identified by the column and row headers. If your data can be expressed in units (milliseconds, liters), put the unit of measurement

---

[5]Exhibit 3.1 is a good example of an APA style table except that it is not double-spaced. Make sure that your tables are double-spaced.

EXHIBIT **3.1**   An Example of a Table

Table 2

Mean Differences in Reaction Time (in ms) Between No-Noise and Noise Conditions

Noise level (dB)	Mean difference[a]	t
	Simple RTs	
60	-7.21_z (9)[b]	2.62*
70	-7.45_z (8)	3.55**
80	-9.15_z (10)	4.49**
90	-9.72_z (9)	3.85**
	Choice RTs	
60	-11.05_y (5)	2.82*
70	-11.92_y (9)	9.90****
80	-4.91_x (10)	3.61**
90	0.33_w (10)	1.41

Note. This table is made up. If it had been previously published, we would have cited the study here. Numbers having different subscripts differ significantly at $p < .01$ by t test.
[a]Negative numbers indicate noise RT was slower than no-noise RT.
[b]Number in parentheses is number of participants in each condition.
*$p < 0.5$. **$p < .01$. ****$p < .0001$.

in parentheses. Italicize the table title and capitalize the first letter of each major word. Place the table caption above the table. Thus, as you can see from Exhibit 3.1, the top of a table might look like this:

Table 2

Mean Differences in Reaction Time (in ms) Between No-Noise and Noise Conditions

The column and row headings tell the reader what the data in the table represent. The left-most column heading identifies the major manipulated variable (i.e., noise level). Under that column header are the row headings. The row headings label the levels (amounts) of the major manipulated variable (i.e., 60 dB). Other column headings specify levels of other manipulated variables, or different measured variables (e.g., "Mean difference").

Often, your tables will have three horizontal lines. Near the top of the table, put a horizontal line right below the table caption to separate it from the column headings. Next, put a line right below the column headings to separate them from the body of the table. Finally, put a line at the bottom of the body of the table to separate the table body from the explanatory notes. Use other horizontal lines sparingly. Do not use vertical lines.

If there are decimal points, the decimal points of the numbers in a column should line up with each other. Write out numbers to two decimal places, except when the data are integers or percentages (see 7.2.6).

TABLE 3.1 Superscripts for Probabilities of Two- and
One-Tailed Statistical Tests

$p <$	Two-tailed	One-tailed
.05	*	†
.01	**	††
.001	***	†††
.0001	****	††††

Set any notes that you have at the bottom of the table in unindented paragraphs. The first paragraph would be *general notes* relating to the entire table (e.g., "Numbers having different subscripts differ significantly at $p < .01$ by t test."). Start this general notes section with the italicized word *Note* followed by a period. Make each note a complete sentence, and end each note with a period (see Exhibit 3.1).

Your second paragraph would start on a new line, and would be *specific notes* applying to particular entries, columns, or rows (e.g., "[a]Negative indicates noise RT was slower than control RT."). Identify those notes, both in the table in the notes, with superscript letters (e.g.,[a]).

The third paragraph would start on a new line and would be *probability notes*. You use probability notes when you use symbols, such as asterisks (*) and daggers (†) to indicate that a result is statistically significant. Probability notes spell out the connection between your symbols (e.g.,*) and the significance level (e.g., $p < .05$) they represent. Table 3.1 shows a common way of using superscripts to express probability levels. Exhibit 3.1 provides an example of probability notes in action.

3.6.6 When to Use Figures

A figure is a picture you use to help your reader see the point you are trying to make. In the Results section, figures can be very useful for helping your reader see the shape of a relationship between two variables, for helping your reader understand an interaction among variables, and for presenting a very large number of data points. You might also use a figure in the Method section to illustrate anything that would otherwise be hard to describe, such as what the apparatus or stimuli looked like.

3.6.7 Creating Figures

As was the case with tables, the following applies.

- Your reader should be able to understand your figures without reading the accompanying text.
- Figures should do more than duplicate information already in text.

■ The text should draw the reader's attention to the important aspects of your figure.

■ The text should refer to the figure by number (e.g., "As can be seen in Figure 1, . . .").

In referring to figures, note three points. First, regardless of whether your "figure" is a graph, a photo, or a diagram, always refer to it by the word "Figure" followed by the figure number. Second, as was the case with tables, it is important to refer to the correct figure number because the figure is not next to the text to which it refers. Instead, the figures are put, one per page, on the pages after the figure captions—and the figure captions are put on the page after the tables (which, in turn, are put after the References). Third, software packages, such as Excel, SPSS, and DeltaGraph can help you construct graphs. However, when using such programs, realize that (a) using them may be extremely time-consuming, (b) using them may result in figures that violate APA standards, and (c) using them to construct appropriate graphs is easier if you know the terminology associated with the four parts of a graph:

1. the graph's axes—the "x" (horizontal) axis and the "y" (vertical) axis
2. the data—the data points and lines joining them or the bars representing them
3. the figure legend—a box within the figure that describes what the bar shadings, symbols, or lines represent
4. the figure caption—a heading that includes the figure's number, the figure's title, and explanations of what lines, symbols, and abbreviations represent—if those explanations are necessary for understanding the figure and those explanations could not fit in the legend box

We will now discuss each of these four components. To follow this discussion, you may find it helpful to refer to Exhibit 3.2.

Axes. Choose scale values for each axis that spread out the data and allow the figure to fit comfortably on one page. Your figure should be wider than it is tall: Ideally, it would be only about two-thirds as tall as it is wide.

Make the horizontal axis by drawing a line that starts near the left-hand, bottom side of the page and goes straight across toward the right-hand, bottom side. If you conducted an experiment, this horizontal axis will represent your independent variable. If you conducted a nonexperimental study, this horizontal axis will represent your predictor variable. Starting at the far left end of that line, draw a straight line up toward the top of the page. Make this vertical line about two-thirds as long as your horizontal axis. This vertical line, your vertical axis, will represent your dependent (measured) variable. Thus far, your graph has two lines for the two axes. The two axes are two sides of an incomplete rectangle. Complete the rectangle (add the top and the right side)—realizing that, for your final draft, you may decide to remove the lines that completed the rectangle.[6] This rectangular box will separate any points, lines, or bars

---

[6]If you are making a scatterplot or a bar graph, you will remove both the line that forms the top of the rectangle and the line that forms the right side of the rectangle from the final draft of your figure. If you are making a line graph and the final graph looks better without those two lines, remove them.

EXHIBIT **3.2**   An Example of a Line Graph

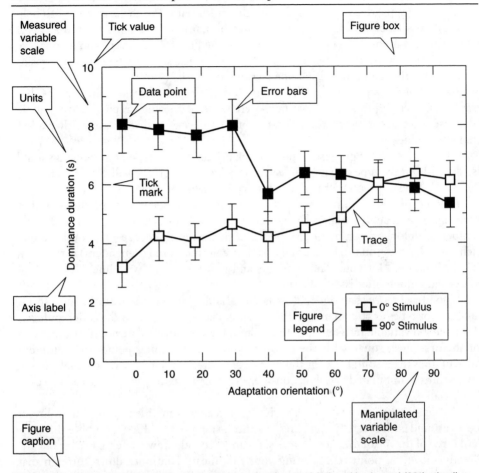

Figure 2. Mean duration of binocular-rivalry dominance of vertical (0°) and horizontal (90°) stimuli following adaptation to a monocular grating of various orientations. Vertical lines show ±1 standard error of the mean.

that represent your data from the (a) axis labels (e.g., "Dominance duration" and "Adaptation orientation"), which describe the measurable characteristic that each axis represents, and (b) axis scale values (e.g., "0"), which are numbers or other labels that help the reader understand what the marks on an axis indicate.

Inside that box, place *tick marks:* small marks that will be used to indicate values of the variables on your axes (see Exhibit 3.2). Then, place the numbers corresponding to the tick marks on the outside of the box. Print those numbers (called "scale values") in their normal orientation.

You now need axis labels to help the reader understand what those numbers represent. The two axis labels should be meaningful but brief. To make the labels meaningful, let the reader know the units to which the numbers are referring (e.g., meters, milligrams, decibels) by including that information in the axis labels. To help make the axis labels brief, try to abbreviate the name of the units (to see a list of abbreviations for common units, see 3.6.8). Put the unit abbreviation—or, if you were unable to use an abbreviation, the unit—in parentheses. Once you have your axis labels, center them and print each one parallel to its axis.

Data. For your purposes, there are three main types of graphs: line graphs, bar graphs, and scatterplots. We have purposely omitted the pie graph because people often use a pie graph when their point would be clearer had they used either a bar graph or a table.

The three types of graphs are not interchangeable. The type of graph you should use depends on the type of data you have. In the next section, we will show you how to choose the type of graph that matches the type of data you have.

Line graphs. Use a line graph when you have conducted an experiment and at least one manipulated variable has continuous, numerical values (e.g., drug dosage, number of onlookers, or, as in Exhibit 3.2, orientation in degrees). If you have one such variable, put it on the horizontal axis. Put your measured (dependent) variable on the vertical axis. Plot your data as points and join the points with lines. Each set of points and joining lines is called a *trace*.

If you have more than one manipulated variable, put the one with the most levels (amounts or types of treatment) on the horizontal axis. Distinguish the different levels of the second variable by using different shapes for each level's data points (e.g., circles for the first level, squares for the second level) and by joining points with different kinds of lines (e.g., solid lines for the first level, dotted lines for the other level). If you have a third manipulated variable, consider drawing a separate graph for each level of that variable.

If your data are means, you can give your reader some idea of the variability of scores around each mean by engaging in a three-step process. First, compute the standard error of the mean *(SE)* for your first mean.[7] Second, draw a line that starts one SE directly above the point representing your first mean, continues down through that point, and stops one standard error below that point. (You should now have a line that is 2 *SEs* in length and has the mean as its midpoint.) This line is an error bar. Third, draw error bars for each of your means. To see what these standard error lines look like, refer back to Exhibit 3.2.

Bar graphs. Use a bar graph when you have conducted a study and all your predictor variables are discrete and nonnumerical (e.g., different kinds—rather than amounts—of treatments, or, as in Exhibit 3.3, experimental vs. control). The measured (dependent) variable will be on the vertical axis. If you have one manipulated (independent) variable, that variable will be on the horizontal axis. If you have two manipulated variables, only one can be on the horizontal axis. The levels of the other one will have to be expressed by differently shaded bars (e.g., black, white, gray). To determine

---

[7]The standard error is the standard deviation of the scores making up the mean divided by the square root of the number of scores making up the mean.

EXHIBIT **3.3**   An Example of a Bar Graph Showing an Interaction

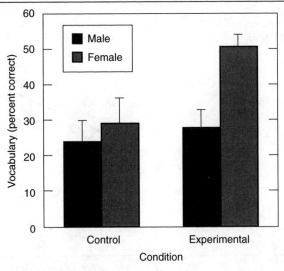

Figure 3. Mean percent-correct words in experimental and control groups as a function of sex. Vertical lines show 1 standard error of the mean.

which manipulated variable you should express with bars, make one graph putting one manipulated variable on the horizontal axis and make another graph putting the other manipulated variable on the horizontal axis. Then, compare the graphs to see which graph makes your conclusions clearer.[8]

When working with your bars, obey the following three rules. First, do not distinguish the levels of the other manipulated variables by using differently colored (e.g., red, purple, green) bars. Instead, use differently shaded bars (e.g., black, white, gray). Second, do not use diagonal lines to shade the bars; diagonal lines will create the illusion that your bars are tilted. Third, do not add 3-D effects: Those effects make it more difficult for readers to understand your graph. Instead, add standard error lines above the bars to show the variability in your data (see Exhibit 3.3).

Scatterplots. If you do not have a manipulated variable, you may want to use a scatterplot (also called a scattergram). A scatterplot is especially useful when you have given two tests to your participants. Put the variable you consider the predictor variable on the horizontal axis and put the criterion variable on the vertical axis. Then, use dots to plot your data on the graph. If you want to provide more information than what a swarm of dots can convey, add a regression line to your scatterplot (see Exhibit 3.4 on page 76).

---

[8]Sometimes, changing which variable you put on the horizontal axis will make no difference in how easy your graph is to read; other times, changing which variable you put on the horizontal axis can make your graph much easier to grasp. To see examples of both cases, go to our website (http://www.writingforpsychology.com).

EXHIBIT **3.4**   An Example of a Scatterplot

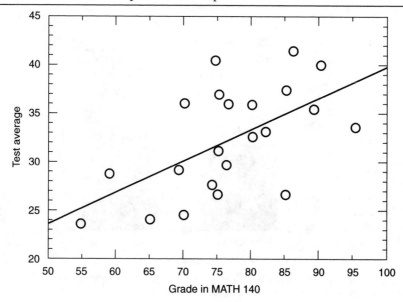

Figure 4. Scatterplot of grades in MATH 140 and average of the PSYC-311 tests. The line is the best-fitting regression line. Its equation is: $Y = 23.59 + 1.63X$; $R^2 = .22$.

Legend. In the figure's legend (the box inside the figure, see Exhibit 3.2), provide explanatory information to help the reader understand any abbreviations, bar shadings, symbols, and lines that you are using. The legend should be contained within the borders of the graph (see the legend in Exhibit 3.2). If there is not enough room within the borders of the graph to write out all the necessary explanatory information, place the explanatory information in the figure caption instead (e.g., if, for Exhibit 3.2, we had been unable to fit "unfilled squares designate the 0° stimulus; filled squares designate the 90° stimulus" in the legend, we would put that information in the figure caption [the figure's heading]).

Figure caption. APA manuscript style requires that manuscript figure captions all appear together on a new page following the tables. This new page must have the centered label: Figure Captions. However, your professor may allow you to deviate from APA manuscript style and put each figure caption under its figure, as we have done in Exhibit 3.2.

Regardless of whether you put the caption under the figure or on a separate "Figure Captions" page, start the caption on the far left margin and treat the caption like an unindented paragraph. Realize that there are two parts to every figure caption.

The first part of the caption is the figure number ending with a period (e.g., "*Figure 1.*"). Note that this first part is italicized.

The second part of the caption is the figure title. In the title, describe the figure in a brief sentence or phrase, capitalizing only the first letter. Note that the figure title is not italicized.

Right after this second part, some figure captions contain a third part. This third part consists of information that the reader needs to understand the figure, such as what the different lines, symbols, and abbreviations represent. Ideally, you would put that information not in the caption but in the legend. Sometimes, however, information vital to understanding your figure will not fit in the legend. For example, in Exhibit 3.2, because the explanation of the vertical lines would not fit in the legend, that explanation was added to the caption.

3.6.8 Units

Both the American Psychological Association and the international scientific community use the metric system. Specifically, they conform to a set of metric system standards called the International System of Units (SI). Units of measurement in any part of your report should almost always be expressed using SI. If you originally took your measurements in non-SI units (e.g., inches), you can report those measurements in non-SI units—but you must also report the measurements in SI units (e.g., centimeters). To be more precise, you "must report the SI equivalents in parentheses immediately after the nonmetric units" (APA, 2001, p. 130). In the rare instances in which non-SI units of measurement are universally used (e.g., decibels), you can use the non-SI unit.

Regardless of whether you use an SI or non-SI unit, abbreviate the unit (to see how to abbreviate some common units, see Table 3.2 on page 78). When abbreviating the units, omit periods from the abbreviation—unless you need the period to make it clear that you are abbreviating a unit rather than writing out a word. For example, if you did not put a period after "in," readers might think you were typing the preposition "in" rather than abbreviating "inches."

You may find that some SI units are too big or too small for your purposes. For example, suppose that you were trying to report the smallest bump that participants could reliably detect in an otherwise flat surface. Putting the size of this bump in meters (e.g., ".0005 m") would be awkward and hard to understand. Put the size of the bump in millimeters instead (e.g., .5 mm). Table 3.3 (on page 78) can help you find a unit that best allows you to express your measurements.

3.7 Discussion

The Discussion follows immediately after the Results and starts with the centered heading: Discussion. In the Discussion, you review your findings and show how they relate to the literature. The Discussion provides you with the opportunity to interpret, reinterpret, qualify, and explore the theoretical importance of your results. If your Discussion makes up less than one fourth of the body of your paper, be concerned: You may not have thought enough about your results. However, do not ramble on merely to lengthen this section: Ultimately, your discussion section will be judged not on how long it is but on how well organized and meaningful it is.

TABLE 3.2 Some Common SI and Non-SI Units and Their Abbreviations*

Quantity	Unit	Abbreviation	SI Unit
Acceleration	meter per second squared	m/s^2	same
Angle	radian	rad	same
Area	square meter	m^2	same
Concentration	molecules per cubic meter	mol/m^3	same
Density	kilogram per cubic meter	kg/m^3	same
Electric current	ampere	A	same
Electric potential	volt	V	same
Electric resistance	ohm	Ω	same
Force	newton	N	same
Frequency	hertz	Hz	same
Length	meter	m	same
Luminance	candela per square meter	cd/m^2	same
Mass	kilogram	kg	same
Power	watt	W	same
Pressure	pascal	Pa	same
Sound pressure level	decibel	dB	N/m^2
Temperature	degree Celsius	°C	°Kelvin
Time	second	s	same
Velocity	meter per second	m/s	same
Visual angle	degree	°	radian
Volume	cubic meter	m^3	same
Weight	see Mass		

*If you need help making these abbreviations in your word processor, see our website (http://www.writingforpsychology.com).

TABLE 3.3 Common SI Prefixes

Factor	1 ×	Prefix	Symbol	Example
billion times	10^9	giga	G	Gb (gigabyte)
million times	10^6	mega	M	MV (megavolt)
thousand times	10^3	kilo	k	kHz (kilohertz)
one tenth	10^{-1}	deci	d	dB (decibel)
one hundredth	10^{-2}	centi	c	cm (centimeter)
one thousandth	10^{-3}	milli	m	mA (milliamp)
one millionth	10^{-6}	micro	μ	μm (micrometer)
one billionth	10^{-9}	nano	n	nm (nanometer)

Remember that you have taken your reader on a journey though the Introduction, Method, and Results. In the Discussion, you should convince your reader that the journey was worthwhile because you have arrived somewhere interesting.

3.7.1 Briefly Restate the Results

To convince your reader of the journey's importance, you must start by telling your reader whether you found what you expected to find. Therefore, begin the Discussion by letting the reader know whether your results are consistent with your original hypothesis. Briefly inform the reader whether the obtained results are (a) statistically significant and consistent with your hypothesis, (b) statistically significant but inconsistent with your hypothesis, or (c) not statistically significant.

To keep your description of the results brief, (a) leave out means, probability values, and other numbers, and (b) focus solely on whether the results support the hypothesis. However, do not be so brief that you fail to remind the reader what it was you set out to test. Do not make a vague statement like, "The results of this study confirm the hypothesis." Instead, say something specific like this:

> As predicted, when students rated the likeability of a person described by a list of adjectives, they rated the person more favorably when the most positive adjective was the first item on the list than when that adjective was the last item on the list.

After relating the results to the hypothesis, you should relate the results to the work of other researchers—a step that often involves reviewing some of the literature you discussed in the introduction. If other researchers have found similar results, explain how your work supports and extends their findings. If other researchers obtained different results, explain why your findings are different from theirs. In short, explain whether your study filled the hole in the literature that you identified in the introduction.

3.7.2 State Qualifications and Reservations

If the results of your study were significant, at least three major questions arise (see 5.9). First, can the results be generalized to a broader population? For example, if your results were based on a sample of students, those results might not generalize to all adults. Second, are the methods you used to measure and manipulate variables valid? For example, if you timed your participants with a stopwatch to induce stress, is this time pressure a valid manipulation of stress? Third, can you legitimately make a cause-effect statement from your results? You probably cannot if there are any other variables that vary along with the manipulated variables (see 5.9.1).

Although you should mention limits on the generalizability and validity of your results, try to be positive. Otherwise, your readers (including the professor grading your report) will feel that they have been taken for a ride rather than taken on a useful journey. Therefore, instead of downplaying your research because you studied only students, for example, you could suggest that students are more suspicious of psychological testing than other people, so any effect that students show is likely to be even stronger in other people. Similarly, rather than deriding your study because you used a weak stressor, you could say that the effects of stress on performance must be quite strong if a weak stressor managed to produce a significant effect.

You should mention any defects in the method or design of the study (e.g., some participants did not follow instructions, the measuring device was difficult to use, the apparatus was unreliable). Do not dwell on these defects, however, unless they were systematic. If the defects were unsystematic, they reduced the chances of obtaining significant results. Consequently, the fact that you obtained significant results in spite of these unsystematic defects is a tribute to the strength of the hypothesis.

If the method or design defects were systematic (e.g., only participants in the experimental group misinterpreted the instructions, the difficulty in using the measuring device led to more errors in one condition than in the others, the apparatus was unreliable for only one of the conditions), you should admit that those errors make it impossible for you to come to a firm conclusion about the effect of your treatment. For example, suppose you found that students using mnemonic techniques (your manipulated variable) recalled more words (your measured variable) than students who did not use such techniques. However, suppose that you also discovered that you tested the mnemonic group in a quiet room and the control group in a noisy room. In that case, you should admit that your experiment is flawed. Point out that the mnemonic technique may not have increased learning in the experimental group; instead, the noise may have decreased learning in the control group. In short, if there are alternative explanations for your results, you should tell the reader about these alternative explanations.

If your results were not significant, there are going to be a variety of possible explanations for your results. Spend part of your Discussion considering why you obtained nonsignificant results. You can guard against making the reader feel that your study has arrived at a dead end if you write about the validity and potency of your manipulations and measures and how they could be improved in future studies.

3.7.3 State the Theoretical Importance

Once you have satisfied the reader that your results should be taken seriously, you can go on to discuss the implications your results have for theory. When discussing these implications, some speculation is allowed. However, such speculation should be (a) closely related to your results, rather than wild speculation; (b) brief, rather than long-winded; and (c) clearly indicated as speculation, rather than being disguised as fact.

3.7.4 Conclude

Sometimes, your last paragraph will be a brief mention of the practical implications of your results or some suggestions for future research. You should always end by stating a conclusion that will make readers believe that your report has important implications for theory, research, or practice. The following are examples of how you might begin your concluding paragraph:

- The present findings suggest a _____ explanation for _____.
- The present findings lend new support for a _____ explanation of _____.
- The present findings go beyond previous explanations of _____.
- The effects reported in this article have two important practical implications.
- Practitioners should be aware of [these findings] when they _____.
- Two important findings from this study are _____.
- Results from the current study suggest several promising directions for future research.
- The results raise serious questions about _____ [explanation/ theory].
- This study is an important step in understanding _____.
- The results presented here should lead psychologists to take a serious look at _____ and its potential impact on _____.
- Future research should [be like my study but make the following changes].

The conclusion can be longer than a paragraph. In journal articles, the conclusion is often several paragraphs long and labeled with a subheading titled "Conclusions." If you are writing a long report, you will probably have more than a one-paragraph conclusion. However, if your report is as short as the typical student research report, you can probably conclude with a single paragraph.

3.8 References

Every journal article you cite in your paper should appear in the Reference section. The citations should be in alphabetical order according to the last name of the work's primary author. The Reference section should start on a new page with the centered heading: References. The format is demonstrated in both the Reference section of the sample term paper (2.11) and the sample research report (3.12). The rules for the Reference page are set out in 4.9, and a checklist for the Reference section is provided in 4.10.4.

3.9 Appendixes

In published articles, appendixes are rare. When an appendix appears in a published article, it is used to present important material, such as unpublished test materials and details of especially constructed equipment that, if presented in the paper's method section, would interrupt the paper's flow. In student reports, on the other hand, appendixes are much more common. Students are often required to prepare appendixes that contain exhibits documenting what either the students or the participants did: raw data, stimulus materials, questionnaires, consent forms, data summary sheets, and statistical calculations. Raw data should be presented in a table, using the same directions as for tables in the text (see 3.6.5). The only difference is that, rather than being labeled with a number (e.g., "Table 1"), each data table will be labeled with a capital letter (e. g., "A" if the table is in Appendix A, "B" if it is in Appendix B), followed by a number (e.g., "Table A1" for the first table in Appendix A, "Table A2" for the second table in Appendix A).

Your appendix will begin on a new page after the references. If you have only one appendix, it will have the centered heading "Appendix." If you have more than one, the heading for the first one will be "Appendix A"; the heading for the second one will be "Appendix B." Unless your professor states otherwise, appendixes must be referred to in the body of your paper. For example, suppose you had appendixes that contained (a) data about your three participants' vision from their eye doctors, (b) your three participants' scores on the task ("raw data") that you later analyzed, and (c) analysis of variance summary tables for all four measured variables. You would need to refer to all three appendixes. You might refer to them as follows:

```
    The participants were three men with normal visual
    acuity. Appendix A presents the details of their optometric
    characteristics.

                          Results

        Raw data for the three participants are presented in
    Tables B1, B2, and B3. . . . Analysis of variance summary
    tables for reaction times to hits, misses, false alarms,
    and correct rejections are shown in Tables C1-C4
    respectively. Consistent with the hypothesis . . .
```

3.10 Author Note

If your professor wants an Author Note (a note that contains your name and affiliation, acknowledgments, and information about how to contact you), start the Author Note on the page following the appendixes (if you do not have appendixes, start the Author Note on the page following the references) using the centered heading: Author Note. For your paper, the most important aspects of the Author Note are disclosures about (a) who, if anyone, helped you on the paper and (b) what part, if any, of the paper has been used in another class. To write an Author Note, follow the example in the sample paper (3.12). (If you need more help on writing your Author Note, see 2.9.)

3.11 Tense

If you are writing a report on a study you performed, most of your report involves describing what you did or reporting on what others did. Therefore, for most of the report, use the past tense. Use the present tense only when you are (a) referring to an existing, permanent condition, (b) referring to conclusions, or (c) referring to other parts of your report (e.g., a figure).

- Jones (1994) *found* [past tense] . . .
- Smith (1990) *argued* that attribution *is* [present tense for a situation that exists and will continue to exist] internal . . .
- As can be seen in Figure 3 [present tense for part of a report], the means *differ* [present tense for an existing and continuing condition] . . .
- In conclusion, X *appears* [present tense for conclusion] to affect Y.

If you are writing a proposal, you are proposing what you will do, so you will use the future tense much more than in a report. For example, whereas the Method section of your report should be in the past tense (e.g., "Participants read a list of 10 traits."), the Method section of your proposal should be in the future tense (e. g., "Participants will read a list of 10 traits."). For more information about tense, see 6.1.3.

3.12 Sample Research Report

Imagine that you are sitting quietly in class one day, waiting for the lecture to begin. However, instead of announcing the day's lecture topic, the professor announces that the day will be devoted to conducting an experiment. Then, your professor asks you to take out pens and paper. The professor tells you that a list of 12 digits will be read aloud, and after 30 seconds, you are to write down as many as you can remember in order. Then, the instructor repeats the procedure with a list of 12 letters. The professor then hands out the lists and asks you to count how many entries you matched on each list. Next, the numbers of digits and letters that each student recalled are collated and a statistical test is performed. Finally, the instructor tells the class that a report, in APA style, on the experiment just conducted is worth 20% of the course grade and is due in a week.

At first, such a writing assignment might seem overwhelming. Eventually, however, you might come up with something resembling the following report. Your report should differ from our report in only three significant respects. First, we have annotated our report with footnotes so you can appreciate particular points. In your own reports, do not use footnotes. Second, we have used only old references. In your own reports, cite current research. Third, we have not double-spaced and not used 12-point font so that the book will cost less. In your own reports, double-space everything and use a 12-point font.

Running[9] head: DIGITS VS. LETTERS IN SERIAL RECALL[10]

Memory for Digits and Letters in a Serial Recall Task[11]

Ann A. Student[12]

Alpha University

---

[9]Ann is using APA copy style (also called APA manuscript format). If your instructor wants you to use published format, see Appendix A. If your instructor asks you to also add a cover sheet, do what your professor asks.

[10]Ann was able to verify that her running head was short enough (had fewer than 51 characters, including spaces) by using the "Word count" feature of her word-processing software.

[11]The first three words of the title became the short title. Also, note that, for the title, if a word has fewer than four letters and is (a) a preposition (e.g., "of" and "in"), (b) an article (e.g., "a"), or (c) a conjunction (e.g., "and"), then that word is not capitalized.

[12]Include your middle initial. Do not include the word "by."

Abstract[13]

The[14] experimenter read a 12-digit list and then a 12-letter list to a class of 72 students (50 women and 22 men, mean age = 20.4 years) to test the hypothesis that letters would be more easily recalled than digits. The results did not support the hypothesis: Letters were not recalled significantly more than digits, $t(71) = -1.21$, $p = .60$.[15] Perhaps letter stimuli have no memory advantage, or perhaps design problems, such as digits always being presented first, having a small sample size, or using only one set of letters, obscured the effect.[16]

---

[13]Begin the Abstract on page 2. Announce it with the centered heading "Abstract."

[14]Do not indent the Abstract (but indent all other paragraphs).

[15]Double-space your entire paper.

[16]In only 93 words, Ann stated her hypothesis and described her method, participants, findings (including significance levels), and conclusions.

Memory for Digits and Letters in a Serial Recall Task[17]

Ebbinghaus[18] (cited in Woodworth & Schlossberg, 1954)[19] considered memory[20] to consist of the formation of associations between stimuli. In attempting to test the capacity of memory, researchers should therefore control prior associations between stimuli.[21]

Ebbinghaus controlled for prior associations by inventing nonsense syllables and discarding any that reminded him of real words, were well-known initials, or had any emotional tone. When Ebbinghaus memorized a list of nonsense syllables, he seemed to be tapping pure memory, uncontaminated by any prior associations. However, prior associations may contaminate current memory tests.[22, 23]

One current memory test[24] is rote memory for digits. Rote memory for digits is sometimes treated as a test of

---

[17]The introduction begins on a new page. Its "heading" is the paper's title.

[18]According to the *Publication Manual*, when you cite a source you have not read, you name the source, but you do not date it.

[19]Note the use of a secondary citation. Ann will not put Ebbinghaus in her reference list because she did not read Ebbinghaus's work.

[20]The first sentence introduces the general area of investigation. (For more on beginning the introduction, see 3.4.1.)

[21]This sentence prepares the reader for the next paragraph. (For more tips on helping the reader navigate your paper, see 6.4.2.)

[22]The first two paragraphs briefly set the theoretical scene (as we advised in 3.4.1).

[23]The last sentence of this paragraph introduces the next paragraph.

[24]Repeating a phrase from the previous paragraph helps the reader make a connection to the previous paragraph.

pure memory and is incorporated into IQ tests (Wechsler, 1939). The usual method is to present a few digits on the first trial and then to increase the number until learners reach their limit and cannot repeat all of the digits (Woodworth & Schlossburg, 1954).[25]

Rote memory for words or letters is less commonly tested. The reasons for not using such stimuli follow from the work of Hilgard and Bower (1966), who established (a) that individuals have prior associations to words and letters and (b) that one individual may have a stronger prior association to a particular word or letter than another individual. The problem of individuals having prior associations to word and letter stimuli cannot be solved by using nonsense syllables. Glaze (1928)[26] found[27] that using nonsense syllables did not entirely eliminate prior associations and thus associative value.[28]

Even though the associative strength of letter stimuli is weaker for some individuals than for others, the average

---

[25]Note that "&" instead of "and" is used to join authors' names inside parentheses.

[26]Whenever possible, you should use recent citations. This paper's sources would have been recent enough about 40 years ago.

[27]Ann used the past tense because Glaze's study was performed in the past and it can be tied to a specific date (1928). In most of your paper, you will use the past tense.

[28]Always review the literature. This paragraph and the previous one provide a brief review of the relevant literature.

associative strength of letter stimuli should be stronger
than the average associative strength of digits. Letters
can be formed into words, rich with associative strength,
whereas[29] digits can be formed only into numbers, poor in
associative strength.[30] Consequently, if no other variable
is operating to favor the retention of digits,[31] people
should have better recall for letters than for digits.
Therefore, I[32] predicted that when participants try to
memorize a set of digits and a set of letters, participants
will[33] remember more letters than digits.[34]

---

[29]Ann wisely used "whereas" instead of "while" so that readers would know she meant "but" rather than "during."

[30]Ann used parallel structure to help the reader note and remember the difference between the rich associative strength of words and the poor associative strength of numbers. (For more on what parallel structure is and how you can use it to improve your writing, see 6.4.3.)

[31]Admit flaws in your argument, questionable assumptions you are making, and qualifications to your argument before your readers think they have discovered a problem that you overlooked.

[32]The use of "I" is proper. The experiment did not make the prediction. "We" did not make the prediction. Ann made the prediction—and said so.

[33]One of the few times to use the future tense in a research report is when stating your prediction about what will happen. Note, however, that because Ann made the prediction in the past, Ann wrote, "I predicted."

[34]The last paragraph of the Introduction develops the logic of the study and ends by stating the hypothesis. (For more about how to write the last part of your Introduction, see 3.4.2.) Note also that a main problem students have with the Introduction is organizing it. To make sure that your Introduction is organized, outline it. To help the reader see that your Introduction is organized, use some of the techniques Ann used (see footnotes 20, 21, 23, 24, 28, and 30).

Method[35]

Participants[36]

Seventy-two[37] members of an introductory psychology class (50 women and 22 men,[38] mean age = 20.4 years,[39] *SD* = 2.1) participated voluntarily as part of a class exercise. All participants were treated in accordance with the "Ethical Principles of Psychologists and Code of Conduct" (American Psychological Association, 2002).[40]

Materials[41]

We selected two lists that excluded meaningful combinations.[42] The list of letters was[43] *G, U, X, K, P, M,*

---

[35]The Method section does not usually start on a new page. Note that its heading is centered but not italicized.

[36]When studying humans, use the term "participants" to acknowledge participation rather than the term "subjects." Note that major sections, such as Method, Results, and Discussion, begin with centered headings. Subdivisions within these sections have italicized headings (e.g., *"Participants"*) that start on the left margin. Note that the section's text is not on the same line as the heading. Instead, it begins as an independent paragraph one double-spaced line below and five spaces to the right of the heading.

[37]Usually, numbers 10 and above should not be written out but should instead be expressed in digits. However, any number starting a sentence must be spelled out rather than expressed in numerals.

[38]Do not use the term "females." Furthermore, do not use one term (e.g., "girls") to describe female participants while using a nonequivalent term (e.g., "men") to describe male participants. (For more tips on avoiding sexist language, see 1.3.4.)

[39]According to the *Publication Manual*, you must be specific about the age of your participants.

[40]According to the *Publication Manual*, you must state that participants were treated ethically.

[41]If the experiment had used any specialized equipment (not standard laboratory equipment such as stopwatches), Ann might have added an Apparatus section. The Apparatus section, like the Materials section, would probably have come before the Procedure section.

[42]Always mention any steps you took to improve the validity of your study. These steps not only boost your credibility but also help others replicate your study.

[43]Note that "list" is the subject of the sentence. It is singular and requires a singular verb. Therefore, Ann wrote that the list "was" rather than that the list "were." In other words, "of letters" is a prepositional phrase, not the subject of the sentence.

B, T, C, S, L, F. The list of digits was 3, 5, 9, 4, 1, 0, 5, 3, 6, 2, 5, 0.[44]

Procedure

The experimenter read the set of 12 digits at 1 digit per s. After another 30 s,[45] the experimenter asked the class to write down as many digits as they could remember, in order. The experimenter then read the set of 12 letters and asked the class to write down as many letters as they could remember, in order.[46] Finally, learners scored their own lists, giving themselves one point for each item that they had recalled in the correct position. They summed the number correct for each list to get a total for each list.[47]

Thus, the design was within-subjects with two levels (letters vs. digits). The dependent measure was how many items were correctly remembered from each list.[48]

---

[44]If including the materials had taken up much more space, Ann would have probably put them in an appendix.

[45]Abbreviate standard units and omit periods. (For more on abbreviations, see 3.6.8.)

[46]Note that the Procedure section is organized around time—what happened first, what happened second, and so on.

[47]Ann needed to provide this information so that (a) readers could understand how Ann obtained the scores that were entered into the analysis, (b) other researchers could replicate the study, and (c) readers could evaluate the possibility that the results would have been different if someone other than the learner had scored the recall. Sometimes, an author will put this information in a separate section called "Data scoring."

[48]Ann could have put the last two sentences in a separate Design section or in the Participants section.

Results

The number of items correctly remembered from each list was analyzed using a within-subjects *t* test and an alpha level of .05.[49] The hypothesis was not supported: Participants did not recall significantly more letters ($M = 6.22$, $SD = 7.92$) than digits ($M = 6.44$, $SD = 8.04$),[50] $t(71) = -1.21$.[51, 52]

Discussion

The results failed to confirm the hypothesis that letters would be easier to remember than digits.[53, 54] There are at least four explanations for the failure to confirm the hypothesis.

First, perhaps the hypothesis that letters are better recalled than digits is wrong. Letters may not be better recalled than digits because any associative advantages letter stimuli might enjoy are offset by other advantages

---

[49]State the significance (alpha) level of your statistical test(s) (see 3.6.1).

[50]Note the use of summary statistics describing the typical score (usually using means) and the spread of the distribution (often using standard deviations). Note also that the abbreviations for these statistics are italicized. These descriptive statistics are included to (a) help the reader understand the pattern of the results and to (b) help investigators who might want to include your study in their meta-analysis of related studies.

[51]Confine your evaluation of the results to a statistical evaluation; do not discuss methodological problems that may account for the results. Such discussions belong in the Discussion.

[52]There is no need for either a table or figure of these results because Ann has only two means to discuss. With such simple results, the reader does not need a table or figure to understand the results. However, your professor may still require you to make a table or figure to give you practice in making tables or graphs.

[53]The first sentence summarizes the results (3.7.1).

[54]Note that participants actually recalled more digits than letters. However, because the difference was not significant, Ann wisely does not discuss the difference as though it were significant (3.6.1).

of digit stimuli. For example, digits may be easier to recall because (a) there are fewer digits than letters (10 as opposed to 26) and (b) digits are more commonly used in isolation than letters.

Second, although letters, as a rule, have more associative strength than digits, perhaps this general rule did not hold for the carefully selected list used in this experiment. It seems likely that a set of letters such as *U N I V X Y Z B S* would be relatively easy for some people to remember. Future research should take into account a wider range of possible association values in the letters (cf. Glaze, 1928).[55]

Third, even if most people show a memory advantage for letters over numbers, this advantage might not have held for the particular participants in this study. University students may be more experienced than the general population at remembering numbers.[56]

---

[55]The abbreviation "cf." means "compare." The abbreviation is used because the comment is inside parentheses. (For more on abbreviations, see 7.2.5.)

[56]As we stressed in 3.7.2, point out weaknesses and limitations of your study.

Fourth, procedural problems in this study could have obscured the advantage of memory for letters. For example, the experimenter always presented letters second. Consequently, participants could have experienced fatigue that reduced their recall for letters (see Woodworth & Schlosberg, 1954, for a review of fatigue effects). In addition, the sample size of 72[57] may have been insufficient to detect the superior recall for letters, especially if the effect is small.[58]

The question about the advantage of letter stimuli in memory is still open. Researchers could seek a more definitive answer by modifying this study (a) to include larger and more varied samples of both learners and of stimuli and (b) to balance order of presentation of letter and digit stimuli. From this experiment, however, we can tentatively conclude[59] that any effect of letters being better recalled than digits is weak.[60]

---

[57]Usually, numbers above 10 are expressed using digits.

[58]Normally, if you have nonsignificant results, you need to discuss the statistical power of your study. However, Ann did not have the statistical background to present detailed information about power.

[59]Note use of present tense for conclusions. (For more on tense, see 3.11 and footnotes 27 and 33.)

[60]Despite the nonsignificant results, Ann has come up with a conclusion likely to reassure a reader that he or she has learned something useful from reading the report.

Memory for Digits   11

References[61]

[62]American Psychological Association.[63] (2002). Ethical
principles of psychologists and code of conduct.
American Psychologist,[64] *57*,[65] 1060-1073.

Glaze, J. A. (1928). The association value of nonsense
syllables.[66] *Journal of Genetic Psychology, 35*, 225-269.

[67]Hilgard, E.,[68] & Bower, G. H. (1966). *Theories of
learning*. New York: Appleton-Century-Crofts.

Wechsler, D. (1939). *The measurement of adult
intelligence*.[69] Baltimore: Williams & Wilkins.

Woodworth, R. S., & Schlossberg, H. (1954). *Experimental
psychology* (rev. ed.).[70] London: Methuen.[71]

---

[61]Start the reference list on a new page and center the heading ("References"). (For more on the reference list, see 4.9.1.)

[62]In the Reference section, the indenting style is the opposite of the indenting for the rest of the paper. Specifically, APA advocates "hanging indent style" in which the first line of a reference is not indented, but additional lines are indented five spaces. To see how to program your word processor to make hanging indents, see the Chapter 4 section of our website.

[63]This is an example of a reference for which the author is an organization.

[64]All major words in a journal name are capitalized; the entire journal name is italicized.

[65]Volume number and journal title are italicized.

[66]Usually, only the first letter of the first word of the title of an article is capitalized. The article title is not italicized.

[67]List references in alphabetical order according to the last name of the first author. Thus, this reference comes after, rather than before, Glaze.

[68]In the reference section, always use a comma between authors' names—even when you have only two authors.

[69]Usually, only the first letter of the first word of a book title is capitalized. However, the entire title is always italicized.

[70]The title of the book is italicized, but not the information in parentheses informing the reader that it is a revised edition.

[71]The reference list for this paper is weak: The references are out of date and only one is a journal article reporting on an empirical study.

Memory for Digits   12

Author Note[72]

Ann A. Student, an undergraduate student at Alpha University.[73]

I thank[74] M. I. Tuder for guiding my thinking on this topic and I. M. Goode for commenting on previous drafts.

Correspondence concerning this article should be addressed to I. B. Professor, Department of Psychology, Alpha University, Alpha, CA 97804. E-mail: myprof@alpha.edu

---

[72]The author note will often be the last page of your paper.

[73]We realize that the first line of the Author Note is not a sentence, much less a paragraph. It is, however, in the form prescribed by the *Publication Manual*.

[74]Thank anyone who gives you general or editorial help. (For more on giving proper credit and on academic honesty, see 1.2.4.)

3.13   Report and Proposal Content Checklist

—— My title is simple and to the point. It contains the names of the relevant variables (in an experiment, the independent and dependent variables; in a correlational study, the predictor and criterion variables).

—— My Abstract is a brief summary of the following sections of my paper: the Introduction—what I studied and why, the Participants section— who the participants were, the Procedure section—what the participants did, the Results section—whether the data supported the hypothesis, and the Discussion section—the meaning of the results.

—— I cited any source from which I got ideas—even if I did not directly quote that source.

—— My citations are free of the following common content errors:
  —— When citing authors, I limited myself to stating authors' last names. I did not mention authors' first names, professional titles (e.g., "Dr."), or professional affiliations.
  —— When citing sources, I used parentheses. I did not use footnotes to cite sources.
  —— I did not mention any article titles in the text of my paper.

—— Most of my citations are from recent journal articles describing actual research studies rather than from secondhand sources (textbooks, magazines, etc.).

Introduction

—— The beginning of my introduction illustrates why my topic area is important.

—— I cited several studies related to my topic.

—— I explained why testing my hypothesis is important: I showed how my study builds on previous work or fills a gap in previous work.

—— I explained why I believe that the hypothesis might be true. To make the logic behind my hypothesis clear, I explained relevant concepts and theories.

—— My hypothesis is clearly stated.

—— My Introduction foreshadows the rest of the paper (especially the essence of the Method section).

Method

—— I divided the Method section into at least two subsections (Participants and Procedure).

—— I specified how I selected or recruited my sample.

___ I indicated how participants were compensated (if they were compensated).

___ I included the number of participants of each gender,

___ I specified the age of participants (average age and either standard deviation or range of ages), and

___ I included other demographic characteristics, when appropriate.

___ I specified the number of participants who dropped out of the study or whose data was not analyzed and the reasons for not having data from all my participants.

___ I explained how participants were assigned to condition.

___ I made it clear that participants were treated ethically.

___ If I used standard laboratory equipment, I identified the manufacturer and model number.

___ If I borrowed questions from other sources, I made that clear—and cited those sources.

___ I focused on what happened to participants and what participants did—and presented the information in order from the first thing that happened to the last thing that happened.

___ It is clear how (under what conditions) I tested each participant.

___ It is clear how I turned each participant's response into a score.

___ It is clear what I did to reduce researcher bias.

___ It is clear how a control or comparison group ruled out an alternative explanation for a difference between groups.

___ It is clear that the measure being used is reliable and valid because
   ___ If I used a published measure, I cited evidence of the measure's reliability and validity.
   ___ If I collected data related to the measure's reliability or validity, I reported those data. For example, if I had data related to the extent to which two different observers' scores agreed when scoring the same response, I reported those data.

___ It is clear from my paper that my study is a good way to test my hypothesis.

Results

___ I included enough information about descriptive statistics to help readers know more than just the outcome of the statistical significance test. For example, if I used a t test, I presented means and standard deviations for the two conditions.

___ I determined my professor's views about reporting analyses beyond that of significance tests. Thus, I know whether my professor required me to follow the *Publication Manual*'s suggestions that I include a confidence interval, or report an estimate of effect size, such as Cohen's *d* (e.g., "$F(2,46) = 3.85$, $p < .05$, $d = .27$").

___ I made it clear to the reader what data I used in the analyses (how behaviors were turned into scores), if it was not obvious or if I did not include this information in the Method section.

___ I explained what analyses I used on those data.

___ I specified what significance level I used (if I used a significance test).

___ I explained why I did that analysis.

___ I indicated which groups scored significantly higher (I usually did this by including, in the text, average scores for my different groups. The summary statistics I included in text (averages) were usually sufficient to help the reader see the pattern in my data. However, I used a table or a graph if (a) I had more than four conditions, or (b) my professor required one.).

___ I indicated whether the results support my hypothesis.

___ If I used tables, I made sure that each table added meaningful information beyond that which was presented in the text of my Results section.

___ I made sure that each table was referred to in the text of my paper (e.g., "As Table 1 indicates,").

Discussion

___ My first sentence summarizes the results as they relate to my hypothesis.

___ I compared my Discussion against the citation checklist.

___ I interpreted my results in the context of the theory, past research, and practical issues that I noted in my Introduction. For example, I compared my results to what other researchers found.

___ I tried to explain results that did not fit my predictions.

___ I addressed alternative explanations for my results. I tried to rule out these alternative explanations, but when I could not, I admitted that I could not.

___ I pointed out the weaknesses and limitations of my study. I even sketched out future research that researchers could do to correct these weaknesses or overcome these limitations.

___ If I believed I could make a case for generalizing my results (I had a representative sample, the results were similar to what others had found, etc.), I made such a case.

___ I treated nonsignificant results as inconclusive.

___ I did not use nonsignificant results as proof that a treatment had no effect.

___ I did not use nonsignificant results that were almost significant as evidence that the treatment had an effect.

___ I ended with a brief paragraph that restates the main findings and highlights how those findings both fill a gap in existing research and suggest directions for future research.

References

___ All the references in this section are also cited in my paper. If a reference was not cited, I either added that citation to the body of my paper or I deleted the reference.

___ All the sources cited in my paper are also listed in this section except for "personal communication" citations (see 4.3.3), original works that I did not read, but which I learned about through a secondary source (see 4.3.2), and ancient works, such as the Bible.

3.14 Summary

1. The sections of a research report or proposal should appear in this order: Title, Abstract, Introduction, Method, Results, Discussion, References, Appendixes (optional), Author Note, Tables (optional), Figure Caption page (optional), and Figures (optional).

2. The title should be short. For an experiment, it should usually include the independent variable(s) and the dependent variable.

3. The Abstract is a short, unindented paragraph that summarizes the paper.

4. In the Introduction (the "why" section of the paper), you should introduce and state the hypothesis.

5. The Method section (the "how" section of the paper) usually has at least two subsections: a "Participants" section (called a "Subjects" section if you studied nonhuman animals), and a "Procedure" section.

6. In the Results section, for each analysis, tell the reader what the analysis was, why you did it, and whether the results of that analysis support your hypothesis.

7. You may be able to present your results without a figure or a table. If you have a table or a figure, refer to it in text.

8. Line graphs are usually best when you are summarizing the results of an experiment in which you manipulated the amount of a variable. If, on the other hand, your experiment involves comparing different kinds of treatments or

comparing a treatment group to a control group, you should probably use a bar graph. Scatterplots are most appropriate when your study does not involve manipulating a variable (e.g., you correlated scores on two tests).

9. Usually, units of measurement in any part of your report must be expressed in metric units.

10. Begin the Discussion by relating the results to the hypothesis. Next, relate your results to previous research. Then, discuss limitations of your study that may qualify your conclusions. Finally, discuss the implications of your study for future research.

11. All the sources in your reference list should be cited in your paper. To see an example of how to format your references, see either the term paper's references (2.11) or the sample research report's references (3.12). To learn more about formatting your reference page, see 4.9.

12. If your professor wants an Author Note, start the Author Note on the page following the appendixes using the centered heading: Author Note. (If you do not have appendixes, start the Author Note on the page following the references.)

CHAPTER

4

Finding, Reading, Citing, and Referencing Sources

To write a strong paper, you must show that your claims are solid and relevant. You show your claims are solid by supporting them with recent evidence from high-quality sources. You show that your claims are relevant by showing how your work builds on what others have done. Put another way, sources are the raw material from which you build your paper. You must find, extract, refine, cite, and reference that raw material. Thus, to write a strong paper, you must first find high-quality sources so that you can base your paper on the best information available. Next, you must extract material that provides solid support for your claim. Then, you must refine that material: Quoting it is not enough. Finally, you must correctly cite and reference your sources so that you show how your work builds on the work of others.

4.1 Finding Information

4.1.1 Starting Your Search

Your professor will expect you to read current journal articles related to your paper's topic. There are two strategies you can use to find current articles.

The first strategy is to use *Psychological Abstracts, PsycINFO, Social Science Index, Current Contents, Educational Resources Information Center (ERIC), Social Science Citation Index*, or some other database designed to help psychological researchers find recent articles on a topic. The key to using these databases is to know what search terms you should use. You can find the right search terms by using the *Psychological Thesaurus*.

Many of these databases come in either a printed version (e.g., *Psychological Abstracts*) or a computerized version (e.g., *PsycINFO*). If you have the choice, try to use the computerized version. The computerized databases can get you the information you want faster. For example, suppose you are not sure that you are using the right search term. If you are using *PsycINFO*, the computerized version of *Psychological Abstracts*, you just enter whatever term you are using, select the "Index Terms" search field and the computer will automatically convert your term into several appropriate search terms and conduct a search under those terms. If, on the other hand, you are using *Psychological Abstracts*, you need to find your library's copy of the *Thesaurus* (that volume will usually be near the *Abstracts*), look up the term in the Thesaurus, find the appropriate search terms, and then search the Abstracts using those search terms. The biggest advantage of computer searches, however, is when you want to search for more than one term at a time. For example, on a computer, in less than a minute you can find all the review papers on recovered memory of sexual abuse among males that were published in APA journals between 1993 and 2006.

Four problems sometimes crop up in computerized searches. First, you may actually get too many references. In that case, see Table 4.1.

Second, you may have too few references. If that is the case, see Table 4.2 (page 104) or consult a reference librarian.

Third, your library will probably not have all the references you have found. Fortunately, you can obtain most of those articles through interlibrary loan. Unfortunately, interlibrary loan takes time—so if you put off your library search you may be in trouble: Searches delayed are often searches denied.

Fourth, you may be tempted to read abstracts of articles (especially if you are using *PsycINFO*, which gives you abstracts rather than entire articles) rather than reading the actual articles. Although reading abstracts can help you separate out the articles that are relevant to your paper from the articles that are irrelevant, you will not get enough detail from the abstract to allow you to analyze the article. You will learn far more if you read the papers themselves. Therefore, when the online abstract of an article suggests that the article is relevant to your paper, take the time to find and read the entire article.

In addition to using databases, there is a second strategy for finding journal articles—consulting secondhand sources. As we will discuss in the next section, a secondhand source such as a chapter in a textbook, a chapter in the *Annual Review of*

T A B L E **4.1**   What to Do If a *PsycINFO or PsycARTICLES* Search Produces Too Many Sources*

Modify Your Quick Search	Example
Limit your search to a publication type.	Under the "Publication Type" menu, scroll down and select "All Journals."
Limit your search to peer reviewed journals.	Check off option "Peer Reviewed," or under "Publication Type" scroll down and select "Peer Reviewed Journal."
Limit the number of articles by selecting specfic publication dates.	Next to "Published Date," fill in the date boxes.
Limit your search to a specific population.	Select a specific age group (e.g., "Child-hood") or population group (e.g., "Human" or "Male") by scrolling down and selecting your choice on the appropriate menu.

Conduct a Fielded Search	Example
Narrow your search by adding a search term.	• 1st search term: "Alzheimer's." • Select **"and"** in the scroll bar located below "Look for." • 2nd search term: "resilience."
Limit your search by excluding concepts.	• 1st search term: "Alzheimer's." • Select **"not"** in the scroll bar located below "Look for." • 2nd search term: "depression."
Limit the search fields.	Instead of searching "any field," select "Title" or "Author."
Limit your search to journals.	Under the "Publication Type" menu, scroll down and select "All Journals."
Limit your search to peer reviewed journals	Check off option "Peer Reviewed," or under "Publication Type" scroll down and select "Peer Reviewed Journal."
Limit your search to a specific journal.	Type in the journal's name next to "Publica-tion Name" (e.g., *Developmental Psychology* or other journals your library has).
Limit the number of years or months searched.	Next to "Published Date," fill in the date boxes.

*Most of this advice is also relevant for computer searches in EBSCO, *ERIC*, and other databases.

TABLE 4.2   What to Do If a *PsycINFO* or *PsycARTICLES* Search Retrieves an Insufficient Number of Sources*

Expanding Either a Quick Search or a Fielded Search	Example
Expand your search by selecting additional publication types.	Select "All" under "Publication Type."
Combine search terms with the word "or."	Search term: "aging OR older."
Conduct a truncated search by adding an "*" following the stem of your search term.	A search for "moral*" will find articles that include "moral," "moralistic," and "morality."

Special Tip for Expanding a Fielded Search	Example
In addition to the above tips, expand your search to include similar search terms by checking "Also search for related words."	If your search term is "aging," the search will include similar terms that are contained in APA's *Psychological Thesaurus* such as "older," "elderly," and "mature."

*Most of this advice is also relevant for computer searches in EBSCO, *ERIC*, and other databases.

Psychology, or a review article in a journal such as *Psychological Science*, will describe and reference relevant articles.

4.1.2 Using One Reference to Find More References

Once you find one relevant article, you can use that article to find other relevant articles. Imagine that you have only found one reference for your assignment: Researcher (2006). When you read Researcher's paper, you may discover that the topic was first identified by Originator (1986), that much of the important work was conducted by Refiner (2003), and that some current work is also being done by Current (in press). You can find these sources from Researcher's reference list.[1] Originator (1986), Refiner (2003), and Current (in press) may have other useful sources in their reference lists.

Although looking at reference lists can educate you about the history of the topic, it will not get you the recent references you need. Fortunately, there are two ways that an older reference can lead to newer references.

First, you can use an older article to get leads to recent articles. To illustrate, suppose Refiner (2003) is a particularly important paper for your assignment. In that case, you could probably find recent, related articles by doing either a *PsycINFO*

---

[1]If the reference list refers to a website that no longer exists, you may be able to find that website by looking it up at http://web.archive.org.

citation search or a *Social Science Citation Index* search. To do a citation search in *PsycINFO*, you would click on "citation search" and then type in the Refiner (2003) reference in the "search" box. You would then get a list of papers that cited Refiner (2003). If Innovator (2007) and Novel (2007) are on that list, those papers are probably relevant to your assignment. If they are, their reference lists may lead you to still more references. To do a *Social Science Citation Index* search, you would go to the most recent volume (e.g., the 2007 volume) of *Social Science Citation Index* and look up Refiner (2003). The index will give you a list of papers written in that year whose authors cited Refiner (2003).

Second, you can search for recent work by the researcher who wrote the original article. A search for other articles written by the same researcher (e.g., "[name of author of original article] in AU") will probably lead you to other relevant articles because the researcher probably did not immediately abandon a line of fruitful research. In addition to tracking down that researcher's published papers, you may want to track down that researcher's website. The author's website may provide links to relevant unpublished work (e.g., papers written by the author or by the author's graduate students) and to the websites of other researchers doing work relevant to the topic.

4.1.3 Reading the Right Stuff

An important part of understanding your assignment is understanding what sources your professor will accept. Most professors, as well as the editors of the *Publication Manual*, expect that you will read, cite, and reference *empirical articles* (articles in which authors report their own research) from high-quality journals. Unfortunately, students often violate this expectation. These violations come in three forms.

The most serious violation is reading an article in a magazine (e.g., *Psychology Today*, *Time*, *Newsweek*) rather than a journal article. (If you are unsure of the difference between magazines and journals, see Table 4.3, page 106.) At worst, magazine articles may misrepresent and misinterpret research findings. At best, magazine articles provide few details about how the research was conducted. In any case, reading secondhand accounts of research in magazine articles does not help you develop the ability to read and critique the firsthand accounts of research that you find in empirical journal articles.

The second most serious violation is reading review articles (in which authors discuss other people's research) instead of reading empirical articles (in which researchers provide firsthand reports of their own research).[2] Although review articles integrate many research studies, they are still secondhand accounts of research. These secondhand accounts may be slanted by their authors' theoretical positions. Furthermore, reading secondhand accounts of research does not give you practice in critiquing firsthand accounts of research studies. (To learn about a few of the journals that specialize in firsthand accounts of research, see Table 4.4, page 106.)

---

[2]Your professor may want you to read review articles in addition to—but not instead of—empirical articles. Note also that because a review article will cite and reference empirical articles, a recent review article may help you find relevant empirical articles.

TABLE **4.3** How Psychological Journals Differ From Magazines

Journal Articles	Magazines
Follow APA format. For example, they have an Abstract and a Reference list.	Do not follow APA format.
Usually list reviewers or consulting editors—and their professional (usually university) affiliation inside the front or back cover. Most of these individuals will have Ph.D.s.	List the magazine staff (but no affiliations) somewhere in the first few pages of the publication. It is likely that none of these individuals will have Ph.D.s.
Usually have instructions for how to submit papers for publication.	Usually do not provide instructions on how to submit articles.
The title of the journal often includes the word "Journal," "Research," or "Bulletin." If the publisher is not the American Psychological Association, the American Psychological Society, or another scientific organization, the journal describes itself (usually on the cover, inside the cover, or on a page before the articles start) as the journal of a certain scientific society or organization.	The title usually does not include the word "Journal." The magazine is rarely affiliated with a professional organization. For example, *Psychology Today* is not affiliated with any group of professional psychologists.
In journals, there are no discontinuous pages for an article: Once a reader starts an article, the reader does not have to skip any page to continue reading the article.	Articles in magazines often have discontinuous pages: To continue reading an article, the reader may have to skip over pages of ads, or the reader may have to follow instructions such as "continued on page 121."
Journals have a more serious look: They usually do not have color pictures. Ads are usually for professional books and other products of interest only to professionals in the field. There are no ads for consumer products.	Most magazines are designed to attract a popular audience. The overall impression is less serious than a professional journal. The magazine contains many glossy pages, color pictures, and ads for commercial products.

TABLE **4.4** A Sample of Journals That Publish Research Articles

Journal	Brief Description
American Education Research Journal	Reports research in education.
Behavioral Neuroscience	Emphasizes biological basis of behavior. Some of the articles are difficult to understand if you do not have a background in chemistry and endocrinology.
Developmental Psychology	Primarily reports research relating to child and adolescent development.

TABLE 4.4   A Sample of Journals That Publish Research Articles—*continued*

Journal	Brief Description
Journal of Abnormal Psychology	Articles focus on the treatment and diagnosis of psychopathology. Occasionally reports experimental studies on humans or animals related to emotion or pathology. Sometimes reports studies that test hypotheses derived from psychological theories.
Journal of Applied Behavior Analysis	Articles report a sizable effect on an important behavior, usually employing a single-participant design.
Journal of Applied Psychology	Reports research relating to industry, government, health, education, consumer affairs, and other applied areas.
Journal of Comparative Psychology	Articles may include both laboratory and field observation of species. Emphasis is on relating findings to the theory of evolution.
Journal of Counseling Psychology	Publishes research articles evaluating the effectiveness of (a) counseling and (b) techniques for selecting and training counselors.
Journals of Experimental Psychology	Publishes research on fundamental mechanisms and processes. There are four different journals:
	Journal of Experimental Psychology: General
	Journal of Experimental Psychology: Animal Behavior Processes
	Journal of Experimental Psychology: Learning, Memory, and Cognition
	Journal of Experimental Psychology: Human Perception and Performance
Journal of Experimental Social Psychology	Almost all articles report the results of social psychological experiments.
Journal of Personality and Social Psychology	Contains three sections: (a) attitudes and social cognition, (b) interpersonal relations and group processes, and (c) personality and individual differences.
Journal of Social Psychology	Source of relatively short articles.
Memory and Cognition	A good source of articles in human experimental psychology. See also *Journal of Experimental Psychology: Learning, Memory, and Cognition.*
Personality and Social Psychology Bulletin	Contains short articles that are often easy to understand.
Psychological Assessment: A Journal of Consulting and Clinical Psychology	Publishes research that assesses the validity of a variety of tests and measures.
Psychological Record	Source of short articles.
Psychology and Aging	Source of easy-to-read articles on physiological and behavioral aspects of aging during older adulthood.

The third most serious violation is failing to use articles from high-quality journals. There are three main reasons that students fail to use articles from elite journals.

First, students may not appreciate that journals vary in quality. Journals vary in quality because journals vary in how likely they are to accept an article. For journals that most professors consider high quality (typically journals sponsored by APA or American Psychological Society [APS]), many manuscripts are submitted but few are published. Usually, manuscripts are rejected because the study had methodological flaws or the study was not considered as important as the studies that were published. Whereas the articles that are published in a high-quality journal have survived a rigorous screening process, articles published in journals that professors consider low quality (typically, journals not sponsored by a professional psychological organization and publishing the majority of the manuscripts submitted to it) have not been as extensively prescreened. [3]

Second, students may fail to use articles from a high-quality journal because they are using Internet sources instead of journal articles. Unfortunately, the Internet is often a questionable source. Some of the information presented as fact on the Internet has little research support, and much of it is not of sufficient quality to be published in a reputable academic journal. Although there is some trustworthy information on the Internet, that information is usually trustworthy because it already appeared in a reputable, reviewed, printed journal.

Third, students may not use an article from a high-quality journal because they do not see how that article is relevant to their paper. Thus, students investigating a specific topic (e.g., discrimination against students who smoke) often fail to realize that articles in an elite journal that study a more general topic (e.g., discrimination) as well as articles that study a slightly different topic (e.g., discrimination against lesbians) are probably relevant to their particular topic. As a result, students may ignore a journal article published in a highly regarded journal that discovers a general principle (e.g., a way to reduce discrimination) but treasure an article in a lower-quality journal that applies that general principle to a specific case (e.g., seeing whether that principle works to reduce discrimination against people who smoke).

In short, your sources should include articles from elite journals. The following three tips will help you include such articles.

1. Realize that the particular phenomenon you are investigating probably represents a particular example of a more general phenomenon. Consequently, principles that affect other attitudes also affect the attitude you are studying; principles that affect other behaviors probably also affect the behavior you are investigating. Therefore, do not exclude an article from your paper merely because it does not study exactly the same behavior, attitude, or population that you are investigating.

---

[3]Usually, the organization sponsoring the journal will be prominently mentioned on either the front or the back of the journal's cover.

2. If you find an article that does examine the behavior or attitude you are focusing on, check its reference list for articles from elite journals that investigated a more general topic.

3. Make sure that at least some of your sources come from journals sponsored by APA or APS.

4.2 Reading

4.2.1 Read Purposefully

As we have discussed, you should find recent journal articles that contain firsthand research. Before you start reading those articles, be sure you are clear about the questions you are trying to answer. Your questions should relate to your thesis statement (if you are writing a term paper) or to your hypothesis (if you are writing a research report). Focusing on the questions you are trying to answer will help you decide which articles to read: You will know, after reading an article's Abstract, whether you should read the rest of that article. As you read the article, continue to focus on the question you want to answer. Focusing on the questions you are trying to answer will help you take useful notes on the article.

4.2.2 Take Notes

Before you start taking notes on the article, record the full reference as it should appear in your paper's reference list (to see how to format a reference in APA style, see 4.9.11). Recording the full reference will allow you to return to the source if you need to and prevent you from needing to return to the source (often the night before the paper is due) merely to complete your reference page.

Before you take notes, you may also want to spend some time deciding how you are going to take notes. For example, you might decide to use a note-taking system like the one in Exhibit 4.1 (page 110).

Before you take notes, read through the article at least once, understand the article, and reflect on how it relates to your paper. Taking many notes while you are reading an article for the first time is often just a substitute for thinking about what you are reading. At best, you have merely copied material. At worst, you may be setting yourself up to plagiarize.

To avoid plagiarizing, be sure (a) to place quotation marks around any paragraphs, sentences, or even phrases of three or more words that you copy and (b) to note the page number. To prevent yourself from merely copying information, use a system of note taking that encourages you to think. The following system might work for you: Precede each "fact" you note with an S if it is the author's own idea, conclusion, theory, or opinion (S because the author Stated it); a C if it is another's fact the author has Cited; or an R if it is a Result of the author's research. Alternatively, you might try using Exhibit 4.1 as a guide for note taking. Using a system like the one described in

EXHIBIT **4.1**   Note-Taking System to Encourage Critical Thinking

1. APA style reference of the article

2. Short description of study
   a. Type of study (correlational/experimental)
   b. The results support (do not support) my hypothesis/thesis because
   c. This study is related to the following other studies
   d. I will use this study in my paper to
   e. The study's main strength is
   f. The study's main weakness is

3. In-depth analysis
   Measure
       Consistency with definition
       Evidence of validity
       Potential for bias
   Manipulation
       Strength
       Potential for bias
        Standardization
        Blind/masked
   Sample
       Size
       Age
       Gender composition
       Diversity

   Were the author's cause-effect statements justifiable (see 5.9.1)?
   Were the author's generalizations justified (see 5.9.5)?
   Were null results properly interpreted (see 5.9.2)?
   What other explanations are there for the results?

4. Notes taken from individual pages of the source

Source page number	Note from that page	Type of note (Q = quote, P = paraphrase, SU = summary, MR = my reaction)	Reason for note I took that note because _____ (e.g., the passage supports [contradicts] my thesis).

Exhibit 4.1 will help you spot common flaws in research. (For more help on spotting flaws in research, see Chapter 5.)

4.2.3 Reread

You will have to read articles more than once. Your job is not to scan them but to dissect them. Many professors spend hours studying a single article. Do not expect that you can gain an in-depth understanding faster than professors can. To help you understand what you will get by reading an article more than once, study Table 4.5. As you can see from studying Table 4.5, the first time through the article, your focus is on

TABLE **4.5** What to Look for in a Journal Article

	First Time Through	Second Time Through
Introduction	Why do we care about this area of research? Do I understand the theory or the studies that set up this research? If not, what references do I need to read? What are the hypotheses? Why do the authors expect their hypotheses to be supported? If this study cures a weakness in previous research, what was wrong with previous research? If this study fills a gap in previous research, what was that gap?	Do I agree with their arguments? Does the hypothesis really follow from theory or previous research? If they had obtained different results, what would they have changed in their introduction?
Method	How were participants selected? What was the age and gender composition of the sample? What population did the sample represent? What was done to the participants? If there were manipulated variables, how were those variables manipulated? What did participants do? What was the measured variable? What was the design? Do I understand how the study's method allowed the researcher to test the hypothesis?	Are there any reasons to expect that the researchers might have obtained different results with a different population of participants? Were groups equivalent before the study began? Were there enough participants? Was there a problem with participants dropping out of the study? Are there any variables that the researchers should have controlled or manipulated? If I had been a participant, would I have guessed the hypothesis? Would I have taken the task seriously? Were the control groups adequate? Would it have been better to use a different measure?
Results	How were participants' responses turned into the scores used in the analyses? What are the average scores for the different groups? Do the results support the hypothesis?	Do the statistics directly test the predictions made in the introduction? Do the statistical tests match up with the verbal descriptions? That is, if the authors say that Group 1 scored better than Group 2, do they have an analysis that directly compares Group 1 against Group 2? Are the statistics appropriate? Did they correctly report their null (nonsignificant) results as failing to reject the null hypothesis?

(continued)

TABLE **4.5**   What to Look for in a Journal Article—*continued*

	First Time Through	**Second Time Through**
Discussion	Do they think the results matched their predictions? How do they explain any discrepancies? What additional studies do they recommend?	What are other explanations for the results? The other explanation could come from (a) a problem with their study that the authors did not mention or from (b) a theory or hypothesis that the author did not mention. Are there additional studies I would recommend? Did the authors make cause-effect statements on the basis of correlational evidence? Did the authors state something that was not supported by the results? For example, did they treat a nonsignificant result as significant or talk about a comparison that they did not statistically test?

understanding what the author is saying. The second time through, your focus is on questioning what the author is saying.

4.2.4 Revise Your Notes

Revising your notes before you start writing can help you in at least three ways. First, it will help you understand the material better. Whereas your original notes will probably consist largely of copied phrases, your rewritten notes should consist of paraphrases, summaries, and critiques. Second, it will help you organize your paper. Third, it will help you see relationships among studies. For example, reorganizing your original notes using the scheme presented in Exhibit 4.2 should help you organize your paper and help you get insights into how studies fit together.

4.3 Citing

Whenever you put information from your notes on a source into the text of your paper, you must accompany that information with a *citation* to that source. Usually, your citation will consist of the last names of the source's authors and the source's year of publication. In most cases, that information will be enough to achieve the main goal of most citations: to provide the reader with enough information about the source that the reader can use your citation to find the complete *reference* to the source in your reference list (see 4.9).

EXHIBIT **4.2**   A System to Help See Connections Among Studies

	Research Study	
	Study 1	Study 2
Reference (in APA style) Type of study (experimental vs. correlational) Measures used Sample (number and type of participants) Precautions used to prevent bias Results of study (supported hypothesis, contradicted hypothesis, or null results)		

You must take thorough notes so that you can support the claims you will make in your paper. Whenever you make a claim, you should provide evidence (e.g., a study, a statistic) to support your claim. When you provide evidence, you must cite the source of that evidence, unless (a) your evidence is a well-known fact or (b) your paper is the source of that evidence (e.g., it was reported in your Results section).

You must also use citations whenever you present someone else's ideas (e.g., words, concepts, criticisms, theories, methods). If you fail to give a source's authors credit for their ideas, you are guilty of plagiarism. To avoid plagiarism, (a) if you borrowed ideas from a source, cite that source—even if you did not quote that source; and (b) if you are in doubt about whether to cite a source, cite it.

4.3.1 Choosing a Citation Type

In psychology papers, you do not use footnotes to cite your sources. Instead, you have a choice between two citation types: *name* citations and *parenthetical* citations.

If you use a name citation, you will probably make the author's(s') last name(s) the subject of the sentence. Right after the names, put the year of publication. Enclose that year—but not the name(s)—in parentheses. Thus, you might write, "Jones (2006) noted that the studies failing to find a significant effect had insufficient power." If you wanted to use a name citation without making the author(s) the subject of the sentence, you might write, "According to Jones (2006), the studies failing to find a significant effect had insufficient power."

In a parenthetical citation, you provide the same information as a name citation: The difference is that both the author's(s') last name(s) and the year of publication are in parentheses. Thus, you might write, "The studies failing to find a significant effect had insufficient power (Jones, 2006)."

In your paper, you should use both name and parenthetical citations for two reasons. First, varying your citation type creates variety in your sentence structure, thereby making your paper more interesting to read. Second, varying your citation type is often necessary because the two citation types accomplish different goals. Consequently, as you will see in the next section, a citation type that works well with one citation may be awkward with another citation.

Use a name citation when you are going to paraphrase extensively, such as when you are introducing a study that is important to your paper. A sentence such as "Smith (2005) conducted an experiment on the problem of response bias in psychological tests" lets the reader know that the rest of what follows refers to Smith's experiment (e.g., "She tested 20 people . . ." refers to what Smith did in her experiment). You may also want to use a name citation when introducing a work by a well-known author. In such a case, a name citation would assist readers who are already familiar with the work of the person you are citing by providing them with a clue about what they are about to read. For example, if you write, "Piaget (1953) stated," sophisticated readers will anticipate the particular points of Piaget's theory that you are going to outline.

When using name citations, the authors' names must fit into the grammar of the sentence. Thus, if you have more than one author, verbs relating to what the authors did must be plural rather than singular. Examples of common errors are "Smith and Brown (1967) *states*," or "Brown et al. (1978) *states*." The correct forms are "Smith and Brown (1967) state," and "Brown et al. (1978) state" (et al. means "and others"; see 4.4.3 and 4.4.4).

Unlike name citations, parenthetical citations come after the information to which they refer. A parenthetical citation is particularly useful when you want the reader to focus on the results of a study rather than on who performed the study. By putting the author's name last, you imply that the findings would hold regardless of who did the study. To illustrate, compare "According to Wiseman (1969), IQ and socioeconomic class are correlated" with "IQ and socioeconomic class are correlated (Wiseman, 1969)."

Parenthetical citations also make it easy to cite related studies. To see the superiority of parenthetical citations over name citations for describing related studies, suppose you had used name citations to describe the following studies:

✗ Wiseman (1969) did a study in which he found IQ and socioeconomic class to be correlated. Harris (1975) confirmed this in another study. Finally, Jones and Smith (1977) uncovered the same relationship in a more recent study.

Using parenthetical citations allows you to convey the same information much more efficiently, as you can see from the following example:

✔ Many studies have found that IQ and socioeconomic class are correlated (e.g., Harris, 1975; Jones & Smith, 1977; Wiseman, 1969).[4]

Using parenthetical citations also allows you to show the reader how related studies fit together. In the next example, note how using parenthetical citations summarizes

---

[4]Note that the citations are not in order by date. Instead, they are in alphabetical order according to the last name of each article's first author. To learn more about how to sequence a series of citations, see 4.5.1.

the common information, yet preserves the detail that the studies were conducted in different countries:

✔ Researchers have found that the relationship between IQ and socioeconomic status exists in American (Wiseman, 1969), Australian (Jones & Smith, 1977), and British (Harris, 1975) samples.

There is one serious limitation of parenthetical citations: Each one applies only to the sentence to which it is appended. As a result, when you need to repeat a particular citation in the same paragraph, parenthetical citations can be awkward. To illustrate, consider the following passage:

✗ The phenomenon of blindsight can have three alternative explanations (Ptito, Fortin, & Ptito, 2001). First, light scattered from one part of the retina to an intact part could allow observers to detect a stimulus (Ptito et al., 2001). Second, detection could be accomplished by small areas of residual function (Ptito et al., 2001). Third, blindsight might simply represent a conservative response criterion for near-threshold vision (Ptito et al., 2001).

Unfortunately, some students, in trying to avoid the awkwardness of repeating the same parenthetical citation make a worse mistake: They commit plagiarism. To illustrate, consider the following passage:

✗ The phenomenon of blindsight can have three alternative explanations. First, light scattered from one part of the retina to an intact part could allow observers to detect a stimulus (Ptito, Fortin, & Ptito, 2001). Second, detection could be accomplished by small areas of residual function (Ptito et al., 2001). Third, blindsight might simply represent a conservative response criterion for near-threshold vision (Ptito et al., 2001).

A professor would want the student to provide a citation for the first sentence because it is a statement of fact that needs to be supported. Given the repeated citation of Ptito et al. (2001), the professor would suspect that the first sentence was plagiarized from that source.

Trying to avoid repeating the same parenthetical citation can lead to even more blatant citation problems. To illustrate, imagine that the student has not read Fendrich, Wessinger, and Gazzaniga (2001) but did see it cited in Ptito et al. (2001). Furthermore, imagine that, to minimize repeating Ptito et al., the student wrote the following passage:

✗ The phenomenon of blindsight can have three alternative explanations. First, light scattered from one part of the retina to an intact part could allow observers to detect a stimulus (Ptito, Fortin, & Ptito, 2001). Second, detection could be accomplished by small areas of residual function

> (Fendrich, Wessinger, & Gazzaniga, 2001). Third, blindsight might simply represent a conservative response criterion for near-threshold vision (Ptito et al., 2001).

As before, the first sentence needs a citation because it is a statement that needs to be supported. In addition, the third sentence has an inappropriate citation: The student is citing a source the student has not read.

To avoid the plagiarism and awkwardness problems caused by repeating a particular parenthetical citation in the same paragraph, reorganize the paragraph to use a single name citation. By so rewriting the previous passages, you might write the following paragraph:

✔ Ptito, Fortin, and Ptito (2001) listed three alternative explanations for blindsight. First, light scattered from one part of the retina to an intact part could allow observers to detect a stimulus. Second, detection could be accomplished by small areas of residual function. Third, blindsight might simply represent a conservative response criterion for near-threshold vision.

4.3.2 Citing From Secondary Sources

Citing from secondary sources refers to citing what one person has done or said after reading a second person's account of what the first person did or said. As a student, you may be tempted to use secondary citations for two reasons. First, after reading a secondhand account of an article and therefore believing you already know what the article is about, it may be hard to motivate yourself to track down the article. Second, reading about an article in a magazine, newspaper, or textbook is easier than reading the original article.

Although you might be tempted to use a secondary source, resist temptation. Instead, read, study, understand, and cite the original source. The only times APA journal editors will allow you to cite secondhand, hearsay evidence are when the primary source is in a foreign language or when the primary source is unavailable. The rationale for editors' distrust of secondhand sources is clear: A secondhand account is an incomplete account—and it may also be an inaccurate account.

Your teacher may be more lenient than a journal editor. You might ask your teacher if you can use one or two secondary sources. If you are allowed to use secondary sources, name the original source and then cite the secondary source. For example, if you read about Original's work in Interpreter's article, then your citation would be

> Original (as cited in Interpreter, 2005) found . . .

In your reference section, you would not mention "Original." Instead, you would provide a reference only to the article you read (i.e., Interpreter, 2005).

To reiterate a point that is very important if you are to benefit from (and do well on) your assignment, do not substitute secondary sources for primary sources. Take the time to find the original article, even if you have to get it from interlibrary loan.

4.3.3 Citing Personal Communications

From a lecture, a conversation, an e-mail, an online news group, or an online bulletin board, you may get an idea from someone and put it in your paper. If so, give that person credit by using a *personal communication* citation. For such a citation, write the person's initials, last name, the words "personal communication," and the date the communication occurred:

✔ I. B. Hepfl (personal communication, May 13, 2006) [name citation] told me

✔ . . . is an alternative explanation (I. B. Hepfl, personal communication, May 13, 2006) [parenthetical citation].

Note that personal communication citations will not be listed in your references because the reader will be unable to access that lecture, conversation, or electronic communication. Note also that most of your citations should be from sources that could be accessed by either visiting a major university library or by logging on to a reputable electronic database such as *PsycARTICLES*.

4.3.4 Citing Information Obtained From the Internet

Although you can use the Internet to retrieve articles that appear in paper journals (by using *PsycARTICLES, Proquest, InfoTrac® College Edition*, and other full text article retrieval services), you can also use the Internet to retrieve information that has never appeared in a paper journal. For example, you may find information on an individual's or an organization's website. However, be very skeptical about information from such a source. The information on the website may not have been evaluated by outside experts. Even if an Internet source does report original research, a paper journal's description of the same research may provide a more complete and more permanently retrievable source.

If the Internet source is still available on the Internet, you would cite it like any other source (to learn how to cite sources, see 4.4). Thus, if you were citing a 2007 work by Jolley, your citation would be (Jolley, 2007), regardless of whether the work was a book, journal article, or Internet source. Because of websites such as http://www.archive.org that back up and preserve copies of websites, if a source was once on the Internet, that source probably can still be retrieved today. If, however, the source is no longer available on the Internet, cite and reference it as you would a personal communication (to learn how to cite personal communications, see 4.3.3).

4.4 Formatting Individual Citations

Citations point readers to the sources of your ideas. Usually, your sources will be research articles. The value of the source is based on the quality of the research, not the personality, fame, or status of the person doing the research. Therefore, the citation will not include the author's title (e.g., Dr., Professor), the author's first name, the author's affiliation (e.g., Harvard), or any other author information that is irrelevant to evaluating the research (e.g., the author's hometown). Instead, citations usually include only two things: (a) the author's(s') last name(s) followed by (b) the year the source was published.

Usually, providing the author's last name is straightforward, especially when the work has one author. When the work has two to five authors, providing the authors' last names is still straightforward. The only added difficulty is that you have to make sure that you put the authors in the correct order (on the first page of a published article, the authors will be listed in order below the title). We will illustrate what to do in more complicated cases (e.g., no author, six or more authors) in the next section. However, before you try to absorb all the specific rules of citations, realize that most of those rules boil down to one general rule: A citation must be complete enough to allow the reader to find the reference in your reference list.

Like providing the author's last name, providing the year of publication is usually straightforward. There are probably only six situations in which you will not just put down the year. First, as previously discussed, you put the precise date for personal communication citations (e.g., September 15, 2005). Second, if the original source is dated differently from its translation, you separate the original year from the translation year with a slash (e.g., Kant, 1781/1965). Third, if the article has not yet been published, you put "in press" (e.g., Jones, in press) for the date. Fourth, if the work has no documented publication date, you put "n.d." (no date) for the date (e.g., Smith, n.d.). Fifth, if you are using a name citation for an article more than once in the same paragraph, you can omit the year the second time you mention the article—unless leaving off the date would prevent readers from knowing which article you meant. For example, if your reference list contains three articles by Jones, the citation "Jones" would not tell the reader which article you meant. Sixth, if you have two or more citations from the same author published in the same year, you add an "a" after the year for the first reference (e.g., Williams, 2005a) and a "b" after the year for the second reference (see 4.5.2).

4.4.1 Work by One Author

```
Crovitz (1964) found . . .
. . . was found (Crovitz, 1964).[5]
. . . was found (Anonymous, 2006).[6]
. . . was found (Clarion University, 2006).[7]
```

---

[5]It does not matter whether the person's full name is Danny Crovitz, Danny Crovitz, Jr., or Daniel Crovitz III: The last name is Crovitz, and the last name is the only name you put in the citation.

[6]If the author is officially listed as "Anonymous," then "Anonymous" takes the place of the author's last name.

[7]If the author is an organization, the organization's name takes the place of the author's last name.

4.4.2 Work by Two Authors

Always include the first author's last name, the second author's last name, and the year the work was published—and include them in that order. To join the authors' names, use the word "and" when you are using a name citation, but use an ampersand ("&") when the authors' names are in parentheses. Note that neither the "and" nor the "&" are preceded by a comma.

```
Spear and Ganz (1975) found . . .
    . . . was found (Spear & Ganz, 1975).
```

4.4.3 Work by Three, Four, or Five Authors

The first time you cite such a source, list all of the authors' last names. Separate the authors' names with commas. Thus, there will be a comma between the first and second authors' names, a comma between the second and third authors' names, and a comma before the final "and" (for a name citation) or "&" (for a parenthetical citation). After the names, put the year the work was published. The publication year will be in parentheses (for a name citation) or preceded by a comma (for a parenthetical citation). If you cite that source again, do not mention all the authors' names. Instead, state only the primary (first) author's last name followed by "et al." and then the year.

```
Spear, Chow, Masland, and Murphy (1972) discovered that . . .
confirmed the well-established effect (Spear et al., 1972).
Also, Spear et al. (1972) commented that . . . have been
found (Burton, Nagshineh, & Ruddock, 1977).
```

Do not replace the authors' names with only the first author's name and "et al." if doing so would make it unclear which reference you were citing. For example, citing "(Wenderoth et al., 1989)" at the end of the following paragraph was a mistake because readers cannot know which of the three Wenderoth references the writer intended to cite.

```
✗  Wenderoth, Johnstone, and van der Zwan (1989) initiated the
   study of the phenomenon when they found. . . . In a
   related study, Wenderoth, van der Zwan, and Johnstone
   (1989) showed. . . . In addition, Wenderoth, Apple, and
   Johnstone (1989) found that. . . . To reconcile these
   disparate findings, one could reinterpret the results of
   Wenderoth et al. (1989).
```

In such cases, the general rule is that you should include the minimum number of authors' names that avoids confusion, then "et al." followed by the publication year. However, note that "et al." means "and others." Therefore, if, after listing the minimum number of authors' names, only one other author is left, do not use "et al." Instead, list all the authors. Thus, in the previous example, the last citation should read, "Wenderoth, van der Zwan, and Johnstone (1989)."

4.4.4 Work by Six or More Authors

Provide the first author's last name followed by "et al." and the date (e.g., Smith et al., 2006), unless that citation could lead readers to more than one reference in your reference list. To illustrate how an "et al." citation could lead to confusion, suppose you referenced 10 seven-author sources that all (a) had Smith as the lead author and (b) were published in 2006. In that case, "Smith et al., 2006" would not tell readers which of the 10 you meant. In such a case, provide the second author's last name as well (Smith, Thomas, et al., 2006). If that citation would still not point to one—and only one—source in your reference list, add the third author's last name (Smith, Thomas, Schadle, et al., 2006). In short, provide the minimum number of authors' names that avoids confusion.

4.4.5 Work by Author Sharing Same Last Name as Another Cited Author

If two first authors share the same last name, use the initials for their first and middle names when you cite their work.

```
G. J. Burton, Nagshineh, and Ruddock (1977) found. . . . H. E.
Burton (1945) set out. . . . R. F. Burton (2006) stated . . .
```

4.4.6 Work With No Author

If the source has no identified author, use the source's title (or, if the title is long, its first few words) in place of the author's last name (e.g., "Keep the Small Fish," 2006). To inform the reader that you are referring to the title of a source, you should differentiate the title from the rest of the text of the sentence. Specifically, if it is the title of an article or the title of a book chapter, enclose the title in quotation marks; if it is the title of any other work (e.g., a title of a book), italicize it.

```
The chapter "Social Psychology" (2006) gave . . .
. . . the common definition ("Social Psychology," 2006).
The book General Psychology (2006) . . .
. . . the common definition (General Psychology, 2006).
```

4.5 Formatting Multiple Citations

Sometimes you will have more than one citation for a statement. In this section, we will show you how to format such citations.

4.5.1 More Than Two Works by Different Authors

Within parentheses, list multiple citations of different authors in alphabetical order according to the primary author's last name. Thus, just as is the case with the reference list, "Alpha & Omega, 2006" would come before "Omega & Alpha, 2006" (for more about ordering citations and references, see 4.9.3). Separate the citations with semicolons.

```
Several studies (Burton et al., 1977; Crovitz, 1964, 1972;
Spear & Ganz, 1975) have found . . .
```

4.5.2 More Than Two Works by the Same Author

Order multiple citations of the same author(s) from oldest to most recent.

```
Crovitz (1964, 1972) found . . .
. . . was found (Crovitz, 1964, 1972).
```

If you refer to works by the same author(s) published in the same year, alphabetize the references on the first word of the title (e.g., if you cited several articles that Kakizaki published in 1950, the one titled "Androgens in action" would come before the one titled "Zebras in zoos"). Once you have ordered those references, put an "a" after the year for the first reference (e.g., Kakizaki, 1950a), a "b" after the year for the second (e.g., Kakizaki, 1950b), and so on until each citation is distinct.

```
Kakizaki (1950a) found that. . . . Kakizaki (1950b) confirmed
his finding. . . . a well-established finding (Kakizaki,
1950a, 1950b).
```

4.6 Paraphrasing

When you paraphrase properly, you take ideas from a source and restate those ideas in your own words. Although you are not using the source's words, you are using the source's ideas. Therefore, when you paraphrase, just as when you quote, you must cite your source. Despite the similarities between paraphrasing and quoting, you should usually try to paraphrase rather than quote because paraphrasing shows that you understand what you have read.

Unfortunately, many students who intend to paraphrase unintentionally plagiarize because they make one of the following three errors. First, some students mistakenly believe that they do not have to cite a source that they do not quote. Do not risk your academic career by making that mistake. Second, sometimes students cannot tell, from their notes, whether they copied or paraphrased material—and they incorrectly assume that they paraphrased the material. Third, some students mistakenly believe that anything other than an exact quote is a paraphrase. They believe that replacing a few words with synonyms counts as a paraphrase or that deleting or moving a few words around counts as a paraphrase. They are wrong: A paraphrase must be in your own words.

To put a passage in your own words, you must first understand the passage. Therefore, before paraphrasing a sentence or passage, read it carefully. Then, put away the passage and try writing a paraphrase in your own words. Then, go back and compare what you have written with the original. If your paraphrase is too close to the original, try again. Otherwise, you will be guilty of plagiarism (see 1.2.4). To be more successful on your second attempt, study the passage again to be sure you understand it. Then, wait until the next day to write your paraphrase. Waiting gives you a chance to forget the original passage's wording (Clarion University of Pennsylvania, n.d.).[8] If your paraphrase still closely resembles the original, consider quoting the original.

4.7 Quoting

There are two main forms of quotation: *embedded quotations* and *block quotations*. Use embedded quotations for short quotations of fewer than 40 words. As we mentioned in Chapter 1, for every 1,000 words (4 pages) in your paper, you should have no more than 50 quoted words. Therefore, if you do quote, try to use short, embedded quotations.

4.7.1 Embedded Quotations

If you use embedded quotations, the following advice will help you format them correctly.

- Provide a normal citation in the appropriate place and enclose the quotation in double quotation marks.

      Jones (1984) argued that both "may follow Morgan's canons"

- Provide the original page number(s) from which the quotation comes. Those page numbers should be put at the end of the quotation and should be enclosed in parentheses.

      Jones (1984) argued that both "may follow Morgan's canons"
      (p. 232).

If you have an Internet source for which you cannot identify the page numbers, count how many paragraphs it comes after a major heading. Then, to help the reader locate the quote, give the heading and the number of paragraphs (abbreviated "para.") that the quote follows the heading. Thus, if you were quoting from the third paragraph of the results section, your citation might be as follows:

      (Merton, 2003, Results section, para. 3)

- Copy the original spelling, punctuation, and wording of the quotation, even if it is incorrect. After any error, put "[sic]" to emphasize that the error is not yours, but instead was present in the original.

      Jones (1984) argued that both "may follow Morgans [sic]
      canons" (p. 232).

---

[8]This citation is unusual because the author is an organization (Clarion University) and the publication does not have a date ("n.d." means "no date").

- Use ellipses (three dots) to indicate omission of material from within the original quotation. Add the usual end-of-sentence mark (e.g., period, question mark) to the end of an ellipsis if the quotation resumes on the following sentence.

  Jones (1984) argued that "lower-level judgments, . . . may follow Morgans [sic] canons" (p. 232).

- Use brackets [thus] to indicate any material you have inserted into the quotation to make it fit into the sense of your text.

  Jones (1984) argued that "lower-level judgments, . . . [arguing that both] may follow Morgans [sic] canons" (p. 232).

- Use single quotation marks to indicate quotation marks within the quotation.

  Jones (1984) applied "the term 'perception,' . . . to [both] aesthetic judgments, . . . [and] to lower-level judgments, . . . [arguing that both] may follow Morgans [sic] canons" (p. 232).

- The first letter of a quotation may be capitalized if what follows forms a complete sentence of its own.

- To highlight particular words in a quotation that are important for your argument, place them in italics. Follow the italicized words with [italics added].

- If a period is next to the closing (right) quotation mark, the period should be inside the quotation mark—even if the period has nothing to do with the quote.

- If a comma is next to the right (closing) quotation mark, the comma should be inside the quotation mark—even if the comma has nothing to do with the quote.

- If the quotation itself ends with a question mark or exclamation mark, enclose the question mark or exclamation point within the quotation marks. If, on the other hand, the sentence, rather than the quotation, contains the question mark or exclamation point, then put the question mark or exclamation point outside of the quotation marks.

To understand these rules, study the following examples:

✔ He argued, "The term 'perception,' *when applied to aesthetic judgments* [italics added], must be distinguished from the term applied to lower-level judgments" (Jones, 1984, p. 232), but he went on to . . .

✔ Jones (1984) applied "the term 'perception,' . . . . to [both] aesthetic judgments, . . . [and] to lower-level judgments, ... [arguing that both] may follow Morgans [sic] canons" (p. 232).

4.7.2 Block Quotations

If your quotation is 40 words or more, use a block quotation. To format block quotations, use most of the same principles you would use if you had an embedded quotation. The difference is that instead of using quotation marks to identify the material you are quoting, you will use indentation. Specifically, indent all lines of the first paragraph of the quotation by about five characters from the left margin so that the first paragraph of the quote forms a block of text.

If your quote is longer than a paragraph, signal the start of each subsequent paragraph by indenting the first line of that paragraph by five more spaces than the lines immediately above and below it. Thus, if you were quoting three consecutive paragraphs, you should start every line of the quote five spaces from the left margin except for the first line of the second paragraph and the first line of the third paragraph, both of which you should start 10 spaces from the left margin.

End each block quotation by citing the quotation's source. Specifically, after the final period of a blocked quotation, enclose the last name(s) of the author(s), the publication year, and page number(s) of the quote in parentheses, as we have done in Exhibit 4.3.

4.8 Deciding What to Reference

Your references should be a list of all the retrievable sources (except for major classical works such as the Bible or Homer's Odyssey) that you cited in text. You must exclude any source that you did not cite in text—even if you read that source. In addition, as you will see in the next sections, you must exclude two types of cited sources from your reference list: (a) sources that readers cannot retrieve and (b) sources that you, rather than actually reading, read about in another source.

4.8.1 Referencing Nonstandard Sources

Personal communications, such as conversations, letters, and e-mails, do not appear in the reference list because there is no easy way to allow a reader to obtain a copy. Messages

EXHIBIT **4.3**   An Example of a Section of a Paper That Contains
a Block Quotation

```
    When astronomers try to explain visual perception, their
explanations can be confusing, as the following quote illustrates.

    Mach bands are present because cones do not operate independently.
    One cone "knows" what its neighbor is seeing [italics added] and
    responds both to the amount of light falling on it and the
    adjacent receptors. At the high contrast bright boundary . . . a
    bright stripe [is visible] where the image becomes dark [and vice
    versa]. (Lynch & Livingston, 1995, p. 225)

    This explanation is confusing because cones neither see nor know
what other cones are doing . . .
```

---

posted to newsgroups, discussion groups, and electronic mailing lists are also usually considered personal communications. Thus, such messages usually would not appear in your reference list. However, you may put such a message in your reference list if you are reasonably confident that the reader will be able to access that message.

4.8.2 Referencing Secondary Sources

You reference only sources you actually cited and read. Therefore, if, rather than reading the original work, you read about the work only in a secondary source, you reference only the secondary source. The only mention of the original work will be in the text's citation (see 4.3.2). As we stated earlier, you should try to read the original work whenever possible. Usually, your professor will expect your paper to be based on journal articles you read—not on journal articles you read about in secondary sources such as magazines, newspapers, encyclopedias, or textbooks. If you cite any secondary sources, most of those citations should probably be limited to the first paragraph of your Introduction.

4.9 Formatting References

In the next few sections, you will learn how to format the major types of references. We did not provide you with every type of reference for two reasons. First, because at least 75% of your references should be journal articles, we focused on teaching you how to format journal articles. Second, we could not provide an example of every type of reference: The *Publication Manual* lists 95 different reference types—and warns that it has not included every reference type. Therefore, you may run into a reference that is outside the guidelines we list. In that case, do not panic. Your professor will probably not penalize you for mistakes in referencing some obscure reference type. Most teachers are delighted when students can reference journal articles correctly. We would be shocked if your professor penalized you for having a comma out of place in a reference to an anonymous, reprinted article in a United Nations technical report. However, if you are extremely concerned about perfectly formatting the reference for an unconventional source, see the *Publication Manual* or use APA's *Style Helper.*[9]

4.9.1 Starting the Reference Page

Begin your list of references on a new page with a centered heading: References. Realize that you will probably not be able to complete your references unless you have the following four pieces of information for each reference:

1. who the author(s) is (are),
2. what the title of the work is,

---

[9]Both the *Manual* and *Style Helper* can be ordered from APA's website (http://www.apastyle.org).

3. when the work was published or presented, and
4. where the work was published or presented (for a conference presentation, the name of the conference and the name of the city in which the conference was held; for a book, the name of the publisher and the name of the city in which the publisher is located; for a journal article, the name of the journal, the volume number of that journal, and the page numbers).

4.9.2 Form of Each Reference

Do not indent the first line of each reference. Instead, start the first line of each reference at the left margin. Subsequent lines for that reference should be indented five spaces. This indentation style is called "hanging indent." If you are having trouble indenting references in this way, go to the "help" menu of your word-processing program and look up "hanging indent."[10] If your reference has a single author, the beginning of your reference will probably adhere to the following format:

1. Author's last name, comma, *one space*, first initial, period, *one space*, second initial, period, *one space*

   Example: Fehr, B. F.

2. Date in parentheses followed by a period and *one space*

   Example: (1999).

3. Title of the source followed by a period.

   Example: Laypeople's conceptions of commitment.

If the source is a book, its title is italicized. Because the source above is not italicized, you know that "Laypeople's conceptions of commitment" does not refer to a book title.

After providing the author's name ("who"), the publication date ("when"), and work's title ("what"), you need to provide the publication data ("where"). For a book (see 4.9.8), stating the "where" may be as simple as stating the name of the city where the publisher is located followed by a colon, the publisher's name, and a period (e.g., "New York: Wiley."). For a book chapter (see 4.9.9), stating the publication data is more involved because you must specify what book the chapter is in, on what pages in that book the chapter is in, as well as providing the publisher's name and address (e.g., "In *Applied multiple regression/correlation analysis for the behavioral sciences* (pp. 73–122). New York: Wiley."). For a journal article (see 4.9.10), stating the publication data involves stating the title of the journal [italicized] followed by a comma, the volume number [italicized] followed by a comma, and the first page of the article followed by a hyphen followed by the last page of the article followed by a period (e.g., "*Journal of*

---

[10]Do *not* make hanging indents by inserting returns at the end of each line and tabs at the beginning. You will be sorry if you do! Instead, ensure that each reference is a single paragraph, free of returns, and use your word processor's margins to make the hanging indent. For more help on getting your word processor to make hanging indents, go to http://www.writingforpsychology.com.

Personality and Social Psychology, 76, 90–103.”). If you accessed your source from the Internet (see 4.9.12), you will probably end your reference with a statement of when you retrieved the source and where in cyberspace (the database or the URL) you retrieved it (e.g., “Retrieved June 15, 2006, from PsycARTICLES database.” or “Retrieved June 15, 2006, from http://faculty.washington.edu/agg/bytopic.htm”).

4.9.3 Order

References must be in alphabetical order according to the primary (first) author’s last name. Thus, Alpha, Z. would come before Beta, A. If different authors have the same last name, break the tie by looking at initials. Thus, Burton, H. E. (1945) would come before Burton, R. F. (2003). For references with the same first author, alphabetize on the second author. Thus, Wenderoth, P., Johnstone, S., & van der Zwan, R. (1989) comes before Wenderoth, P., & van der Zwan, R. (1989). For references with the same author(s), put the oldest references first. Thus, Lehmkuhle, R. T., & Fox, S. L. (1962) comes before Lehmkuhle, R. T., & Fox, S. L. (1994). For references with the same author(s) and year, alphabetize on the first word of the title (ignoring “a” and “the”), and distinguish references by single, lowercase letters immediately after the year. Thus, to distinguish the two articles that Kakizaki published in 1950, the one listed first in the reference list would be Kakizaki, S. (1950a), whereas the one listed second would be Kakizaki, S. (1950b).

With compound names (such as von Helmholtz, van der Zwan), check the author’s own reference list to see where the author’s name appears (in van der Zwan’s case, it is with the Vs). If you cannot find the author’s name in the author’s own reference list, alphabetize on the first capitalized part of the name. Put the uncapitalized parts of the name after the initials (e.g., Helmholtz, H. L. von).

Examples.

Burton, G. J., Nagshineh, S., & Ruddock, K. H. (1977). Processing by the human visual system of the light and dark components of the retinal image. *Biological Cybernetics, 27,* 189-197.

Burton, H. E. (1945). The optics of Euclid. *Journal of the Optical Society of America, 35,* 357-372.

Burton, R. F. (1884). *The book of the sword.* London: Chatto & Windus.

Crovitz, H. F. (1972). Transient binasal hemianopia in a pair of plastic soupspoons. *Psychonomic Science, 28,* 234.

Helmholtz, H. L. von (1962). *Handbook of physiological optics* (3rd ed.) (J. P. C. Southall, Trans.). New York: Dover. (Original work published 1910)

Kakizaki, S. (1950a). The effects of preceding conditions upon binocular rivalry (I.). *Japanese Journal of Psychology, 20*(2), 24-32.

Kakizaki, S. (1950b). The effects of preceding conditions upon binocular rivalry (II.). *Japanese Journal of Psychology, 20*(4), 11-17.

Spear, P. D., Chow, K. L., Masland, R. H., & Murphy, E. H. (1972). Ontogenesis of receptive field characteristics of superior colliculus neurons in the rabbit. *Brain Research, 45,* 67-86.

Spear, P. D., & Ganz, L. (1975). Effects of visual cortical lesions following recovery from monocular deprivation in the cat. *Experimental Brain Research, 23,* 181-201.

van der Zwan, R., Wenderoth, P., & Alais, D. (1993). Reduction of a pattern-induced motion aftereffect by binocular rivalry suggests the involvement of extrastriate mechanisms. *Visual Neuroscience, 10,* 703-709.

Wenderoth, P., Johnstone, S., & van der Zwan, R. (1989). Two dimensional tilt illusions induced by orthogonal plaid patterns: Effects of plaid motion, orientation, spatial separation, and spatial frequency. *Perception, 18,* 25-38.

Wenderoth, P., & van der Zwan, R. (1989). The effects of exposure duration and surrounding frames on direct and indirect tilt aftereffects and illusions. *Perception and Psychophysics, 46,* 338-344.

Wenderoth, P., van der Zwan, R., & Johnstone, S. (1989). Orientation illusions induced by briefly flashed plaids. *Perception, 18,* 715-728.

4.9.4 Author Names

Invert authors' names (i.e., put the last name first, then the initials). Separate last names from initials with a comma. Separate initials with a space. Separate different authors' names with a comma. For two or more authors, separate the final name from the rest with a comma then an ampersand (e.g., Burton, G. J., Nagshineh, S., & Ruddock, K. H.; see 4.4.2). Do not use "et al." in the reference list unless you have more than six authors. If there is no identifiable author, put the title of the work in the author position.

Examples.

Benjamin, L. T., Jr. (1988). A history of teaching machines. *American Psychologist, 43,* 703-712.

Crovitz, H. F. (1972). Transient binasal hemianopia in a pair of plastic soupspoons. *Psychonomic Science, 28,* 234.

Helmholtz, H. L. von (1962). *Handbook of physiological optics* (3rd ed.) (J. P. C. Southall, Trans.). New York: Dover. (Original work published 1910)

High-handed professor's comments called hot error. (1985, August 16). *USA Today,* p. 2c.

Social psychology (1995). (17 paragraphs) [CD-ROM] In *Britannica CD 2.0.* Chicago: Encyclopaedia Britannica.

Social psychology (1999). In *The new encyclopaedia Britannica* (Vol. 27, pp. 802-803). Chicago: Encyclopaedia Britannica.

4.9.5 Date of Publication

For most sources, put the year of publication of the reference in parentheses followed by a period. For books, this is the most recent copyright year and is usually found on the page after the title page. For journals, the year is the publication date of the journal. For a book that has been translated into English, put the year of the translation (e.g., Kant, 1965), and then add "(Original work published in [date])" at the end of the reference.

For some sources, you will provide information other than the year of publication. For example, with a daily newspaper article, knowing what year it was published would not be nearly as helpful as providing the date it was published. Therefore, for daily and weekly publications, enclose the year of publication, a comma, and the month and day of publication in parentheses, followed by a period. Thus, a reference for a newspaper article might start as follows: Homichl, J. (2003, July 16). You may use the same procedure for an Internet journal, if the date is provided. Similarly, you may provide the month or season (Winter) of the publication of a newsletter. Finally, if your source is a paper or poster presented at a conference, always follow the year of the conference with a comma and the month the conference was held (e.g., "2003, August").

Thus far, we have discussed cases in which you have access to more information than just the publication year. However, sometimes, you will not even know what year the source will be published. If the source has been published but there is no date, put "n.d." in place of the date. If the source has been accepted for publication, but is not yet published (the delay between article acceptance and publication is often more than a year), use "in press" in place of the date.

Examples.

Honomichl, J. (1990, August 6). Answering machines threaten survey research. *Marketing News,* 11.

Kant, I. (1965). *Critique of pure reason* (N. K. Smith, Trans.). New York: St. Martin's. (Original work published 1781)

Neisser, U. (1984, August). *Ecological movement in cognitive psychology.* Invited address at the annual meeting of the American Psychological Association, Toronto, Canada.

4.9.6 Title

Type the title of the reference exactly as it appears in the original, including the original spelling. Capitalize only the first letter of book, journal article, and book chapter

T A B L E **4.6**   Abbreviations Used in References

Abbreviation	Translation	Usage
2nd	second	No period; same for all numbers
c.	about	When a publication year is uncertain
chap.	chapter	
Ed(s).	Editor(s)	
ed.	Edition	
n.d.	no date	
p.	page	For one-page newspaper or magazine articles
pp.	pages	For book chapters
Rev.	revised	
Trans.	Translator(s)	
Vol.	Volume	When part of a title
Vols.	volumes	When part of publication data
—	to	As in "pp. 22–33"

titles. Capitalize only the first letter of book and book chapter subtitles (the subtitle is what follows a colon or question mark). Italicize book titles and subtitles. End the title section of each reference with a period.

4.9.7 Abbreviations

As you will see in 4.9.8, for books published in the United States, use the two-letter U.S. postal service's abbreviation for that state instead of spelling out the entire state name. In addition, there are other abbreviations you should use in the reference section. The most common of these are listed in Table 4.6.

4.9.8 Book Reference

Usually, fewer than one fourth of your references will be books; most of your references will be journal articles. Usually, books will be the shortest and easiest sources to reference. Like most references, book references start with the author's name (inverted), followed by parentheses enclosing the year the work was published, and a period.

Next comes the book title. Note that the book title is italicized. As a general rule, the first letter of the first word of the book title is the only letter capitalized. The exceptions to this general rule are that you capitalize (a) the first word of a subtitle (which may appear in the title after a colon) and (b) proper nouns (see 6.1.1).

Usually, the book title is immediately followed by a period. If it is not followed immediately by a period, then the book has probably either been through several editions or has been translated. For such a book, there is a parenthesized, nonitalicized phrase telling the reader which edition of the book you are using or who translated the book. Thus, if the title alone would not necessarily lead the reader to the right source (e.g., the book is a revised edition, a third edition, a translation, the second volume, etc.), you need to add information after the title that will help the reader locate the right source. Abbreviate that information and put it in parentheses, in normal, nonitalicized font (Rev. ed., 3rd ed., Trans., Vol. 2).

Next comes the place of publication. If the place is a famous city (e.g., New York, London), the city name is sufficient. If the city is not famous and is in the United States, follow the city name with the two-letter U.S. Postal Service's abbreviation for the state rather than typing out the entire state name (e.g., "PA" instead of "Pennsylvania"). Note that the postal abbreviation is capitalized and does not contain any periods. If the city is not famous and not in the United States, you will usually follow the city name with the country name.

After the publishing location, put a colon and the name of the publisher (e.g., "Pacific Grove, CA: Wadsworth."). In listing the publisher's name, keep it short by omitting the words or abbreviations for "Company" or "Incorporated." Put a period after the publisher's name.

Normally, your reference will end at that period. However, there may be cases in which the year you are citing for the book is quite a bit later than the year the book was originally published. For example, a book may be reprinted over a hundred years after it was first published, or it may be translated into English decades after it was first published. Consequently, your citation date may make it seem like a person who has been dead for years has just published a book. Without an explanation, such a citation date might confuse the reader. Therefore, after the ending period, add a parenthetical explanation such as "(Original work published in 1871)" at the end of the reference.

General form.

Author, I. N. (year). *Book title italicized* (information about specific edition—if needed). Place of publication: Publisher. (Explanatory material—if needed)

Examples.

Alhazen, I. (1989). *The optics of Ibn Al-Haytham: Books I-III: On direct vision* (A. I. Sabra, Trans.). London: The Warburg Institute. (Original work published c. 1024)

Burton, R. F. (1884). *The book of the sword.* London: Chatto & Windus.

Helmholtz, H. L. von (1962). *Handbook of physiological optics* (3rd ed.) (J. P. C. Southall, Trans.). New York: Dover. (Original work published 1910)

Strunk, W., Jr., & White, E. B. (1972). *The elements of style* (2nd ed.). New York: Macmillan.

4.9.9 Book-Chapter Reference

Referencing a specific book chapter involves a few more steps than referencing a book. As with a book reference, provide the author's name (inverted) followed by the year of publication, in parentheses, followed by a period. After that, provide the chapter title—but do not italicize it.

Then, if there is an editor, provide the name of the editor. Three common mistakes students make in formatting the editor information are (a) putting the editor's name where the author's name should be, (b) inverting the editor's name, and (c) not putting "(Ed.)," after the editor's name.

Next, put the book title in italics. After the book title, put a left (opening) parenthesis, then "pp." followed by the number of the first page of the chapter, a hyphen, the number of the last page of the chapter, followed by a right (closing) parenthesis and a period (e.g., "pp. 56–92"). Finally, add the publication information using the same format you would if you were referencing an entire book. Specifically, you put the place of publication followed by a colon, followed by the name of the publisher, followed by a period (e.g., "Belmont, CA: Wadsworth.").

General form.

Author, I. N. (year). Chapter title. In A. N. Editor (Ed.), *Book title italicized* (information about specific edition) (pp. start page-finish page). Place of publication: Publisher.

Examples.

Leibowitz, H. W., Post, R. B., Brandt, T., & Dichgans, J. (1982). Implications of recent developments in dynamic spatial orientation and visual resolution for vehicle guidance. In A. Wertheim, W. Wagenaar, & H. L. Leibowitz (Eds.), *Tutorials in motion perception* (pp. 231-260). New York: Plenum Press.

Westheimer, G. (1981). Visual hyperacuity. In *Progress in sensory physiology* (Vol. 1, pp. 1-30). Berlin: Springer.

4.9.10 Journal-Article Reference

As we mentioned earlier, most of your references should be to journal articles. Fortunately, the general form is not difficult and applies to most journal articles.

General form.

Author, I. N. (year). Article title. *Journal Title Italicized and Capitalized, volume number italicized* (issue number only if each issue begins with page 1), start page-finish page.

Examples.

Fehr, B. F. (1999). Laypeople's conceptions of commitment. *Journal of Personality and Social Psychology, 76,* 90-103.

Spear, P. D., & Ganz, L. (1975). Effects of visual cortical lesions following recovery from monocular deprivation in the cat. *Experimental Brain Research, 23,* 181-201.

van der Zwan, R., Wenderoth, P., & Alais, D. (1993). Reduction of a pattern-induced motion aftereffect by binocular rivalry suggests the involvement of extrastriate mechanisms. *Visual Neuroscience, 10,* 703-709.

Wenderoth, P., Johnstone, S., & van der Zwan, R. (1989). Two dimensional tilt illusions induced by orthogonal plaid patterns: Effects of plaid motion, orientation, spatial separation, and spatial frequency. *Perception, 18,* 25-38.

As you can see, most articles adhere to the following format:

1. Author's last name, comma, first initial, period, second initial, period

   Example: Fehr, B. F.

2. Date in parentheses followed by a period

   Example: (1999).

3. Title of article followed by a period

   Example: Laypeople's conceptions of commitment.

4. Title of journal (italicized) followed by a comma

   Example: *Journal of Personality and Social Psychology,*

5. Volume number (italicized) followed by a comma

   Example: *76,*

6. First page of article followed by a hyphen followed by the last page of the article followed by a period.

   Example: 90-103.

Variations in author's last name come from four cases. First, when there is more than one author, use a comma to separate one author's name from the next author's name. In addition to a comma, use an ampersand (&) to join the last author's name to the list (e.g., "Johnson, L. B., Smith, A. O., & Jones, E. F."). Second, if the original source does not provide an author's middle initial, do not include that author's middle initial. Third, if the article has more than six authors, list only the first six. After the sixth author, place a comma and "et al." Fourth, if no one—not even "Anonymous"—is listed as the author of the source, use the title of the article as the author.

Variations in the date come from three cases. First, magazines, newsletters, and newspapers often provide more detail than the year of publication. For example, Internet journals and newsletters may note the season (2005, Winter) or months (2005, September/October) that they come out, whereas newspapers and magazines may have the exact date (2006, August 26). Second, if the article is not yet published, the phrase "in press" is put in parentheses. Third, if the article has no date, such as some Internet sources, put "n.d." in parentheses rather than the date.

Variations in the rest of the reference are rare. There are, however, four variations you might encounter. First, if you read only the electronic version of a printed article, put "[Electronic version]" after the journal title. Second, if each issue in a journal begins on page 1, then, after the volume number, put the issue number in parentheses. Third, if you are referring to newspapers, use "p." before the page number of an article that appears on a single page (e.g., "p. D4," "p. 5") and use "pp." before the page numbers of an article that appears on multiple pages (e.g., "pp. D4–D6," "pp. 1, 5"). Fourth, if you are referring to an Internet source, you may not have page numbers or volume numbers.

4.9.11 Journal-Article-Abstract Reference

If you have searched sources such as *Psychological Abstracts*, you have access to journal articles' abstracts. If you want to cite one of these articles, you should find and read it. If, however, an abstract is all that is available (e.g., your library does not subscribe to the journal and you cannot obtain it from interlibrary loan), cite the Abstract using the following format:

General form.

Author, I. N. (year). Article title. *Journal Title Italicized and Capitalized, volume number italicized* (issue number if each issue begins with page 1), start page-finish page. Abstract obtained from name of source, year of source, publication year of source, volume number, "Abstract No. [abstract number],", and period.

Example.

Lo, T. Y. (1925). Correlation of name and fame. *Chinese Journal of Psychology, 3,* 701. Abstract obtained from *Psychological Abstracts, 1927, 1,* Abstract No. 319.

Usually, if you have access to the entire article, you should read the entire article. You should not merely skim the Abstract. However, if, for some reason, you access the source, but read only the Abstract (e.g., your professor specifically stated that for a particular writing assignment reading Abstracts was all that was required), cite the abstract using the following format:

General form.

Author, I. N. (year). Article title [Abstract]. *Journal Title Italicized and Capitalized, volume number italicized* (issue number if each issue begins with page 1), start page-finish page.

Example.

Spear, P. D., & Ganz, L. (1975). Effects of visual cortical lesions following recovery from monocular deprivation in the cat [Abstract]. *Experimental Brain Research, 23,* 181-201.

4.9.12 Referencing Internet Sources

We have saved Internet referencing for last because it is not much different from referencing any other source. In fact, if you are accessing an electronic version of a published source, often the only difference is that you add "[Electronic version]" after the title. For example, suppose you accessed a PDF copy of a published article from the website of the primary author, a journal, the APA, the APS, or the electronic library reserve your professor set up for your class. In that case, you would include the same reference information as you would for the printed source so that the reader can obtain the information you saw by going to the printed source. Then, you would add "[Electronic version]" after the title to state that you saw an electronic version rather than a printed one: You do not have to pretend that you saw the printed source.

For other Internet sources, usually the main differences are that (a) you need to put the phrase "Retrieved" followed by the date you retrieved the information (e.g., January 14, 2007), followed by a comma and the Uniform Resource Locator (URL; e.g., http://www.writingforpsychology.com),[11] and (b) you do not end your reference with a period. You need to include the date that you retrieved the source because URLs change. You need to include the URL so readers can access the source. You do not end a URL reference with a period because the reader might think the period was part of the URL.

> *Electronic version of a printed book.*
>
> *General form.*
>
> Author, I. N. (year). *Book title italicized* (information about specific edition—if needed) [Electronic version]. Place of publication: Publisher. (Explanatory material—if needed)
>
> *Example.*
>
> Strunk, W., Jr., & White, E. B. (1972). *The elements of style* [Electronic version]. New York: Macmillan.
>
> *Book existing only as an Internet document.*
>
> *General form.*
>
> Author, I. N. (year). *E-title italicized.* Retrieved date (e.g., March 13, 2003), comma, and URL (if it is not possible to avoid an unnecessary line break in the pathname, start the URL on a new line)
>
> *Example.*
>
> American Psychological Association (2003). *Electronic references.* Retrieved January 8, 2006, from http://www.apastyle.org/elecref.html

---

[11]Note that the URL should not be underlined. Unfortunately, your word-processing software may automatically underline it. To learn how to turn off that feature, see our website (http://www.writingforpsychology.com).

Electronic version of a book chapter from a printed book.

General form.

Author, I. N. (year). Chapter title. In A. N. Editor (Ed.), *Book title italicized* (information about specific edition) (pp. start page-finish page) [Electronic version]. Place of publication: Publisher.

Example.

Strunk, W., Jr., & White, E. B. (1972). Elementary principles of composition. In *The elements of style* (pp. 15-33)[Electronic version]. New York: Macmillan.

Book chapters from a document existing only on the Internet.

General form.

Author, I. N. (year). Title of e-chapter. In A. N. Editor (Ed.) *E-title italicized.* Retrieved date, comma, from URL

Examples.

Dennett, D. C. (1994). Consciousness in human and robot minds. In S. Harnad (Ed.), *CogPrint: Cognitive sciences eprint archive.* Retrieved July 15, 2006, from http://cogprints.soton.ac.uk/archives/comp/papers/199803/199803001/doc.html/concrobt.htm

Wagon-wheel effect (2005). In *Wikipedia: The free encyclopedia.* Retrieved December 1, 2005, from http://en.wikipedia.org/wiki/Wagon-wheel_effect

Journal articles. There are two main types of electronic journal articles: (a) articles from journals that exist only electronically (e.g., *Psycoloquy*), and (b) articles from conventional paper journals that are reproduced electronically (e.g., the electronic version of *American Psychologist*). For an Internet-only journal, use the following format.

General form.

Author, I. N. (year). Article title. *Electronic Journal Title Italicized and Capitalized, volume number italicized,* article number (if available). Retrieved date, comma, from URL

Examples.

Forgie, M. L. (1995). Are ovarian secretions all that females "need"? Commentary on Fitch & Denenberg on sexbrain. *Psycoloquy, 6,* Retrieved June 27, 2006, from ftp://ftp.princeton.edu/pub/harnad/Psycoloquy/1995.volume.6/psyc.95.6.22.sex-brain.3.forgie

Hoffman. W. C. (1998). The topology of wholes, parts and their perception-cognition: Commentary on Latimer

& Stevens on Part-Whole-Perception. *Psycoloquy, 9.*
Retrieved September 10, 2006, from http://www.ai.
univie.ac.at/archives/Psycoloquy/1998.V9/0003.html

O'Shea, R. P., & Corballis, P. M. (2003). Binocular rivalry
in split-brain observers. *Journal of Vision, 3,* 610-615.
Retrieved January 3, 2006, from
http://www. journalofvision.org/3/10/3/

If you saw the electronic version of a printed journal article from any source other than a database, reference it as you would a conventional journal article. The only difference is that you put "[Electronic version]" after the title.

Example.

Greenwald, A. G., & Farnham, S. D. (2000). Using the
Implicit Association Test to measure self-esteem and
self-concept [Electronic version]. *Journal of
Personality and Social Psychology, 79,* 1022-1038.

If you retrieved the article from a database, your citation would reflect that fact. Note that you do not put "[Electronic version]" in such a citation.

Example.

Greenwald, A. G., & Farnham, S. D. (2000). Using the
Implicit Association Test to measure self-esteem and
self-concept. *Journal of Personality and Social
Psychology, 79,* 1022-1038. Retrieved July 28, 2006, from
PsycARTICLES database.

Journal article abstracts. If you try to retrieve an article from the Internet, you may be able to retrieve only the article's abstract. If you want to cite that article, you should find and read it. If, however, you can access only the abstract (e.g., your library does not subscribe to the journal and you cannot obtain it from interlibrary loan), cite the abstract using the following format:

General form.

Author, I. N. (year). Article title. *Journal Title Italicized and Capitalized, volume number italicized* (issue number if each issue begins with page 1), start page-finish page. Abstract retrieved from date, comma, and URL or name of source. If the source is a URL, there is not a period at the end of the reference. If the source is a database, there is a period.

Examples.

Greenwald, A. G., & Farnham, S. D. (2000). Using the
Implicit Association Test to measure self-esteem and

self-concept. *Journal of Personality and Social Psychology, 79*, 1022-1038. Abstract retrieved July 28, 2006, from http://faculty.washington.edu/agg/bytopic.htm

Greenwald, A. G., & Farnham, S. D. (2000). Using the Implicit Association Test to measure self-esteem and self-concept. *Journal of Personality and Social Psychology, 79*, 1022-1038. Abstract retrieved July 28, 2006, from *PsycINFO* database.

4.10   Checklists

4.10.1 Academic Honesty Checklist

___ I cited any source from which I got ideas—even if I did not directly quote that source.

___ When I summarized or paraphrased from a source, I cited that source.

___ If I had any paragraph without a citation (a) in any section of my term paper or (b) in the Introduction or Discussion sections of my research proposal or report, I went back to my notes to make sure that I had not left out a citation.

___ I double-checked my notes and my sources to make sure that I had neither inadvertently quoted someone nor had a paraphrase that was almost identical to the source quotation.

___ If I had any doubt about whether to cite a source, I cited it.

___ If I took words from a source, I made it clear that I was quoting that source.

___ If I got ideas or quotes from an informal source, I cited that source as a personal communication (see 4.3.3).

___ If a source was not the original report of a study, I admitted it.

___ If I read a secondary source instead of the original article, I made it clear that I had read only the secondary source by correctly citing (4.3.2) and referencing (4.8.2) that secondary source.

___ If I read only the Abstract, I made it clear that I did not read the entire article (4.9.11).

___ If I read a theoretical or review article, I made it clear that the article was not an empirical article. In other words, for review articles, I wrote "(for a review, see Smith, 2006)" and for theoretical articles, I wrote "Smith (2006) argued" rather than "Smith found."

4.10.2 Formatting Citations Checklist

___ When citing sources, I did not use footnotes; mention article titles; or mention authors' first names, professional titles (e.g., "Dr."), or professional affiliations.

___ If I used a name citation, I put only the date in parentheses (e.g., "Jolley and Mitchell (2007) argued that . . .").

___ If I used a parenthetical citation, I put the authors' names and the date in parentheses, and I separated the last author's name from the date with a comma: "Some have argued that . . . (Jolley & Mitchell, 2007)."

___ If I used a name citation for a multiple-author source, I used "and" to connect authors' last names; however, if I used a parenthetical citation for a multiple-author citation, I used "&" to connect authors' last names.

___ If I cited several articles within one set of parentheses, I listed the articles in alphabetical order, and I separated the articles from each other with semicolons: "(Brickner, 1980; Jolley, 2007; Mitchell, 2006; Ostrom, 1965; Pusateri, 1995; Williams, 1992)."

___ If the paper had more than six authors, I listed only the first author's last name followed immediately (with no comma) by "et al." (e.g., Glick et al., 2006).

___ If I discussed a paper with three to five authors, I mentioned all the authors' last names the first time I cited that paper.

___ If I discussed a paper with three to five authors and had already cited the paper, I used the first author's last name, followed immediately (with no comma) by "et al." (e.g., First et al., 1996).

___ I checked all my citations that used the phrase "et al." to make sure that I had (a) correctly used such citations and (b) correctly punctuated such citations.

___ I did not overuse "et al." citations.

___ I listed all authors' names the first time I introduced a paper with fewer than six authors.

___ I never used "et al." with a two-author paper.

___ I correctly punctuated my "et al." citations: I never put a period after "et" (e.g., I wrote "et al." instead of "et. al."), and I never put a comma between the first author's last name and "et al." (e.g., I wrote "First et al." instead of "First, et al.").

___ I listed the page number of the source from which I got the quote. (If there is no page number, as in a website, see 4.9.12. If it is a quotation from a classic work, see 4.8.)

___ I used the short quote format for quotations under 40 words (see 4.7.1), but used the block quote format for quotations of 40 or more words (see 4.7.2).

4.10.3 Finding and Using Sources Checklist

___ My citations are recent (most were published within the last 2 years).

___ My citations are from journal articles describing actual research studies rather than from secondhand sources (e.g., textbooks, magazines, newspapers).

___ If my professor required the paper to have a certain number of sources, I met that requirement. For example, if my professor required a minimum of five sources, I cited at least five empirical articles published in refereed journals.

___ Rather than quoting, I paraphrased, summarized, interpreted, and critiqued. As a result, I limited quotes to fewer than 50 words for every 950 of my own.

___ I paraphrased and summarized empirical research reports in a way that makes it clear that (a) I read them rather than skimmed their abstracts and that (b) I understood them.

___ I showed, through my paraphrases and summaries of those articles, how the different articles fit together—and how they related to the main point of my paper.

___ I commented on weaknesses I found in published research. If I had trouble finding weaknesses, I consulted Chapter 5.

4.10.4 Reference Page Checklist

___ My reference section starts on a separate page. The centered heading "References" is at the top of that page.

___ Everything is double-spaced.

___ The first line of each reference is not indented. Instead, it begins at the left margin.

___ When a reference takes up more than one line, I indented those additional lines five spaces.

___ My references are listed in alphabetical order (according to the last name of the first author).

___ Each reference begins with the authors' last names and initials, followed by the year of publication (in parentheses), and then a period.

___ Every reference ends with a period—except for (a) those ending with a URL and (b) those ending with a parenthetical explanation about the work's original source.

___ If a source had more than one author, I separated authors' names with commas.

___ I italicized only book titles, names of journals, and the volume numbers of journal articles.

___ I capitalized only the following parts of article and book titles: the first word of the title, the first word following a colon, and proper nouns (see 6.1.1).

___ When citing journal articles, I avoided both the word "pages" and the abbreviation "pp."

___ If a book was published in the United States, I abbreviated, rather than wrote out, the name of the state. I used the same state abbreviations (e.g., PA for Pennsylvania) that the U.S. Postal Service uses. I remembered that these abbreviations are capitalized and do not contain periods.

___ I tried to find a print version of any article that I found on the Internet because the print version may be easier for readers to locate and the text of the print version will not change.

___ If I did not find a print version, I checked to make sure that the URL worked.

___ I turned off the "auto-underline" feature of my word-processing software so that the URL was not underlined.

___ I made sure that all URLs in my paper and in my reference section were in the same color (black), font size (12-point), and style (not underlined) as regular text.

___ All the references in this section are also cited in my paper. If a reference was not cited, either I added that citation to the body of my paper or I deleted the reference.

___ All the sources cited in my paper are also listed in this section except for "personal communication" citations (see 4.3.3), original works that I did not read but instead learned about through a secondary source (see 4.3.2), and classical works (e.g., the Bible).

4.11 Summary

1. You need to find good sources to write a good paper. Good sources will usually be research articles published in scientific journals.

2. It is vital to cite and to reference your sources correctly.

3. One source may give you leads to other sources (see 4.1.2).

4. Computerized databases can help you find sources. If you have trouble finding enough sources, consult Table 4.2.

5. When you find a source, read it, reread it, and take notes on it. Your notes should include an APA style reference to the source, your critical comments

on the source, and quotation marks around any words you are copying from the source.

6. When you get an idea from a source, you must cite that source. When you paraphrase from a source, you must cite that source. When you quote a source, you must cite that source. When you are not sure about whether you should cite a source, cite that source.

7. Short quotations (fewer than 40 words) are formatted differently than longer quotations (see 4.7).

8. Use a personal communication citation (4.3.3) to give credit for ideas that you acquired through informal sources. Do not put these personal communications in your reference list.

9. When citing, do not provide any information about the authors except for their last names—unless you have more than one author with the same last name (in that case, see 4.4.5). Do not mention authors' first names, titles, or professional affiliations.

10. There are two types of citations: name citations and parenthetical citations. Use a name citation when you are going to paraphrase extensively from a single source. Use parenthetical citations to show the reader how related studies fit together. Do not use footnotes to cite a source.

11. When using a name citation, put the date in parentheses. When using a name citation for a paper with two authors, connect the last names with the word "and." When using a name citation for a paper with three to five authors, use a comma between all the authors' names and add the word "and" before the last author's name.

12. When using a parenthetical citation for a paper with two authors, connect the last names with the symbol "&" and separate the last name from the date with a comma. When using a parenthetical citation for a paper with three to five authors, use a comma between all the authors' names and add the symbol "&" before the last author's name.

13. When citing several articles within one set of parentheses, (a) put the articles in alphabetical order and (b) separate the articles from each other with semicolons.

14. When citing a source with six or more authors, provide only the primary author's last name followed immediately (with no comma) by "et al." (e.g., Glick et al., 2006).

15. When citing a source with three to five authors that was cited earlier in the paper, use the primary author's last name, followed immediately (with no comma) by "et al." (e.g., Lead et al., 1996).

16. The Reference section starts on a separate page titled "References."

17. All the sources listed in the references should be (a) cited in the paper and (b) in alphabetical order according to the last name of the primary author (see 4.9.3).

18. The first line of each reference starts at the left margin. The rest of the reference is indented five spaces.

19. Each reference begins with the authors' last names and initials, followed by the year of publication (in parentheses), and then a period. Separate last names from initials with a comma. Separate initials with a space. Separate different authors' names with a comma. For two or more authors, separate the final name from the rest with a comma then an ampersand (e.g., Burton, G. J. , Nagshineh, S., & Ruddock, K. H.).

20. Below is an example of a journal-article reference (for more see 4.9.10):

    Spear, P. D., & Ganz, L. (1975). Effects of visual cortical lesions following recovery from monocular deprivation in the cat. *Experimental Brain Research, 23,* 181-201.

21. Below is an example of a book reference (for more, see 4.9.8):

    Strunk, W., Jr., & White, E. B. (1972). *The elements of style* (2nd ed.). New York: Macmillan.

22. Below is an example of a reference from a book chapter (for more, see 4.9.9):

    Westheimer, G. (1981). Visual hyperacuity. In *Progress in sensory physiology* (Vol. 1) (pp. 1-30). Berlin: Springer.

23. Below is an example of a reference from an Internet source (for more, see 4.9.12):

    Hoffman. W. C. (1998). The topology of wholes, parts and their perception-cognition: Commentary on Latimer & Stevens on Part-Whole-Perception. *Psycoloquy, 9.* Retrieved September 10, 2001, from http://www.ai.univie.ac.at/archives/Psycoloquy/ 1998.V9/0003.html

CHAPTER

5

Making Your Case: A Guide to Skeptical Reading and Logical Writing

When you read sources that you will use in your paper, you want to know when authors are making arguments that do not logically follow from their earlier statements, and you want to know when authors are making claims that do not follow from the evidence. When your professor reads your paper, you do not want your professor to write any of the following comments on your paper: "illogical," "not true," "not fair," "does not follow," "not necessarily," "unsupported assertion," "the evidence does not support that claim," or "that is only one interpretation." Instead, you want your professor to recognize that you have accomplished two competing tasks: (a) making a strong case in support of your claims and (b) acknowledging the case against your claims. In this chapter, we will help you refine two abilities that will enable you to defend your claims fairly and forcefully: the ability to evaluate arguments and the ability to interpret evidence.

5.1 Theses

In a term paper, your job is to answer a question. Your professor may give you a question (e.g., "Does wisdom increase with age?"), or only a general topic (e.g., "Your term paper should deal with an issue related to wisdom.") from which you have to generate the question. Your answer to the question, the answer that you believe to be true, is your *thesis*.

In one sense, defending your thesis is like taking one side of a debate. You may remember participating in a classroom debate in which you defended one side of a question (e.g., "Is it better to be a lion or a lamb?"). Each side of this debate (i.e., "It is better to be a lion than a lamb," and "It is better to be a lamb than a lion") would constitute a thesis. However, there is an important difference between taking one side in a debate and defending a thesis: In a debate, it does not matter whether the assertion is actually true; in a term paper, the truth does matter. Thus, in a term paper, propose a thesis that, based on your careful examination of the published literature, appears to be true.

Table 5.1 lists some thesis statements. To introduce such theses into a paper, precede each thesis with words such as "In this paper, I will argue that . . ." Although you should believe that your thesis is true, your thesis should be one that some reasonable people might disagree with—before they read your paper. Thus, your thesis statement should not fall into any of the following types of unarguable assertions: (a) a well-documented fact, (b) an extremely vague statement, or (c) a *tautology:* a statement that must, according to rules of logic, be true—often because the statement involves essentially defining a term with itself (e.g., "a reinforcer is something that reinforces"). In Table 5.2, you can see examples of assertions that are not good thesis statements because they fail the test of allowing a reasonable person to disagree with them.

Although your paper's thesis is a statement that some of your readers may disagree with as they start reading the paper, your goal is that all your readers will agree with

T A B L E **5.1**   Examples of Legitimate (Although Not Necessarily Correct) Thesis Statements

---

Human handedness is learned.

There is no intellectual decline in old age.

Situational factors determine more of human behavior than personality.

The research on this particular topic (e.g., the efficacy of drugs for treating depression) is beset with methodological problems preventing any firm conclusion.

Human perception is not affected by expectations or prior knowledge but is instead completely stimulus driven. That is, numerous raw sensory data are combined to create our perception of the entire stimulus.

IQ tests accurately measure mental ability.

TABLE **5.2**   Examples of Unacceptable Thesis Statements

Assertion	Problem
Approximately 10% of humans are left-handed.	It is a statement of fact.
Performance on speeded tasks declines in old age.	It is a statement of fact.
IQ tests measure IQ.	This is a tautology.
Situations are important in human behavior.	All behavior occurs within situations. Consequently, this assertion is too vague to allow disagreement.
Some human perceptions are not affected by prior expectations or knowledge but are instead solely the result of combining the raw data coming from the senses.	This fails on two counts: (a) it is a statement of fact, and (b) it is vague.

your thesis by the time they reach the end of the paper. To convince your audience, you must make a strong argument in support of your thesis statement.

To make a strong argument, you must convince your readers (a) that your argument follows logically from the *premises*—statements, assumptions, and beliefs—on which it is based and (b) that those premises are probably true. When both of these conditions are satisfied, your argument is said to be sound.

To show that your premises are true, you will back up your claims with evidence—and your evidence will usually be a citation of someone else's work. If you do not cite evidence to support a claim, your professor may write "unsupported assertion" or "evidence?" next to your claim.

To show that your conclusion follows logically (validly) from your premises, you must state your premises and, like a district attorney making an opening statement, you must carefully lay out your reasoning. To show all your steps—and to prevent your professor from writing "non sequitur" (does not follow) or "quite a leap" next to your conclusion—you may wish to outline your argument.

One simple strategy for determining whether you have succeeded in both (a) providing evidence for your premises and (b) showing that your conclusion logically follows from your premises is to share your paper with a friend who does not share your thesis. To use more sophisticated strategies, you need to know whether your argument is deductive or inductive.

5.2 Deductive Arguments

In deductive arguments, premises are statements couched in absolute terms (e.g., "all," "every," "always") or in unambiguous comparisons (e.g., "A is bigger than B."). The conclusions that can follow from such premises are determined by the rules of formal logic. The simplest deductive argument is the *syllogism*, in which there are two premises and a conclusion. As you can see from studying Syllogism 1.0, one can construct a sound argument from two true premises (Premises 1 and 2).

Syllogism 1.0   A Valid Syllogism

Premise/ Conclusion	Abstract Form	Marble Example	Theory Example
Premise 1	All As are Bs.	All As (Alicia's marbles) are B (Black).	According to theory X (e.g., terror management theory), A (e.g., reminding participants that they will die) will result in B (increased allegiance to a cultural worldview that explains their existence and gives them hope of existing after death).
Premise 2	T is an A.	T (That marble) is A (Alicia's).	T (This study) will involve A (reminding participants that they will die).
Conclusion	T is a B.	T (That marble) is B (Black).	According to theory X, T (This study) will result in B (increased allegiance to a cultural worldview that explains their existence and gives them hope of existing after death).

There is, however, more to creating a syllogism than putting two premises together. To illustrate, examine an invalid syllogism: Syllogism 2.0.

Syllogism 2.0   An Invalid Syllogism Based on Sound Premises

Premise/ Conclusion	Abstract Form	Marble Example	Psychological Example
Premise 3	All As are Bs.	All As (Alicia's marbles) are B (Black).	According to theory X (e.g., terror management theory), A (e.g., reminding participants that they will die) will result in B (increased allegiance to a cultural worldview that explains their existence and gives them hope of existing after death).
Premise 4	T is a B.	T (That marble) is B (Black).	T (This study) resulted in B (increased allegiance to a cultural worldview that explains their existence and gives them hope of existing after death).

Syllogism 2.0   An Invalid Syllogism Based on Sound Premises—*continued*

Premise/ Conclusion	Abstract Form	Marble Example	Psychological Example
Conclusion	T is an A.	T (That marble) is A (Alicia's).	According to theory X, T (This study) involved A (reminding participants of their own death).
Why conclusion is not necessarily true	Some Bs might not be As. Thus, T could be a B that is not an A.	Some Bs (Black marbles) may not be As (Alicia's). Thus, that marble could be a black marble belonging to someone besides Alicia.	Being reminded that one will die may not be the only way that one might become more committed to a worldview.

Even if an argument is logically valid, it may be untrue. The truth of a logically valid argument depends on the truth of its premises. If either of the premises is untrue, the conclusion may be untrue. Syllogism 3.0 is an example of an argument that is valid but unsound.

Syllogism 3.0   A Logically Valid but Unsound Argument

Premise/Conclusion	Abstract Form	Marble Example
Premise 5	All Bs are As.	All "Bs" (black marbles) are "A" (white).
Premise 6	All Xs are Bs.	All Xs (your marbles) are "B" (black).
Conclusion	All Xs are As.	All Xs (your marbles) are "A" (white).

Unfortunately, students commonly insert two types of unsound deductive arguments into their papers. The first involves stating an untrue premise, such as stating a myth (e.g., "people only use 10% of their brain"), overstating the incidence of a phenomenon (e.g., "everyone believes in God"), or stating that a theory makes a certain claim when the theory does not make that claim. If you insert this first type of unsound deductive argument into your paper, your professor may write "citation?" or "No!" next to your questionable premise.

The second type of unsound deductive argument involves stating, "If A, then C," when "C" does not necessarily follow from "A" alone. This error is usually due to leaving out a premise. For example, a student might write, "If people had more positive attitudes toward children, child abuse would be eliminated." To prevent a professor from responding with "does not follow," "illogical," "not necessarily," or "non sequitur," the student would have to add the premise: "if having positive attitudes toward children eliminates child abuse."

When constructing your own syllogism or when reconstructing someone else's syllogism, follow the model presented in Syllogism 4.0. That is, precede premises with the word "If," separate each premise with the word "and," and precede the conclusion with the word "then." Adding "If" to the premises raises the possibility that the premises might be wrong. Adding "and" reminds you that all your premises must be correct to make a valid argument. Careful reading of the literature on a topic will be required to convince yourself, and careful reporting of that literature will be required to convince your reader, that all your premises are correct.

Syllogism 4.0   Expressed in Sentences (reading down)

Premise 7	If all Bs are As, *and*	If all learning phenomena show acquisition curves, *and*
Premise 8	if all Xs are Bs, *then,*	if handedness is a learning phenomenon, *then,*
Conclusion	all Xs are As.	handedness will show an acquisition curve.

In conclusion, whether you are writing a term paper or a research paper, you should know about deductive arguments. If you are writing a term paper, you may want to structure your term paper in the form of a syllogism (for an example, see Syllogism 4.0). If you are writing a research paper, you will probably want to use a deductive argument to justify your hypothesis (for an example, see Syllogism 1.0).

5.3 Inductive Arguments

When you make a deductive argument, (a) you are usually applying a general rule to a specific case (e.g., how a theory applies to a particular situation) and (b) your premises are couched in absolute terms. On the other hand, when you make an inductive argument, (a) you are usually forming a general rule from observing some specific cases (e.g., determining what most people believe from a poll of a few people) and (b) at least one of your premises is couched in relative (e.g., "some," "most," "usually") rather than in absolute terms. If you make an inductive argument, beware of three errors.

First, beware of overstating the frequency of an observed event. For example, if you have evidence that some people in a sample had been sexually abused, do not write, "most people in the sample had been sexually abused."

Second, realize that if the evidence for your conclusion is from a sample (e.g., a poll of individuals, a personal experience), the validity of your conclusion will depend on the extent to which the sample is representative. Thus, whereas a large, random sample would provide a solid basis for estimating the frequency of abuse, your personal experiences would not provide a solid basis for estimating the frequency of abuse.

Third, realize that even when your observations are accurate and your sample is representative, your conclusion may be wrong for three reasons. First, samples do not reflect their populations perfectly. Second, rules that worked in the past may not hold in the future. Third, more than one rule may fit the data. To illustrate that you may not find out until too late that a rule that fits the existing data is incorrect, consider the classic story of the "inductive turkey." The turkey is greeted every morning by the nice farmer who gives the turkey corn. The turkey induces that this kind treatment will always be the case. On Thanksgiving morning, however, the turkey finds that inductive reasoning has a fatal flaw.

Although you should be cautious about all conclusions from inductive arguments, you should be especially careful about arguments from analogy. In one form of argument by analogy, people argue that (a) X and Y are similar because they are known to share certain properties (e.g., humans and nonhuman animals have brains and learn), (b) it is now known that X has certain property (e.g., humans have abstract thought), and (c) because Y is similar to X, Y also has this property (e.g., nonhuman animals have abstract thought).

In another form of this argument, people argue that because Y (e.g., handedness) has several characteristics of X (learned behavior), Y is an X. For example, they may argue that handedness is a learned behavior because it shares several characteristics of learned behavior: it takes time to develop, it may be exhibited in one situation but not in another, and it exhibits spontaneous recovery. The more similarities people find between Y and X, the better their case that Y probably belongs to the X category. However, they can never prove that Y is a member of the X category (e.g., ants have many similarities to humans but ants are not humans).

In summary, arguments by analogy can lead to interesting insights (e.g., modern cognitive psychology has benefited from comparing human memory to computer memory) and useful applications (e.g., research on nonhuman animals has been successfully applied to humans). However, because being like something does not make it identical to something, arguments by analogy may lead to false conclusions (e.g., nonhuman animals do not have abstract thought).

5.4 Hypotheses

Your hypothesis should be a prediction about how a measured variable depends on one or more other variables. Table 5.3 provides some examples of hypotheses.

If you think of your hypothesis as the conclusion of a syllogism (see Syllogism 4.0), you will find it easier to write the Introduction of your paper. You will spell out and defend the premises and then explain how the premises lead to the conclusion that

TABLE **5.3** Examples of Hypotheses

Adults over age 65 in good health will score better on the XYZ test of crystallized intelligence than adults between the ages of 25 and 35.

When a person thinks that several others have witnessed an accident, the person will be slower to give help than when the person thinks he or she is alone.

Visual acuity will improve with increases in lighting level.

Performance on the ABC test of IQ will predict school performance.

your hypothesis should be supported. When you write the discussion section, you will again find it useful to think of your hypothesis as the conclusion of a syllogism. For example, suppose your study shows that your hypothesis—the conclusion of your syllogism—is false. In that case, not only would your conclusion be false, but at least one of your premises would be false as well (provided that your syllogism is valid). Thus, in addition to making the case that your study's results really did disprove the hypothesis, you would also discuss the implications of the study for the validity of the premises.

For instance, if your hypothesis was based on Syllogism 4.0, your discussion might make the case that your results not only call into question the conclusion (that handedness shows an acquisition curve) but also call into question the premise that led to that conclusion (that handedness is learned). Similarly, if one of the premises of your syllogism is a core premise of a theory, you would not only argue that your results disprove your hypothesis, but you would also argue that they challenge the validity of that theory.

5.5 Problems in Making Arguments

As we have pointed out, your paper should make a case for your thesis. In the next sections, we will show you what errors to avoid in arguing for your thesis. Note that you should try to catch these errors both when reading and revising your own paper as well as when reading another person's paper. As you will see, these problems in making arguments can be broken down into three categories: (a) not stating an arguable thesis, (b) not making a fair argument, and (c) failing to consider alternative explanations for the evidence.

5.6 Stating an Unarguable Thesis

As we suggested earlier, people sometimes err by choosing to make a case for an uncontestable claim. For example, their claim is a vague statement ("environment has some effect on behavior"), a statement of a well-documented fact ("some responses can be classically conditioned"), a statement of a feeling or opinion ("I feel that shock treatment is morally wrong"), or a tautology (e.g., "effective behavioral treatments are effective"). The problem with tautologies is that, because they are redundant, they are valid even when their premises are questionable. For example, suppose you state the following tautology: "Stereotypes are hateful, inaccurate views of a group held only by extremely prejudiced people. If we stop people from being extremely prejudiced, we will eliminate stereotypes." The reader may disagree with your definitions but, given your definitions, the reader must accept your conclusion.

Sometimes, the reason a reader may disagree with your definitions is that you have defined your terms using a dictionary of English rather than a dictionary of psychology. Your professor, for example, would probably disagree with your definitions if you used a dictionary of English to define any of the following terms: experiment, personality, random, reliable, reinforcement, intelligence, or motivation.

If you find yourself resorting to a dictionary of English to define your argument, stop yourself. Use a reputable dictionary of psychology, such as Reber's (2001) *Penguin Dictionary of Psychology*, instead. However, even a psychological dictionary will not always help you make an appropriate argument. If your instructor posed a topic in which the key issue was one of definition (e.g., "Are recovered memories false memories?"), accepting a particular definition because it was stated in your dictionary would be to miss the point of the assignment. For example, if your dictionary defined recovered memories as real memories, accepting this definition would be to miss the point that some memories may not be accurate. Given your dictionary's definition, the thesis that recovered memories are real would be unarguable.

In summary, you should make a strong case for your thesis. However, you should not make a strong case by improperly defining terms or by stating an unarguable thesis. To avoid having an unarguable thesis, ask yourself what evidence would disprove your thesis. If no pattern of results could disprove your thesis, you need a new thesis.

5.7 Substituting Appeals for Reasoning: Nonobjective Thinking

Once you have a thesis that you can argue, the key is to argue using objective evidence and logical reasoning. Unfortunately, sometimes people substitute appeals to emotion, faith, or authority for logical reasoning.

5.7.1 Appeal to Emotion

An appeal to emotion is to set aside one of the major criteria of the scientific method: objectivity. Zechmeister and Johnson (1992) say that appeals to emotion ask the reader to suspend objectivity and to experience either pity or fear. In a paper arguing for the accuracy of recovered memories, a student might try to evoke pity by writing, "The distress shown by clients as they retrieve these painful memories compels us to believe that the memories are real." Alternatively, a student might try to evoke the fear of being considered insensitive by writing, "Only someone devoid of human feelings could doubt clients as they recall these painful memories."

To make appeal-to-emotion arguments, students commonly ask rhetorical questions. For example, suppose a student posed the following question: "Who could doubt such clients' experiences?" The question is rhetorical because the writer is convinced that the reader will be forced to answer, "Nobody could." Rhetorical questions are out of place in scientific discourse; avoid them.

5.7.2 Appeal to Faith

Like appeals to emotion, appeals to faith set aside objectivity. Imagine a writer asserting that there are fairies at the bottom of the garden, but that the fairies will reveal themselves only to those who believe in them. Further, the writer adds, the fairies will refuse to give any evidence of themselves. Such an appeal to faith would probably be ineffective. Unfortunately, however, if, instead of appealing to faith in fairies, the writer appealed to faith in a particular religious, political, or theoretical position, the writer would sway some readers.

5.7.3 Appeal to Authority

An appeal to authority is made when a well-respected person's name is cited for a particular position. The assumption underlying appeal-to-authority arguments is that any position associated with someone so wonderful must be a correct position.

Do not rely on appeal-to-authority arguments. At best, arguments made by appeal to authority are weak. For example, it would be weak to write, "In his presidential address to the American Psychological Association, Smith (1993) asserted that most repressed memories of childhood sexual abuse surfacing in therapy are examples of false memories." This citation of Smith is weak because there is nothing in the citation to allow the reader to evaluate Smith's opinion that therapist-elicited repressed memories are false memories. For example, there is no discussion of research demonstrating the falsehood of the memories. Consequently, the only reason to believe Smith's opinion rests on Smith's reputation as president of the APA.

5.8 Unfair Arguments

5.8.1 Ad Hominem Arguments

Whereas the writer making an appeal-to-authority argument implies that the reader should believe a position because a person with a good reputation believes in that position, a writer making an *ad hominem* argument implies that the reader should not believe a position because the person advocating the position has a poor reputation. Specifically, whenever a writer attacks the character of the person providing the evidence, the writer has made an ad hominem argument (the English translation of the Latin phrase "ad hominem" is "toward the person"). The assumption underlying ad hominem arguments is that any position associated with someone so disreputable cannot be a correct position. For example, let us say that Jones (1990) has shown that some therapists consistently elicit reports of childhood sexual abuse (e.g., satanic rituals) from clients randomly assigned to them. Ad hominem arguments would include claims that Jones used cocaine or that Jones was a fascist. Ad hominem arguments would not address the quality of Jones's research. Ad hominem arguments are unfair.

5.8.2 Ignoring Contradictory Evidence

Another unfair way for a writer to favor one position at the expense of opposing positions is to ignore any contradictory evidence. For example, you could make a convincing argument that the world is flat if you ignored all the evidence that the world is round. Similarly, you could make a convincing case for the validity of recovered memories by accepting uncritically only papers in which the authors concluded that recovered memories were accurate.

Students are often guilty of not citing and discussing contradictory evidence. To avoid making this error, you must (a) read widely enough on a topic to be able to write about the evidence relating to both your position on an issue as well as to the opposing position, and (b) be open-minded enough to be fair to the opposing position.

5.8.3 Straw Man Arguments

If you cannot be fair to the opposing position, you may be guilty of attacking a *straw man:*[1] a description of the opposing position that is designed to be attacked and defeated. By discrediting the opposing position, writers make their own position appear stronger. For example, suppose that a writer wishes to favor the argument that there have been no reliable demonstrations of repressed memories. The writer could construct a straw man by presenting a weak case for repressed memories. One way to create a weak case would be to build the case using only the most seriously flawed studies the writer could find. The writer would then proceed to demolish the straw man by listing all the methodological flaws.

The straw man argument is likely to surface when students are attacking a theory they do not like. To destroy the theory, they oversimplify it and misstate its premises. Then, the professor, like a referee calling a foul, reprimands the students for attacking a "straw man version" of the theory rather than the theory itself.

Although even some published writers make straw man arguments, resist the temptation to provide weakened and oversimplified versions of positions that disagree with your position. Instead, if you want to demolish an argument opposing yours, make sure you demolish the strongest version of the argument.

5.9 General Errors in Reasoning From Evidence

Thus far, we have discussed errors caused by ignoring the evidence, such as attacking a caricature of an opposing idea rather than the idea itself, attacking the person who proposed an opposing idea rather than the person's idea, and ignoring evidence that favors an opposing idea. That is, we have discussed errors resulting from passion overriding reason. In the next section, we will discuss errors in which the person looks at the evidence but errs by failing to consider alternative explanations for the evidence. Reading this section will help you evaluate other people's published papers as well as help you evaluate drafts of your own papers.

---

[1]The original straw man was a soldier's uniform stuffed with straw that was propped on the battlements of a castle. It was designed to draw the arrows of enemy archers, leaving the real soldiers unharmed. As the soldiers were always dressed as men, it is inaccurate, and possibly disrespectful to women, to use the term "straw *person* argument."

5.9.1 Inferring Causation From Correlation

If you conduct a correlational study or read a report of one, you learn that two variables are related. Unfortunately, you may also jump to the conclusion that the research has also established that the two variables are causally related. In other words, you may label one variable the "cause" and the other the "effect"—despite the fact that you should not make cause-effect statements from correlational studies.

To understand why you should not draw cause-effect conclusions from correlational studies, imagine reading about a correlational study that found a relationship between television watching and depression. Specifically, suppose that a survey found that people who watched more television were more likely to be depressed. You would be tempted to believe that television viewing caused some of those surveyed to become depressed. Yet to do so would be to commit the error of inferring causation from correlation. The reason we cannot infer causation from correlation is that there are numerous explanations for a correlation between two variables. For example, it may be that television watching, rather than being a cause of depression, may be an effect of depression: Perhaps depressed people watch more television because they are more likely to feel that they do not have the energy to do anything else. Alternatively, both television watching and depression may be side effects of some other factor: Perhaps people who lose their jobs or who are not getting enough sleep are more likely to (a) become depressed and (b) have more time to watch television.

To make cause-effect statements, you cannot rely on surveys or other correlational studies. Instead, the only studies that allow causation to be inferred correctly are *experiments*,[2] most of which embody three principles:

1. At least two groups of individuals are formed by random assignment.[3]
2. Each group is treated identically except for the *manipulated variable:* the *independent variable.*[4] Sometimes, the experimental group receives a treatment that contains a moderate or high amount of the manipulated variable, whereas another group, a *control* group, gets no treatment. Usually, however, if there is a control group, either that group will receive a treatment that contains a small amount of the manipulated variable or it will receive a *placebo treatment:* a fake treatment, such as a sugar pill in a drug study, that does not contain any of the manipulated variable.
3. The groups are significantly different in terms of their scores on the *measured variable* (also known as the *dependent variable*).

---

[2]We will not discuss small-n research, quasi-experiments or causal modeling because such techniques are beyond the scope of this book.

[3]We will not consider experiments in which people participate in more than a single experimental condition. Such within-subjects (repeated-measures) experiments have their own specialized procedures that allow causation to be inferred.

[4]Experiments can have more than one manipulated variable. However, for simplicity's sake, we will confine ourselves to the simple, single-factor experiment.

To see how you could do an experiment that incorporated these three principles, imagine that you want to determine whether watching violent television causes children to be aggressive. In that case, you might design the following experiment.

1. Randomly assign children to violent-television-viewing and nonviolent-television-viewing groups. Random assignment might involve flipping a coin for each child: A head means the child goes into the violent-television group, and a tail means the child goes into the nonviolent-television group.

2. Treat the groups identically except that you show one group one television program and the other group a different program (the independent variable manipulation). All children then have an identical session of free play in which an observer counts the number of aggressive acts committed by each child. The number of aggressive acts represents the measured (dependent) variable.

3. Test whether there is a statistically significant (reliable) difference between the two groups' scores. If there is such a difference in behavior, one can conclude that the difference in the content of the two television programs caused the difference in aggressive behavior.

If any one of the three principles is violated, causation usually cannot be inferred. In the next section, we will show you why the first principle, random assignment, is crucial to making cause-effect statements.

If the researcher does not randomly assign participants to groups, the groups may be systematically different even before the treatment is introduced. For example, suppose the researcher decided to assign boys to see the violent program and girls to see the nonviolent program. In that case, skeptics could argue that the difference between the groups' behavior was due to gender rather than to the manipulation. Alternatively, suppose the researcher let all the children who wanted to go first watch the violent program and had the more hesitant children watch the nonviolent program. In that case, skeptics could argue that the difference between groups' behavior was due to personality differences between the groups (e.g., maybe assertive children are more aggressive than reserved children) rather than to the manipulation.

Another form of nonrandom assignment that creates groups that are systematically different before the manipulation is administered is *self-selection:* letting people choose their treatment condition. If the researcher in the television violence study we have been discussing were to let children self-select, the aggressive children might be more likely than less aggressive children to choose to watch the violent television program. Although self-selection might seem far-fetched for the study we are considering, self-selection is a problem with much survey research.

For example, suppose that a survey researcher questions children and finds that children who watch more hours of violent television are more aggressive than children who watch fewer hours of violent television (i.e., aggression and watching violent television are correlated). The researcher should not conclude that watching violent television causes a child to be aggressive because of the problem of self-selection:

Aggressive children may simply choose to watch violent television more than less aggressive children.[5]

Any study that uses self-selection is a correlational study and should not be used as the basis of a cause-effect conclusion. For example, in the 1960s, researchers found that people who smoked were more likely to have heart disease than people who did not smoke. However, that finding was not based on randomly assigning people to smoke. Smoking was not even a manipulated variable. Instead, the smoking and nonsmoking groups were formed by self-selection: People chose either to smoke or to not smoke. Thus, the finding that smokers had more heart disease than nonsmokers was a correlational finding. Such a correlational finding did not establish that smoking had any effect on heart disease. Indeed, in the 1960s, when researchers knew only that smokers were more prone to heart disease than nonsmokers, many reasonable people argued that both smoking and heart disease could be side effects of another variable (e.g., stress may cause people to have heart disease as well as cause people to smoke).

5.9.2 Making Something Out of Nothing: Misinterpreting Null Results

The failure to consider alternative explanations for a correlational finding is one of the most common and one of the most serious reasoning errors that students make. The second most common and second most serious reasoning error is the failure to appreciate that there are alternative explanations for null results.

The failure to find a relationship between two variables is not proof that the two variables are unrelated. Admittedly, one reason a study might fail to find a relationship is that there is no relationship to find. However, there are other reasons for failing to find a relationship. For example, the relationship may be overlooked because the study's measure was not sensitive enough or because, as often occurs in psychological research, the researcher did not study enough participants (Cohen, 1990).

In short, null results are inconclusive. On the one hand, you cannot use them to conclude that your variables are related. On the other hand, you cannot use them to conclude that your variables are unrelated.

5.9.3 Adding Meaning to Significance: Misinterpreting Significant Results

If you observe a relationship between two variables in your study, you need to view that finding with caution. Sometimes, random error makes it appear that two variables are related when, in fact, the variables are not related. Therefore, you need to ask

---

[5]Note that it is self-selection—not the survey instrument itself—that prevents the survey researcher from making valid cause-effect statements. If a questionnaire is used as the dependent measure in an experiment, the experimenter can make a cause-effect statement. For example, in our television violence experiment, we could have used a questionnaire—rather than observation—to measure aggressiveness. We could make a cause-effect statement because, instead of using self-selection, we randomly assigned participants to receive different manipulations.

whether the pattern of results you observed is reliable: If you repeated the study, would you get similar results? The best and most direct evidence for reliability is replication: Others have repeated the study and obtained similar results.

For better or worse, the evidence that psychologists have typically used to evaluate the reliability of a single study is the evidence from statistical significance tests. Significance tests tell you the probability of getting the obtained results if the *null hypothesis* (the null hypothesis is that there is no relationship between the variables) is true.[6] Traditionally, if the chances are less than 5 in 100 ("$p < .05$ [or less]") of getting certain results given that the null hypothesis is true, psychologists have considered the null hypothesis to be false, and therefore have considered the results reliable. That is, they declare such results "statistically significant."

Statistically significant results are not necessarily large. Many statistically significant results, based on huge samples, are small and meaningless. In short, realize that if you want to estimate the size of an effect, you must do more than look at the results of a significance test.

5.9.4 Trusting Labels Too Much: Not Questioning Construct Validity

In addition to questioning the relationship between manipulated and measured variables, you should question the labels that the researchers attached to those variables. For example, suppose that the researchers claim to have manipulated the construct "television violence" and claim to have measured the construct "aggression." They could be wrong on both counts.

The researchers' manipulation would not have *construct validity* if the two programs differed in their excitement level. If the violent program was also more exciting than the other program, the increase in aggression may be from the heightened arousal of children who viewed it rather than from the violence.

The researchers' measure would not have construct validity if it did not accurately measure aggression. For example, if their aggression measure consisted of giving children inkblots to look at and then counting the number of times the children thought that the inkblots looked like animals, you should question the construct validity of the aggression measure. The measure does not match up closely with definitions of aggression, and there is no evidence that it correlates with valid measures of aggression. If the measure was how aggressive the researchers thought the inkblot responses were, you would also question the measure's validity on the grounds that it was not objective and therefore allowed the researchers to bias the results.

In many studies, you should be concerned about the potential for *researcher bias:* the researcher behaving differently in different conditions of the study, thereby influencing the behavior of the participants (to favor the researcher's hypothesis). Research has shown researcher bias to be quite subtle and to occur despite the researcher's best intentions (Rosenthal, 1966).

---

[6]As Cohen (1994) pointed out, significance tests do not tell us what we really want to know: how likely it is, given these results, that the null hypothesis is true.

In many studies, you may also need to decide whether the results may be due to *participant bias:* participants guessing the hypothesis and altering their behavior either to favor or to refute the hypothesis. Participant bias is often a problem in research that asks participants to fill out a scale or to answer a question. In such research, it is easy for participants to give a researcher the answers they think the researcher wants to hear.

Researcher bias and participant bias are often serious threats to research in clinical psychology. For example, suppose that people suffering from depression are randomly assigned either to take a particular treatment (e.g., a new drug or a new therapy) or to take a control treatment (a capsule containing an inert substance or an ineffective therapy). If the researcher knows which people are receiving the treatment and which are receiving the control, the researcher might behave more cheerily to those receiving the treatment than to those receiving the control—and that cheeriness might improve the treatment group's mood. In such a case, the study's construct validity would be ruined by researcher bias. If the participants know whether they have received the treatment, those receiving the treatment might cheer up because they expect the treatment to work, whereas those receiving the control might despair. In that case, participant bias would poison the study's construct validity.

One popular way to deal with both participant and researcher bias has been to run *double-blind* (also called *double-masked*) studies, in which the experimenter and the participants are kept ignorant of (are blind to) which group is which. For example, in a drug study, the primary investigator might have assigned a code to each bottle of pills. The participants and the research assistants who interacted with the participants would know the pill's code number (e.g., X3987), but would not know whether the pill contained a drug or whether it was only a placebo.

5.9.5 Not Questioning Generalizations

In addition to questioning the study's construct validity, you should question the study's *external validity:* the degree to which the results of the study can be generalized to different settings and different participants. One clue to the extent to which the results can be generalized will come from the Participants section. If the participants constitute a large, representative sample (e.g., a large random sample) of a broad population, you can be more confident that the results will generalize to people beyond the participants of that particular study than if the participants were not a representative sample of that population. Note, however, that if only two of the participants in this representative sample were Asian Americans, you have little evidence that the results generalize to Asian Americans.

In evaluating generalizations, be cautious, but not cynical; you should neither unquestionably accept them nor unquestionably reject them. Be cautious by realizing that any generalization beyond the evidence may be wrong: The only way to be sure that the results generalize to a particular group or setting is to repeat the study with that particular group or setting. However, do not be so cynical that you completely reject any generalization that goes beyond the immediate study. It is often reasonable to make tentative generalizations.

For example, given that almost all research results obtained in a lab setting also hold in field settings, it is usually reasonable to generalize from the lab to the field. Similarly, given that most relationships found with one group also can be found with a different group, generalizing the results to a group that was not adequately sampled may be reasonable. To reject such a generalization, you should do more than say that no generalization is possible because the particular group has not been sampled. Instead, you should have a logical explanation of how differences between that particular group and the group studied would prevent the results from applying to that particular group.

5.10   Critical Thinking Checklist

____ I did not substitute a tautology (see 5.1) for a claim.

____ I used accepted definitions of terms.

____ My arguments were logical.

____ I identified my premises and, when possible, used evidence to make the case that they were true.

____ I made sure that my conclusion followed logically from my premises.

____ I avoided appeals to emotion, faith, and authority.

____ I dealt fairly with opposing positions.

____ I did not engage in ad hominem attacks on proponents of opposing positions.

____ I did not attack a straw man version of the opposing position.

____ I did not ignore evidence that appeared to support an opposing position: I either showed how that evidence, when properly interpreted, was consistent with my claims, or I qualified my claims to be consistent with that evidence.

____ I considered alternative explanations for findings.

____ I did not interpret correlational evidence as proving causality.

____ I did not use the fact that studies failed to find differences as proof that differences did not exist.

____ I questioned whether the measures and manipulations really reflected the labels that the researcher gave them.

____ I considered explanations, other than the ones provided by the authors, for the obtained results.

____ I was careful when accepting generalizations from a study, especially when there was reason to believe that the sample was biased.

5.11 Summary

1. If you are writing a term paper, state an arguable thesis (see 5.1 and 5.6).

2. Use sound (accurate) premises. Once you have sound premises, you can focus on demonstrating that your argument is *valid* (the conclusion follows logically from your premises).

3. Decide whether your argument is inductive or deductive. The simplest deductive argument is the *syllogism*, in which there are two premises and a conclusion. In deductive arguments, premises are statements about the world couched in absolute terms (e.g., "all," "every," "always") or in unambiguous comparisons (e.g., "A is bigger than B."). In deductive arguments, if the premises are true and the reasoning is valid, the conclusion must be true. In inductive arguments, premises are statements about the world couched in relative terms (e.g., "few," "some," "most"). Often, inductive reasoning involves generalizing from observed instances. Such generalizations may turn out to be false.

4. If you are making a case for a hypothesis, you may want to make your case using a syllogism.

5. Avoid appeals to emotion or authority.

6. Deal with evidence that contradicts your argument.

7. Avoid unfair tactics, such as ad hominem arguments (5.8.1) or straw man arguments (5.8.3).

8. Avoid common errors in reasoning from evidence include inferring a cause-effect relationship from a correlational study, uncritically generalizing the results from a study that used a biased sample, and uncritically accepting the labels that a researcher gives to the measures and manipulations.

9. Recognize that although you cannot safely infer causation from a correlational study, you can reasonably infer causation from an experiment (see 5.9.1).

10. Recognize that null results are inconclusive.

11. Recognize that statistically significant results are not necessarily large or important.

12. Assess a study's construct validity. Did the researcher (a) use commonly accepted measures and manipulations and (b) take steps, such as using "blind" procedures, to decrease both participant bias and researcher bias?

13. Be cautious about generalizing. Although there is always some risk in generalizing the results of a study, you can be more confident that the results apply to a larger group if the study looked at a large random sample of participants from that group.

CHAPTER

6

Writing the Wrongs: How to Avoid Gruesome Grammar, Putrid Punctuation, and Saggy Style

Writing a paper is like driving passengers to a destination. In addition to knowing where you are going, you should know enough about the

1. components of a car (parts of speech) and how they work together (basic grammar) to get in and start the car

2. controls (punctuation) to keep the car going, to steer, and to brake

3. rules of the road (usage) so you drive on the correct side of the road and respect other road users

4. passengers' preferences and the car's handling characteristics (style) to drive with care, and, possibly, with flair

If you spend a little time studying this chapter, you will be able to understand most of the comments that the *Publication Manual* makes about writing, as well as the comments that your professor or writing center may make about your paper. If you spend a moderate amount of time studying this chapter, you will be able to write competently. If you spend a great deal of time studying this chapter and practicing what it preaches, you will be able to express your ideas with style and flair.

6.1 Elements of Grammar

The smallest unit of writing is the word. Types of words include nouns, pronouns, verbs, articles, adjectives, adverbs, prepositions, conjunctions, and relative pronouns. To illustrate the different parts of speech, we will analyze a sentence written by McDougall (1914):

```
The department of psychology that is of primary importance
for the social sciences is that which deals with the springs
of human action. (pp. 2-3)
```

6.1.1 Nouns

Nouns are names: person names, place names, object names, and concept names (e.g., freedom). Here is McDougall's sentence with the nouns printed in bold italics:

```
The department of psychology that is of primary importance
for the social sciences is that which deals with the springs
of human action.
```

Nouns have a property called *number*, meaning they can be *singular* or *plural*. Singular nouns refer to just one of the named thing (e.g., "department"); plural nouns refer to two or more of the named thing (e.g., "sciences"). Most plurals are formed simply by adding *s*, *es*, or *en* to the end of a singular noun (e.g., "cats," "foxes," "oxen"). However, not all plurals are formed so simply. Nouns derived from Greek or Latin may have singulars ending with *on* or *us* (e.g., criterion, stimulus) and plurals ending with *a* and *i*, respectively (e.g., criteria, stimuli). To use the correct plural form of these and other irregular nouns, you must memorize the plural form (e.g., geese). The six most misused plurals are listed in Table 6.1. Memorize these six. In addition, when proofing your paper, consult Appendix B to check for other tricky plurals.

Be alert not only to nouns that have unusual plural forms, but also to nouns that are singular even though they refer to more than one person. For example, "everybody," "everyone," and "anyone" are all singular. Similarly, *collective nouns*, nouns that stand for groups (e.g., "team," "university," "family"), are treated as singular—if you are treating the group as a single unit. Thus, you should write, "The family was interviewed together."

Sometimes, students have trouble deciding whether a percentage (e.g., 33%) or fraction (e.g., one in three) is singular or plural. At first, it seems contradictory to treat "33%" as plural but to treat "one in three" as singular. The key is to realize that, in the first case, you are discussing more than one unit (the units being percents), whereas in the second case you are discussing one unit (e.g., the unit being thirds). Once you accept that it is the number of units that determine whether a percentage or fraction is

TABLE **6.1** Six Tricky Plurals

Singular	Plural	Examples
criterion	criteria	One criterion of good writing is correct use of plural words. There are several other criteria, including correct punctuation and grammar.
datum	data	A datum for each individual was the time taken for his or her first correct response. These data were analyzed using *t* tests.
hypothesis	hypotheses	Hypothesis 1 was supported, but the other hypotheses were not.
medium	media ("Mediums" refers to psychics.)	The most influential medium is television. Other media such as magazines, newspapers, and radio cannot combine moving images and sound.
phenomenon	phenomena	One learning phenomenon is spontaneous recovery. There are three other important learning phenomena.
stimulus	stimuli	Each stimulus was displayed in a circular field. The six stimuli occurred in a random order.

singular or plural, the rule is simple: If you are referring to one unit (e.g., "one percent" or "one in three"), use the singular; if you are referring to more than one unit (e.g., "33%," "two in three"), use the plural.

Sometimes, students have trouble deciding what to do when two nouns are connected in a sentence. However, you will not have that problem if you follow two rules. First, when "and" joins two singular nouns, treat the nouns as plural (e.g., "Smith and Brown provide a useful definition"). Second, when "or" or "nor" joins two nouns, use the form required by the noun closer to the verb (e.g., "Either they or I *am* correct," "Neither she nor they *are* correct").

The final problem students have with nouns is that they do not capitalize *proper nouns:* names of particular people, events, organizations, languages, buildings, countries, and racial groups. Remember to capitalize all proper nouns (e.g., "Jones," "Pennsylvania," "Asian Americans").

6.1.2 Personal and Impersonal Pronouns

Pronouns are words that substitute for nouns. *Personal pronouns* stand for people (e.g., "her," "him"). *Impersonal pronouns* stand for things (e.g., "it," "this," "that," "these," "those," "either," "neither"). Here is McDougall's sentence with its impersonal pronoun printed in bold italics:

> The department of psychology that is of primary importance for the social sciences is *that* which deals with the springs of human action.

The boldfaced and italicized "that" stands for "the department of psychology."

Personal pronouns have three *persons: first person* (referring to the person[s] speaking [e.g., "I," "me"]), *second person* (referring to the person[s] being spoken to [e.g., "you"]), and *third person* (referring to the person[s] being spoken about [e.g., "she," "he," "him," or "her"]). In addition, personal pronouns also have three *cases: subjective, objective,* and *possessive.*

Subjective means the pronoun is the *subject* (the agent that is the focus) of the sentence (e.g., "*I* calculated"). The subjective pronoun usually comes before the verb. The subjective case is also known as the *nominative* case. "I," "we," "they," "she," and "he," are nominative pronouns. "Who" is also a nominative pronoun: If you can replace the "who" in your sentence with "he" or some other nominative pronoun, you have correctly chosen between "who" and "whom."

Objective means the pronoun is the *object* acted upon in the sentence (e.g., "The idea [subject] surprised [verb] *me* [object]"). The pronoun following the verb is almost always an objective pronoun[1] (e.g., "I [subject] was surprised *by him* [object]"). "Me," "us," "them," "her," and "him" are objective pronouns. "Whom" is also an objective pronoun: If you can replace the "whom" in your sentence with "him," "her," or some other objective pronoun, you have correctly chosen between "who" and "whom."

Possessive means the pronoun owns (possesses) something (e.g., "*Our* argument is"). Note that, whereas the possessive form of a noun has an apostrophe (e.g., Mark's), possessive pronouns, even "its," "whose," "ours," "hers," and "theirs," do not have apostrophes.

Like nouns, pronouns have number. Table 6.2 shows all the possible combinations of person, case, and number for most of the personal pronouns. In formal writing,[2] pronouns must agree in number and gender with the nouns they represent:

✘ The technique is best for disciplining the *child* because *they* learn the consequences of *their* actions [unclear because *child* is singular, but *they* and *their* are plural].

✔ The technique is best for disciplining *children* because *they* learn the consequences of *their* actions [now the noun and pronoun are both plural].

Reading your paper aloud will not be enough to make sure that your nouns agree with your pronouns. Instead, you will have to take at least two additional steps. First, use your word processor's grammar checker to find some of the disagreements.

---

[1]The pronoun following a verb will be an objective pronoun except when the verb is "was," "is," "are," "were," or some other form of the verb "to be." In such cases, you would use a subjective pronoun rather than an objective pronoun. Thus, you would write, "It was she" rather than "It was her."

[2]Unfortunately, in everyday speech, you will often hear people make this grammatical mistake. Consequently, when you read your paper aloud, you may not catch this error because it may not sound wrong to you (unlike many other grammatical mistakes, such as "I were" and "he ain't"). One solution is to use your word processor's search function to find each "their" and verify that each "their" corresponds to a plural noun.

TABLE **6.2**   Subjective, Objective, and Possessive Cases of Personal Pronouns by Person and Number

Person	Subjective (Nominative)	Objective	Possessive
		Singular	
First	I	me	my, mine
Second	you	you	your, yours
Third	he, she	him, her	his, her, hers
	who	whom	whose
		Plural	
First	we	us	our, ours
Second	you	you	your, yours
Third	they	them	their, theirs
	who	whom	whose

Second, use your word processor's "find" command to search for "their" and check to make sure that each "their" refers to a plural noun.

Although you need to be careful whenever you use pronouns, you need to keep three additional cautions in mind when you use the indefinite pronouns "neither" and "either." First, realize that both "neither" and "either" are singular (e.g., "Either is a problem"). Second, realize that "neither" and "either" can be used only when you are referring to two things. If you have three items, use "or" instead of "either" (e.g., "the answer could be A, B, or C") and use "not . . . or" instead of "neither" (e.g., "the answer could not be A, B, or C"). Third, appreciate the intimate relationship between "neither" and "nor": You can use the conjunction "nor" in only two situations: (a) after "neither" or (b) to continue negation started in one clause into the next clause.

✘ There were *neither* colloquialisms, contractions, foreign words, *nor* proper nouns in the list [wrong because *neither* was used to cover more than two things].

✔ There were no colloquialisms, contractions, foreign words, or proper nouns in the list.

✘ Neither Smith (1967) or [wrong because *nor* must be used after *neither*] Jones (1973) explained the phenomenon.

✔ Neither Smith (1967) nor Jones (1973) explained the phenomenon.

✘ Theory Y does not explain paranoia *nor* [*nor* would have been okay if *neither* had come before paranoia] catatonia, *or* [need to use *nor* to show that the theory does *not* deal with mania] deal with mania.

✔ Theory Y does not explain paranoia or catatonia, nor deal
with mania [*nor* continues the negation started in the first clause into
the last clause].

6.1.3 Verbs

Verbs are words that represent actions; they are the "doers" of the sentence. Here is
McDougall's sentence with the verbs italicized (the main verb of the sentence has been
printed in bold italic):

> The department of psychology that *is* of primary importance
> for the social sciences *is* that which *deals* with the springs
> of human action.

Verbs have a property called *tense*. Tense refers to when the action of a verb happened. *Future* tense means the action is going to happen. To form the future tense, put
the word "will" before the verb (e.g., will analyze). *Present* tense means the action is
happening now. *Past* tense means the action happened some time ago. To form the past
tense of regular verbs, put "-ed" on the end of the verb (e.g., analyzed). *Present perfect
tense* means that the event happened in the past at some unknown time and is continuing to occur. To form the present perfect tense, put "have" before the past-tense form
of your verb (e.g., have analyzed). (To learn more about using the right tense, see 2.10
and 3.11.)

In addition to tenses, verbs also have moods. One mood is the *subjunctive* mood,
used to describe something that did not happen. If you use the subjunctive mood in a
sentence, you will use the verb "were," and you will probably begin your sentence with
the word "if " (e.g., "If I were to boil the participants in oil").

Unless a verb is in the subjunctive mood, it must be singular if its subject is singular and must be plural if its subject is plural. If you are using a regular verb in the present tense, finding the verb form that *agrees* with the subject will usually be easy
because *regular* verbs have only two forms for the present tense. One form, with an "s"
at the end (e.g., "agrees"), covers the third person singular ("he agrees," "she agrees").
The other form, without an "s" at the end, covers the other cases ("I agree," "you
agree," "we agree," and "they agree"). Meeting the requirement of subject-verb agreement is more difficult with *irregular* verbs: verbs having more than one form (e.g., the
verb "to be" has "I am," "you/we/they are," and "he/she is").

Verbs also have a property called *voice*. There are two voices: *active* and *passive*. In
the active voice, the subject acts on the object (e.g., "Smith [subject] discovered [active
verb] the phenomenon [object]."). In the passive voice, the subject is acted on by the
object (e.g., "The phenomenon [subject] was discovered [passive verb] by Smith
[object]."). The active voice is more direct and less wordy. Usually, you should use the
active rather than the passive voice. (For more about voice, see 1.3.2.)

Two "almost-verbs" that writers sometimes mistake for verbs are the *infinitive* and
the *present participle*. An infinitive always has the word "to" in front of it (e.g., "to be,"
"to deal"). A present participle is usually produced by adding "-ing" on the end of
the verb's infinitive form (e.g., "being," "dealing"). Neither infinitives nor present

participles can function as verbs: As you can see from the following examples, trying to use these almost-verbs as verbs will cause you to write incomplete sentences.

✗ To be immoral. [not a sentence] What does it mean? . . . This theory dealing with motivation. [not a sentence]

✔ Defining immoral behavior is difficult . . . This theory deals with motivation.

6.1.4 Articles

Articles come before nouns. There are only three: one *definite* article, "the," and two *indefinite* articles, "a" and "an."

■ Use definite articles to (a) refer to a noun you mentioned earlier (e.g., "*The* concept I mentioned earlier") or (b) to indicate that you are referring to one particular noun (e.g., "*The* most important concept for my argument"—there can be only one concept that is most important).

■ Use an indefinite article to indicate that you are not referring to one specific, unique individual entity but instead are referring to one among many possible nouns ("I saw a dog"). Thus, if you write, "*An* important concept for my argument," you are implying that there are other important concepts relating to your argument.

■ "An" is usually used for the indefinite article if the word that follows it begins with a vowel sound (e.g., "an apple"); otherwise, "a" is used (e.g., "a bed"). However, there are exceptions to the "use 'an' before words starting with vowels and 'a' before words starting with consonants" rule. For example, "a" is sometimes used before words beginning with "u" (e.g., "a university"), and "an" is sometimes used before words beginning with "h" (e.g., "an historical event"). You can detect most of the exceptions by reading your sentence aloud: If you have incorrectly applied the rule to an exception (e.g., "an unicorn"), your sentence will probably not sound right.

6.1.5 Adjectives

Adjectives are words that describe nouns and pronouns. Here is McDougall's sentence with the adjectives printed in bold italics:

The department of psychology that is of *primary* importance for the *social* sciences is that which deals with the springs of *human* action.

There are two serious—and avoidable—problems that students have with adjectives. First, students often use too many adjectives because they think that using adjectives will make their writing more powerful. They are wrong. Powerful writing comes from using nouns and verbs that help readers see what the writer is thinking.

Second, students sometimes use adjectives to label people in ways that are offensive. For example, students may use adjectives such as "elderly" or "retarded" in such a way that the individuals being referred to are not seen as individuals, but rather as members of a group possessing only that one characteristic. In the most extreme cases of focusing on one characteristic to the exclusion of every other characteristic, some students err by using an adjective as a noun (e.g., "the elderly," "the depressed"). Do not make that mistake (for more about using inclusive language, see 1.3.4).

6.1.6 Adverbs

Adverbs are words that modify verbs or adjectives. Adverbs usually are formed from an adjective with "-ly" tacked on the end (e.g., "correctly," "effectively," "largely"). We have changed the first part of McDougall's sentence to include an adverb (the word "primarily"):

> The department of psychology that *primarily* deals with the springs of human action . . .

Take care when placing the adverb "only" in a sentence. Usually, that adverb should come after—not before—its verb:

✗ The participant only pressed one button [The participant did nothing else except press one button: The participant did not look at the stimuli, think, or breathe].

✔ The participant pressed only one button.

Be cautious when using adverbs to modify verbs. Sometimes, you can omit the adverb without losing anything (e.g., "analyze" is no less descriptive than "closely analyze"). Sometimes, rather than looking for an adverb to modify the verb, you should look for a better verb (e.g., instead of adding "closely" to "look at," replace "look at" with "inspect," "examine," or "analyze"). If you must use an adverb to modify the verb, use the "-ly" adverb form rather than the adjective form (e.g., "closely" rather than "close"), and place the adverb close to its verb.

Sometimes, rather than use an adverb to modify a verb, you might use an adverb as a transition word. For example, you might use words such as "consequently," "similarly," or "conversely" at the beginning of a sentence to point out the relationship between that sentence and the previous sentence. Even as transition words, however, adverbs can get you in trouble. Thus, the editors of the *Publication Manual* discourage the use of either "importantly" or "interestingly." In addition, they point out that it is wrong to use "hopefully" to mean "it is hoped." Most students would be better off if they never used the word "hopefully."[3]

---

[3]To see how to have Microsoft Word automatically eliminate that word from your paper, see our website.

6.1.7 Prepositions

Prepositions are words, such as "among," "between," "beyond," "during," and "with," that describe the relationship of nouns and pronouns to other words. Some prepositions could be used to describe a cat's location relative to a box (e.g., "in," "on," "near," "behind," "under," "above," "into," and "off"). Many prepositions are short (e.g., "at," "by," "of," "for," and "to"). Here is McDougall's original sentence with the prepositions printed in bold italics:

> The department *of* psychology that is *of* primary importance *for* the social sciences is that which deals *with* the springs *of* human action.

If you put a personal pronoun after a preposition, that pronoun should not be "I," "she," "he," "we," "they," or "who." Instead, that pronoun should be an objective pronoun such as "me," "her," "him," "us," "them," or "whom" (e.g., "to *him*," "between *her* and *me*," "give it to *them*").

If you have a prepositional phrase containing "of," see if you can remove that preposition to create a shorter and more powerful sentence. For example, if you have a possessive prepositional phrase (e.g., "results *of the study*," "origin *of the effect*"), you can eliminate the preposition "of" by adding *apostrophe "s"* ('s) to the phrase's key noun (i.e., "study's results," "effect's origin"). If "of" follows a noun ending in "tion," you may be able to eliminate the "of" by replacing the noun with a verb (e.g., changing "the apparatus for the presentation of stimuli" to "the apparatus presented the stimuli").

See if you can shorten prepositional phrases that (a) begin with the preposition "with" and (b) describe a noun. Often, you will want to replace such phrases with an adjective. Using an adjective is more concise and more powerful than using a prepositional phrase. Thus, writing "the *bloody* knife" puts more emphasis on your description of the knife than writing "the knife *with blood on it*")—a prepositional phrase that emphasizes the noun "knife" but makes your description of the knife seem like an afterthought. Sometimes, however, you may wish to emphasize the noun rather than the words modifying the noun. For example, use prepositional phrases when describing people who have disabilities (e.g., "a person with a disability" rather than "a disabled person") so that the focus is on the person rather than on a label (APA, 2001).

Realize that you may mistakenly use the preposition "between" when you should use the preposition "among"—and vice versa. Most of the time, you should use "between" to distinguish two things and use "among" to distinguish more than two (e.g., "Our choice is between Theory X and Theory Y"; "Our choice is among Theory X, Theory Y, and Theory Z").

6.1.8 Conjunctions

Conjunctions are words that connect other words, phrases, or clauses. The conjunctions you are most familiar with are coordinating conjunctions such as "and," "but," and "or." However, there are many other conjunctions. To illustrate some of the different types of conjunctions, suppose you had two short sentences that you wanted to connect (e.g., "They talked. I walked."). You could connect the sentences using a comma and a coordinating conjunction such as "and" (e.g., "They talked, and I walked."). However, you could also connect the sentences by using either a conjunctive adverb or a subordinating conjunction.

If you use a conjunctive adverb such as "however," "nevertheless," or "moreover" to connect the two sentences, you have two choices. First, you could add the conjunctive adverb to the second sentence (e.g., "They talked. However, I walked."). Second, you could combine the two sentences into one (e.g., "They talked; however, I walked.").

If you use a subordinating conjunction, such as "although," "as," "if," or "when," you must combine the two sentences into one (e.g., "As they talked, I walked.") because you no longer have two independent sentences (for more about sentences, see 6.1.12). If you put a subordinating conjunction in front of the first sentence (e.g., "Although they talked"), your first "sentence" is no longer a complete sentence but instead becomes a sentence fragment. If you put a subordinating conjunction in front of the second sentence (e.g., "As I walked"), your second "sentence" would now be a sentence fragment. In short, when using subordinating conjunctions, be careful not to make a sentence fragment.

If you use the subordinate conjunctions "while" or "since," use them only when referring to time (e.g., "While the experimenter waited, the participant continued with the task"; "Since Freud's seminal works, the idea of the unconscious has gained greater acceptance"). If you are not relating the time sequence of events, replace "while" with either "although" or "whereas" and replace "since" with "because" (i.e., "Although the experimenter waited, the participant continued with the task"; "The idea of the unconscious has gained greater acceptance because of Freud's seminal works").

6.1.9 Relative Pronouns

Relative pronouns refer to pronouns such as "that," "which," "who," "whom," and "whose." A relative pronoun introduces text that describes a noun. Here is McDougall's original sentence with the relative pronouns printed in bold italics:

> The department of psychology *that* is of primary importance for the social sciences is that *which* deals with the springs of human action.

In the next section, we address the three most common questions students have about relative pronouns.

1. *"Should I use 'who' or 'that'?"* Although "that" can be used to refer to humans, skilled writers use "who," "whom," and "whose" to refer to humans (e.g., "It was Piaget *who* first showed . . ."; "Freud is the one to *whom* Jung was referring . . ."; "Spock, *whose* ideas shaped the attitudes of a generation of mothers, asserted . . ."). Reserve "that" for referring to animals and objects (e.g., "The animals *that* were in the experimental group . . ."; "The realization *that* changed our approach . . .").

2. *"Should I use 'who' or 'whom'?"* The key is to realize that "who," like "he," "she," and "we," is a nominative pronoun, whereas "whom," like "him," "her," and "us" is an objective pronoun (see Table 6.2). If you correctly use "he" and "him," you do not need to consult Table 6.2 to determine whether to use "who" or "whom." Instead, you can figure out whether to say "who" or "whom" by saying your sentence aloud. First, say your sentence aloud using a nominative personal pronoun (e.g., "he") instead of "who" or "whom." Then, say the sentence again using an objective personal pronoun (e.g., "him"). If the sentence sounds better using the nominative pronoun ("he first showed"), use "who"; if the sentence sounds better using the objective pronoun ("to him"), use "whom."

3. *"Should I use 'which' or 'that'?*￼ Usually, you should use "that" rather than "which." However, in two situations, you should use "which" instead of "that." First, use "which" when you are introducing a parenthetical (nonessential, nonrestrictive) clause: a clause that could be left out of the sentence without changing the sentence's meaning; a clause that could be set off by parentheses. You can spot such nonrestrictive clauses because they are set off from the rest of the sentence by commas (e.g., "This idea, *which* has been promoted on several previous occasions, is again becoming popular."). Second, use "which" if you would otherwise have to write "that that" (e.g., In our example passage, McDougall wrote, "department . . . is that which" rather than writing, "department . . . is that that.").

6.1.10 Phrases

After the individual word, the next major unit in writing is the phrase. A *phrase* contains more than one word and expresses an element of an idea. *Prepositional phrases* always contain a preposition and either a noun or pronoun. Prepositional phrases may also include an article and an adjective, as you can see from the following examples:

```
The department [phrase] of psychology [prepositional phrase] that
is [phrase] of primary importance [prepositional phrase] for the
social sciences [prepositional phrase] is that [phrase] which
deals [phrase] with the springs [prepositional phrase] of human
action [prepositional phrase].
```

6.1.11 Clauses

After the phrase, the next major unit in writing is the clause. A *clause* contains a subject and a verb. An *independent* clause contains a complete thought and so could stand as a sentence. Note that the first part of the last sentence, "An independent clause contains a complete thought," is an independent clause. A *dependent clause*, although it also has a subject and a verb, does not contain a complete thought, and therefore could not stand as a sentence:

> The department of psychology (that is of primary importance for the social sciences) [dependent clause 1] is that (which deals with the springs of human action) [dependent clause 2].

6.1.12 Sentences

The next major unit in writing is the sentence. A *sentence* contains a subject and a verb, expresses a complete thought, begins with a capital letter, and ends with an end mark (usually a period). Often, a sentence is a single independent clause.

In informal writing, the shortest sentences may contain only a single word: a verb. In such sentences, the subject is implicit (e.g., "Eat."). In formal writing, the subject of a sentence should be explicit (e.g., "*You will* eat."). Furthermore, in formal writing, if the sentence also contains an object (a recipient of the verb's action), the object should be explicit (e.g., "You will eat *11 prunes*.").

When editing your sentences, try to make sure that you have not committed either of the two most serious errors in sentence construction: (a) writing a sentence that is incomplete (a "fragment") and (b) writing a sentence that is too long. The first error, writing an incomplete sentence, rather than a complete sentence, usually occurs when a student does the following:

■ leaves out a verb

■ employs an "almost verb" (e.g., "to deal" or "dealing") rather than a verb (e.g., "deals")

■ turns what would have been an independent sentence (e.g., "I walked.") into a subordinate clause by putting a subordinating conjunction (see 6.1.8) such as "although" or "while" in front of it (e.g., "Although I walked.")

The second error, writing a sentence that is too long, often leads to additional problems. At best, such sentences exceed not only the reader's patience but also the reader's short-term memory capacity. Usually, such long sentences also set up the writer to make at least three additional errors.

First, because there are more nouns, more pronouns, and more verbs, the writer has a greater chance of losing track of whether a particular noun, verb, or pronoun is singular or plural. As a result, the writer is more likely to make (a) more subject-verb agreement errors and (b) more pronoun-noun agreement errors.

Second, because there are more words in the sentence, the writer has a greater chance of putting a pronoun too far from its noun and a modifier too far from what it should modify. If your teacher does not know which noun the pronoun refers to, your teacher may circle the pronoun and write "vague referent"; if your teacher does not know what a modifier is supposed to be modifying, your teacher may circle the modifier and write "misplaced modifier."

Third, because there are more clauses, there is greater potential for making errors in joining clauses. For example, the writer may leave out a comma needed to link a dependent clause to an independent clause. Alternatively, the writer may create a "run-on" sentence (see 6.3.4) by (a) trying to join two related independent clauses using only a comma or (b) by trying to join two unrelated independent clauses with a comma and a conjunction (e.g., "The theory has won wide acceptance, and I will consider methodological errors").

6.1.13 Paragraphs

After the sentence, the next major unit in writing is the paragraph. A *paragraph* expresses one major idea. It must consist of at least two sentences. Although some of your paragraphs may consist of only two sentences, most should be longer: Your average paragraph should consist of about 100 words. If a few of your paragraphs are well under 100 words, do not be concerned. If, on the other hand, any of your paragraphs are well over 100 words (130 words or more), be concerned.[4] Put another way, your paragraphs should usually be shorter than half of a page and should never be longer than one double-spaced page. (To learn more about writing paragraphs, see 6.4.2.)

6.2 Punctuation

6.2.1 End Marks (Periods, Question Marks, Exclamation Points)

In formal writing, you will rarely use a question mark to end a sentence, and you will almost never use an exclamation point to end a sentence. Instead, you will almost always use a period. A period will be the last character of a sentence, with the following exceptions:

- if the last word of the sentence is in quotation marks, in which case the quotation mark ends the sentence
- if the entire sentence is in parentheses, in which case the right parenthesis ends the sentence
- if the sentence is a question, in which case the question mark ends the sentence

6.2.2 Commas

Use a comma in the following situations:

- after transition words such as "however," "consequently," and "furthermore"
- after transition phrases that begin sentences such as "on the other hand," "for example," "consistent with this explanation,"

---

[4]The word count feature of your word processor can tell you how many words are in a paragraph.

■ before conjunctions, such as "and," "but," "for," "nor," "or," "so," and "yet" (e.g., "The participants read the instructions, and the researcher read the instructions aloud"), when those conjunctions connect two independent clauses

■ to segregate elements of lists of three or more, including authors' names (e.g., Jones, Smith, and Taylor)

■ to set off parenthetical phrases or dependent clauses (e.g., "This idea, which Freud originated, has had enormous influence")

■ to connect a dependent clause that starts a sentence (such clauses often start with "if," "although," "as," or "when") to the independent clause that follows it (e.g., "Although rewriting is hard work, it should be done.")

Do not use a comma before a conjunction such as "and," "but," or "or" when the conjunction connects (a) both elements of a two-item list (e.g., "Jones and Smith" or "pears or apples") or (b) a second verb to the subject of the sentence (e.g., "The first researcher greeted the participants and handed out the test booklets").

6.2.3 Semicolons

There are three main uses for semicolons. First, use a semicolon to separate two or more lists of words. In such cases, the semicolon lets readers know when one list stops and another begins.

```
Here is an example list of related terms: conditioned
response, unconditioned response, conditioned stimulus, and
unconditioned stimulus; milligram, gram, and kilogram; and
intelligence quotient, chronological age, and mental age.
```

Second, use a semicolon to connect closely related, independent clauses without using a coordinating conjunction such as "and." For example, you should write

```
Theory A is popular; theory B is not popular.
```

Note that had you used a comma instead of a semicolon to connect the two independent clauses in the previous example, you would have a "run-on" sentence (see 6.3.4).

Third, use a semicolon to connect highly related independent clauses with linking words such as "consequently," "furthermore," "however," "moreover," "therefore," "nevertheless," "indeed," and "thus." Note that you will need to use semicolon *before* the linking word and a comma *after* the linking word (e.g., "; therefore,").

6.2.4 Colons

Use a colon either to introduce a list of items (e.g., "There were four conditions: control, auditory, visual, and olfactory") or to emphasize the final element of a sentence (e.g., "Skinner devoted his life to one concept: operant conditioning"). In either case, you can use a colon only if the clause coming before the colon is an independent clause. That is, if you replace the colon with a period, that period should mark the end of a grammatically intact sentence. If the words in front of the period would not make a sentence, you should not use a colon. Thus, you should never use a colon to separate a verb from its direct object (e.g., it is incorrect to write, "Three reasons are:").

6.2.5 Apostrophes

In informal writing, an apostrophe may signal that some letters have been omitted from a word to form a *contraction* (e.g., "wasn't" is a contraction of "was" and "not," the "o" being the omitted letter). In formal writing, an apostrophe may be used for only one purpose: to signify a possessive (e.g., "the experiment's design"). To form the possessive of a singular noun, add *apostrophe "s"* (e.g., "the theory's assumptions," "the stimulus's duration," "Jones's paper"). To form the possessive of a plural noun ending in *s*, add a final apostrophe (e.g., "these theories' assumptions," "The Joneses' [i.e., Fred and Myrtle's] contribution"). To form the possessive of a plural noun ending in anything other than *s*, add *apostrophe "s"* (e.g., "children's toys," "the stimuli's origin").

Note that apostrophes are not a part of any of the possessive pronouns: my, mine, his, her, hers, yours, ours, theirs, whose, and its. Thus, "it's" is not the possessive form of "it" but rather the contraction for "it is." Because you should write "its" when you mean "belonging to it" and "it is" when you mean "it is," you should never write "it's" in a formal paper.

In conclusion, the big problem students have with apostrophes is that students use them too much. Do not use apostrophes with dates (e.g., write "1950s," not "1950's"). Do not use contractions (e.g., "don't") in your papers—and especially do not use the contractions "it's," "they're," "who's," and "ain't."

6.2.6 Parentheses

Use parentheses to enclose parenthetical material unnecessary for the meaning of the sentence (e.g., this example). Parentheses signal to the reader that the enclosed material could safely be ignored. Each time you use parentheses, ask yourself if the material is vital to the meaning of the sentence. If the material is vital, build it into the sentence. If it is not vital, consider omitting it: Parenthetical asides may distract the reader from your main point. In short, except for citations, you should probably avoid using parentheses.

6.2.7 Dashes

Use *em dashes*—illustrated here—to enclose parenthetical material. Em dashes—given that name because they are the width of a capital letter "M"—create a form of parenthetical comment intermediate in strength between commas and parentheses. Usually, you can make an em dash with your word processor.[5] If you cannot make an

---

[5]In Microsoft Word, you choose "Symbol . . . " under the "Insert" menu and then choose "Special Characters." Alternatively, you can hold down the following three keys at the same time: the "alt" key, the control key, and the minus sign key that is on the number pad.

em dash with your word processor, use two hyphens. Like material set off by parentheses, material set off by an em dash is often material that should be edited or deleted.

6.2.8 Hyphens

Use hyphens only in words that could otherwise be misinterpreted (e.g., "I re-sent your letter" could be interpreted differently from "I resent your letter"). Thus, you may have to use hyphens in some compound words (e.g., if you are describing a woman, "man chasing woman" might be misinterpreted but "man-chasing woman" would not be). You are especially likely to need hyphens with compound words in which the first word is a number (e.g., "The 3-year-olds" has a different meaning from "The 3 year-olds" and "the 10-item lists" has a different meaning from "the 10 item lists").

In short, students tend to overuse hyphens. You will be less likely to overuse hyphens if you (a) do not use hyphens for common phrases (e.g., day care center) and (b) do not use hyphens to keep your right margin even.

6.2.9 Quotation Marks

There are only two reasons to surround words with quotation marks: first, to signal the reader that those words are a brief quotation (see 4.7.1), and second, to signal the reader that you are using the selected word or words in a different way from how the word or words are normally used.

> ✔ Participants waited in an anteroom with two other "participants" [appropriate only if you had previously explained that these two people were actually confederates of the experimenter].

Keep the latter sort of usage to a minimum. For example, you should not write anything like the following:

> ✘ The computer "knew" which alternative the participant had chosen.

If you had written the previous sentence, you would be saying to the reader, "I want you to understand the word 'knew' in a way other than you would normally understand it because I did not bother to find the right word. I hope you can figure out what I meant to say." Rather than telling readers to figure out your unconventional meanings of words, you should make it easy for readers by finding the word you mean:

> ✔ The computer recorded which alternative the participant had chosen.

Students often make mistakes punctuating material in quotation marks. Fortunately, you can avoid most of these mistakes by following one rule: Put commas and periods inside quotation marks but put colons and semicolons outside of quotation marks.

If you are trying to decide where to put question marks in a quoted passage, you need to follow a pair of rules. First, if the question mark is part of the quote (e.g., She said, "What is the rule?"), put the question mark inside the quotation mark. Second, if the question mark is not part of the quote (e.g., What is "Beetlebom's delight"?), put the question mark outside the quotation mark.

6.3 Usage

6.3.1 Know What You Mean

Make sure you know the meaning of all words you use. Be careful when using a thesaurus to find synonyms. Check the dictionary definition of any synonym to ensure that it does not have a different meaning from the one you intend.

Sometimes, students see a similarity between two words and end up using the wrong member of that pair. For example, students often use "affects" when they should use "effects"—and vice versa. To be sure that you are using the right member of these "problem pairs," consult Table 6.3. By consulting Table 6.3, you will avoid common errors such as writing "my analysis infers" and "stress effects memory."

Also, be careful about words and phrases that sound identical. Don't use "their" when you mean "there," "to" when you mean "too," or "would of" when you mean "would have."

T A B L E 6.3   Problem Pairs

Problem Pair	Part of Speech*	Meaning	Example
affect	noun	emotion	The client had depressed *affect*.
affect	verb	influence	Learning the prior list *affected* recall of the test words.
affect	verb	pretend	The client *affected* a cheerful mood.
effect	noun	result	The *effect* of diffusion of responsibility was to delay helping.
effect	verb	bring about	The therapist *effected* a quick recovery in her client.
alternate	verb	change from one to another	The experimenter *alternated* the order in which the stimuli were presented.
alternative	noun	one of two or more possibilities	Choose the correct *alternative*.
alternative	adj	allowing a choice between two or more possibilities	They wanted an *alternative* candidate.

(continued)

TABLE 6.3   Problem Pairs—*continued*

Problem Pair	Part of Speech*	Meaning	Example
amount	noun	how much (refers to an uncountable quantity)	The dependent variable was amount of stress.
number	noun	how many (refers to a countable quantity)	The dependent variable was number of errors.
casual	adj	informal	We will be playing outside, so wear *casual* clothes.
causal	adj	relating to the causes of an effect	They found a *causal* relationship between smoking and cancer.
continually	adv	recurring often	The writer was *continually* interrupted by the telephone.
continuously	adv	without interruption	The noise level was reduced *continuously* until the observer could hear the tone.
dependent variable	noun	a measure of the participant's behavior	The *dependent variable* was the participant's score on the measure.
independent variable	noun	the factor that is manipulated in a study	The *independent variable* was the noise level.
disinterested	adj	impartial, fair, unbiased	Smith, coming from neither side of the controversy, is a *disinterested* judge.
uninterested	adj	without interest, unconcerned	The participant, having just eaten, was *uninterested* in eating more.
experiment	noun	a type of study, usually involving random assignment, that allows researchers to make cause-effect statements	In this *experiment*, participants were randomly assigned to one of three groups.
study	noun	any type of research, including nonexperimental studies, such as survey research	In this *study*, we asked participants about their views.
farther	adj	more distant	Observers judged the distance of the *farther* of the landmarks.
	adv	to a more distant point	Maze-bright rats progressed *farther* in the maze than maze-dull rats.

TABLE 6.3 Problem Pairs—*continued*

Problem Pair	Part of Speech*	Meaning	Example
further	adj	additional	With *further* research, the phenomenon might be explained.
	adv	more	Jones developed the theory *further*.
fewer	adj	fewer in terms of how many (refers to a countable quantity)	Participants made *fewer* errors.
less	adj	less in terms of how much (refers to an uncountable quality)	Participants seemed *less* anxious.
fortuitous	adj	occurring by chance	The meeting between the mail carrier and the sharp-toothed dog was *fortuitous*.
fortunate	adj	lucky	We are *fortunate* to be living in the information age.
gender	noun	masculine vs. feminine	*Gender* refers to the psychological and sociological aspects of being a man or a woman.
sex	noun	boys and men vs. girls and women	*Sex* refers to the biological or sexual aspects of being a man or a woman.
imply	verb	suggest	The author *implied* that previous research was not methodologically sound.
infer	verb	generalize from evidence	From my analysis of the literature, I *inferred* that much of the previous research was not methodologically sound.
insignificant	adj	unimportant	The effect, although statistically significant, was small and *insignificant*.
nonsignificant	adj	not statistically significant	The *nonsignificant* results may have been due to the study's lack of power.
literally	adv	exactly as written	The patient *literally* threw stones inside a glass house (use *literally* only when readers might otherwise think you were writing figuratively).

(continued)

T A B L E 6.3   Problem Pairs—*continued*

Problem Pair	Part of Speech*	Meaning	Example
figuratively	adv	involving a figure of speech	The comedian *figuratively* died during his act (use *figuratively* only when readers might otherwise think you were not using a figure of speech, e.g., if they might otherwise think that the comedian actually died).
method	noun	procedure, technique	We used Donders's subtraction *method*.
methodology	noun	system, or study, of methods	In one class, we studied the *methodology* of single-case designs.
principal	adj	main, first	The *principal* effect of caffeine is stimulation.
principal	noun	director of a school	The *principal* of the school resigned.
principle	noun	law, tenet, rule	Psychologists should understand the *principles* of reinforcement.
reliable	adj	consistent, replicable	Participants' scores on the retest were similar to their original test scores, suggesting that the test is *reliable*.
valid	adj	accurate	Participants' scores on the test predicted their behavior in a real life situation, suggesting that the test is *valid*.
significant	adj	unlikely to be due to chance	The effect, although small, was statistically *significant*.
substantial	adj	large	The difference between carrying 100 pounds and 200 pounds is *substantial*.
use	noun	purpose	One *use of* debriefing is to learn how participants viewed the study.
usage	noun	the manner of using	Word *usage* is discussed in this chapter.

Note: *adj = adjective, adv = adverb.

6.3.2 Complete Comparisons

Relational words describe relations between things (e.g., "different [from]," "similar [to]," "bigger [than]," "oldest [of]," "irrelevant [to]"). The main problem students have in using relational words is that, in trying to be brief, students may not make it clear which two things are being related. For example, a student wrote, "*The participants liked the experiment better than the experimenter.*" The student's sentence was ambiguous because the reader could not know whether (a) participants liked the experiment more than they liked the experimenter or (b) participants liked the experiment more than the experimenter liked the experiment. Note that completing the comparison results in an unambiguous sentence: "The participants liked the experiment more than they liked the experimenter."

6.3.3 Distinguish Comparatives From Superlatives

A *comparative* is an adjective or adverb used to compare two things. It is usually formed either by adding "-er" to an adjective (e.g., "strong" becomes "stronger") or by placing the word *more* before an adverb (e.g., "strongly" becomes "more strongly"), and then adding "than" (e.g., "The mean of group A is *larger than* the mean of group B"; "Participants in the X condition pressed the button *more* rapidly *than* participants in the Y condition").

Use "less" for uncountable qualities (e.g., "less affection"); use "fewer" for countable qualities (e.g., "fewer items"). The word after "less" must always be singular; the word after "fewer" must always be plural.

✘ Theory A has more applications and *less* problems than Theory B.

✔ Theory A has more applications and fewer problems than Theory B.

Note that "different" is not a comparative, so you should not write, "A is different *than* B." Instead, you should write, "A is different *from* B."

A *superlative* is an adjective or adverb used to compare more than two things. It is usually formed by adding "-est" to an adjective or by placing the word "most" before an adverb (e.g., "Of the three groups, participants in A scored the *fewest* hits"; "Of participants in all four conditions, those in B pressed the button *most* rapidly").

6.3.4 Divide Run-On Sentences

There are at least two types of *run-on sentences*. The first occurs when two unrelated independent clauses are fused into one sentence (e.g., "There are problems with classical theories, and Smith proposes a new theory"). Fix such sentences by putting a period at the end of each independent clause. The second, often called a *comma splice*, occurs when two (or more) independent clauses are joined by only a comma. You have three options for fixing comma spliced sentences: (a) replace the comma with a period, (b) replace the comma with a semicolon, or (c) add a conjunction (e.g., "and") after the comma.

✘ The choice among the classical theories is complicated, there are problems with all of them and Smith proposes a new theory that I will discuss.

✔ The choice among the classical theories is complicated; there are problems with all of them. Smith proposes a new theory that I will discuss.

6.3.5 Specify Nonspecific Referents

All sentences you write should be clear. These provide problems. We hope you have recoiled in horror at the second sentence of this paragraph. You should be wondering what we mean by "These" (a *nonspecific referent*). One possibility is that "these" refers to "All sentences," the subject of the first sentence. However, we were referring to "nonspecific referents," the last part of the heading.

Take two steps to avoid problems with nonspecific referents. First, be sure that your sentences stand independently of the previous paragraph, heading, or title. Thus, if, as in our example of a problem sentence ("These provide problems."), you had a pronoun that referred to a noun in a heading, replace the pronoun with the heading's noun ("Nonspecific referents cause problems."). Second, any time you use a pronoun, ensure that the reader knows which noun that pronoun represents.

One way to see whether a pronoun ("a pointing word") could mislead or confuse a reader is to draw an arrow from the potentially ambiguous pointing word (e.g., "this," "that," "they," "it," "those") back to the word or idea to which it refers. If the arrow passes other words that could also fit, you have a problem. Solutions to the problem include the following:

■ replacing the ambiguous pronoun with the noun that the pronoun referred to (e.g., change "it is" to "cognitive dissonance theory is")

■ distinguishing the targeted noun from other nearby nouns by making it the only plural (or only singular) noun near your plural (or singular) pronoun (e.g., change "There were several potential causes of these effects. They include" to "There were several potential causes of this effect. They include")

■ using "who" to refer to humans rather than using "that" (e.g., change "the participants that were most influenced" to "the participants who were most influenced")

■ adding a word or a descriptive phrase after words such as "this" so the reader knows what "this" refers to (e.g., replace "this is" with "this psychoanalytic idea is")

6.3.6 Attribute Humanity Only to Humans

Only humans do such things as point out, argue, or suggest. Do not attribute human abilities to theories, concepts, data, or other nonhuman entities. To attribute human abilities to nonhuman entities is to commit the error of *anthropomorphism*. Next, we show you some examples of anthropomorphism, followed by solutions:

✘ Smith's (1969) theory suggests an alternative explanation.

✔ Smith (1969) suggests an alternative explanation.

✘ This concept favors a different perspective.

✔ Holders of this concept favor a different perspective.

✘ The data speak to my hypothesis.

✔ Figure 1 shows that the data are consistent with my hypothesis.

✘ The results emphasize the connection between temperature and aggression.

✔ The results indicate that there is a relationship between temperature and aggression.

6.4 Writing With Style

6.4.1 Accentuate the Positive

Your English teachers probably taught you not to use a double negative (e.g., "Do not not turn on the light") because a positively worded statement (e.g., "Turn on the light") is easier to understand. What your English teachers might not have taught you is that a positively worded statement is also easier to understand than a single negative, as you can see from studying the following pair of examples:

✘ To create a good test, do not use questions worded negatively.

✔ To create a good test, use positively worded questions.

6.4.2 Point the Way Within and Between Paragraphs

The main idea, the punch line, of every paragraph you write should be expressed in a single sentence called the *topic sentence*. If your paragraph does not have a topic sentence, you may be able to generate one for it by either summarizing the paragraph or by referring to your outline. If you cannot generate a topic sentence for a paragraph, you probably should delete that paragraph from your paper.

A paragraph's topic sentence could be the first sentence of the paragraph (e.g., "Smith and Jones (2003) identified three problems with previous research"). In that case, the rest of the paragraph would develop, defend, or explain the topic sentence.

A paragraph's topic sentence can also be the last sentence of the paragraph, especially if you are presenting an argument or a hypothesis (e.g., "Therefore, previous research is flawed in at least three ways"). In that case, you would start the paragraph with evidence supporting a position and hope that the reader will come to your conclusion before coming to your topic sentence stating that conclusion.

The paragraph's topic sentence, regardless of where it is, helps readers navigate within the paragraph. After helping the reader make it through a paragraph, you must help the reader make it through the next one. You must ensure that each paragraph stands independently of others, yet flows logically and gracefully from the one before it and the one after it.

To ensure that each paragraph makes sense by itself, check any of your paragraphs that begin with the words "This," "These," or "Those" (such pronouns are known as *nonspecific referents;* see 6.3.5). The problem with using nonspecific referents is that such words are meaningless on their own. As a result, using one of these words to start a paragraph makes that paragraph depend on the previous paragraph for its meaning. Therefore, do not use "this" or a similar word in your paragraph's first sentence as shorthand for a concept, idea, study, or criticism stated in a previous paragraph. Instead, restate the concept, idea, study, or criticism.

Starting a new paragraph by restating an idea from the previous paragraph not only helps the new paragraph stand independently, but it also helps readers see connections between adjoining paragraphs. To give the reader even more help, you may, occasionally, put connecting words or connecting phrases such as "In addition to," "Next," "Consequently," or "Although" in front of your restatement. However, be selective in your use of connecting words: If most of your paragraphs start with connecting words, it will hurt the flow of your paper.

Often, the smoothest way to ensure that paragraphs flow is to use the concluding sentence of the previous paragraph to set up the next one. Concluding sentences that accomplish flow look like the following.

> Researchers could use three tactics to overcome these methodological problems. [The next paragraph would begin with a sentence about the first tactic.]

> The range must be limited, however, when adaptation phenomena are considered. [The next paragraph would begin with description of an adaptation phenomenon.]

6.4.3 Use Parallel Construction

You can improve both the flow and the clarity of ideas within a paragraph by using *parallel construction.* Where you have several similar ideas, express them using the same, parallel construction, whether within adjacent phrases, clauses, or sentences:

✘ The participant began each trial with a button press, using the keyboard to give a response, and the trial finished when the participant pressed another button.

✔ The participant began each trial with a button press, gave a response with the keyboard, and finished the trial with another button press.

✔ The participant used key presses to start each trial, give a response, and end a trial.

✘ The results showed no significant differences in the area of anxiety, or regarding depression; psychoses also did not differ.

✔ The results showed no significant differences in anxiety, depression, or psychosis.

6.4.4 Use a Consistent, Formal Tone

Keep a formal tone; avoid clichés or colloquialisms. Use metaphors sparingly, and carry through any you do use.

✘ When all is said and done [cliché 1], the moral of the story [cliché 2] is that the bottom line [cliché 3] of my study is that children trained with the X technique were literally [cliché 4] out of hand [colloquialism 1], so the results are up the creek [colloquialism 2]. . . . When the results were analyzed with a finer-toothed [metaphor 1] statistical test, the hypothesis still lay bleeding on the ground [metaphor 2].

✘ In conclusion, my study showed that children trained with the X technique misbehaved so badly there were no significant results. . . . When the results were analyzed with a finer-toothed statistical test, the only new results combed out were statistical dandruff. [Although the author did not mix two different metaphors, the author used a metaphor that is too informal for scientific writing.]

✔ In conclusion, the unruliness of children trained with the X technique obscured any significant results. . . . When the results were analyzed with a higher-powered test, no new meaningful findings emerged.

6.4.5 Use Small Words and Short Sentences

Obsolescent prolixities are to be eschewed. Note that if you replaced the previous sentence's unfamiliar words with familiar ones and if you changed the previous sentence's voice from passive to active (for more information about voice, see 6.1.3), you could change it to the following useful tip: "Avoid unfamiliar words."

In addition to using simple, short, familiar words, try to keep most of your sentences shorter than 20 words. A good test of a sentence's length is to read your assignment aloud, taking a breath only when you find a period. If you are running out of breath and a period still has not come into sight, the sentence is too long. The solution is to break long sentences into a number of shorter sentences. On the other hand, avoid going to the opposite extreme of using only short sentences; using too many short sentences will make you repeat yourself unnecessarily, will make it hard for you to show the connections between your ideas, and will make your paper sound like a telegram.

6.4.6 Be Precise

Do not try to make your sentences sound less telegraphic by adding adjectives and adverbs. Although you may believe that adding adverbs and adjectives makes your writing more dramatic, your writing will be more powerful if you replace your vague adjectives and imprecise adverbs with numbers. Thus, instead of writing "*numerous times,*" be precise by writing "17 times." Similarly, instead of writing things like "a *relatively large* number of participants" and "a *fairly big* effect," be precise by writing "25 participants" and "a 55% increase."

6.4.7 Be Concise

Another problem with using adjectives and adverbs is that such words are often unnecessary. Consequently, adjectives and adverbs can weaken your sentences by making your sentences wordy. Remember, shorter is often more powerful. Thus, rather than writing "a *disastrous* event," save words—and gain power—by writing "a disaster."

In addition to cutting adjectives and adverbs that dilute your prose, you should cut unnecessary paragraphs, sentences, phrases, and expressions.

- Eliminate paragraphs dealing with material not directly relevant to your paper.
- Replace pairs of sentences that restate one another (i.e., sentences beginning explicitly or implicitly with phrases such as "In other words," "To put it another way") with the better of the two.
- Replace passive sentences (e.g., "The unconscious *was emphasized by* Freud") with active sentences (e.g., "Freud *emphasized* the unconscious").
- Replace nouns trying to do a verb's job (e.g., "We did *a modification of* ") with verbs (e.g., "We *modified*").
- Replace phrases (e.g., "The theory applied *in the context* [phrase 1] *of sensory processes* [phrase 2]") with single words (e.g., "The theory applied to *sensation*").
- Replace wordy prepositional phrases referring to time (e.g., "at the present time") with single words (e.g., "now").
- Replace wordy prepositional phrases for "about" (e.g., "in relation to") with "about."
- Replace wordy expressions (e.g., "despite the fact that") with single words (e.g., "although").
- Replace redundant pairs of words (e.g., "actual fact") with their essential elements (e.g., "fact"). (To see examples of redundant pairs and other multiword expressions that you should replace with single words, see Table 6.4.)

TABLE 6.4   Wordy Expressions to Remove From Your Writing

Replace This	With This
Prepositional phrases about relationships	
in terms of	in, on, about
vis-à-vis	in, on, about
with respect to	in, on, about
in relation to	about
Prepositional phrases about time	
at the present time	now
at this point in time	now
in the process of	now
at that particular time	then
in the near future	soon
Other wordy expressions	
be of the opinion	believe
despite the fact that	although
in spite of the fact that	although
owing to the fact that	because
the reason is because	because
Double trouble: Redundant pairs	
actual fact	fact
close proximity	close
completely unanimous	unanimous
consensus of opinion	consensus
final conclusion	conclusion
future planning	planning
must necessarily	must
new innovation	innovation
reason why	reason
true fact	true
Triple threats	
consensus of opinion	consensus
whether or not	whether

6.4.8 Be Cautious

The good writer obeys all the writing rules—even those that most readers would not mind seeing violated. The good writer realizes that obeying all the rules will not offend anyone, whereas disobeying the rules may offend someone. To make reading an agreeable experience for all readers, the good writer tries to obey even those writing rules that most readers ignore, such as not ending sentences with prepositions and not splitting infinitives.

Do not end any sentence with a preposition. For example, do not write a sentence like the following: "This is an impertinence which I will not put up with." Winston Churchill is reputed to have objected to the rule of not ending sentences with prepositions by saying, "This is an impertinence up with which I will not put." Although Churchill's sentence sounds stilted, realize that his sentence can be rewritten in a way that honors the rule, yet sounds natural: "I will not put up with such impertinence."

Keep infinitives intact. Writers *split infinitives* when they put something, usually an adverb, between the *to* and the *verb* part of an infinitive. A famous phrase from the television series "Star Trek" is an example of a split infinitive (and sexist language): "to boldly go where no man has gone before." You could rewrite the phrase to rejoin the infinitive (and to remove the sexist language): "to go boldly into new frontiers."

6.5 Your Own Style

To resume the analogy we made at the start of this chapter, writers ignorant of grammar and punctuation are like drivers who, although they know the way to their destinations, fail to arrive because they drove on flat tires, ran out of gasoline, or crashed into a pole. Writers ignorant of good usage are like drivers who reach their destinations, but only after running over curbs, grinding the gears, and losing their passengers. Writers ignorant of style are like drivers who reach their destinations, but who make some wrong turns and who circle some blocks several times. Skilled drivers have their own styles: some drive slowly, admiring the view along the way; others drive fast, showing flair and verve. As you master the skills of driving your words, you can develop your own style. Remember, however, that the point is to arrive at your destination with your passengers still on board.

6.6   Checklists

6.6.1 Parts of Speech

___ I put pronouns close to their respective nouns.

___ I made sure that pronouns agreed with their nouns. That is, I do not have a singular pronoun (e.g., "him") referring to a plural noun (e.g., "children").

____ I usually followed the pronoun "this" with a word or phrase that made it clear what the referent was for "this."

____ When referring to humans, I used the pronoun "who" instead of the pronouns "that" or "which."

____ The subjects of my sentences agree with the verbs of my sentences. That is, I do not have a plural noun (data) with a singular verb (is).

____ I made sure I knew what the subject of the sentence was, even if that meant shortening or simplifying that sentence.

____ I remembered that if I had two nouns as subjects and they were joined by the conjunction "and," I used the plural form of the verb. However, if the nouns were joined by the conjunction "or," the noun closest to the verb dictated whether I used the singular or plural form of the verb.

____ I checked Appendix B to make sure that the subject of the sentence was in the form (singular or plural) that I intended—unless I was sure I knew what the singular and plural forms were (e.g., dog, dogs).

____ If I am referring to either (a) a specific event that occurred in the past or (b) a certain study (including the results of my own study), I use the past tense (e.g., "the study found").

____ If I am referring to something that started at some time in the past but continues to the present, I use the present perfect (e.g., "studies have found").

____ I usually use the active voice instead of the passive voice.

____ When possible, I eliminated adverbs.

____ If I need an adverb to modify a verb, I made sure that I used the proper "ly" ending for adverbs rather than using the shorter, adjective form. For example, I wrote that participants "worked quickly" rather than "worked quick."

____ If I used an adverb, I put it next to the verb it was modifying.

6.6.2 Punctuation

____ I used commas at places where I would pause if I were reading my paper aloud—unless another punctuation mark was more appropriate.

____ I used commas between a dependent clause (such clauses often start with "although," "as," "if," or "when") that started a sentence and the independent clause that followed it (e.g., "When he fell, he did not cry").

____ I used commas before a conjunction such as "and" that joined two independent clauses.

____ I used commas between all lists of three or more items—unless the items contained commas.

____ I used semicolons to separate list items when those list items contained commas.

____ I used semicolons to join two independent clauses without a conjunction.

____ I did not overuse apostrophes, quotation marks, parentheses, or hyphens.

____ I do not have any contractions in my paper and I have not used apostrophes with the pronoun "its" or with years (e.g., I wrote "1990s" rather than "1990's.").

____ I used hyphens only when the meaning of a sentence would be unclear without them. For example, I did not use hyphens merely to make my right margins even.

____ I used quotation marks sparingly. I used them only with quotations that were shorter than 40 words or with words that were being used in an unconventional way. Furthermore, I rarely used quotes and I rarely used words in an unconventional way.

____ I put commas and periods inside quotation marks.

6.6.3 Style

____ I outlined my paper.

____ I made sure that all my paragraphs had topic sentences—and I made sure that those topic sentences referred to entries in my outline.

____ I used subheadings.

____ I built bridges between paragraphs by using transition words or repeating key phrases and ideas.

____ I made all my paragraphs shorter than a page, and I kept most of them shorter than half a page.

____ I kept most of my sentences under 20 words.

____ I did not ask the reader questions (e.g., "Who could disagree with that?").

____ I did not end sentences with prepositions.

____ I did not start sentences with coordinating conjunctions such as "and," "but," and "or."

____ I did not split infinitives.

____ I did not use one-word sentences.

____ I did not use one-sentence paragraphs

____ I did not use contractions.

____ I did not use the word "you" to refer to the reader.

____ I did not use exclamation points.

6.7 Summary

1. The main parts of speech are nouns, pronouns, verbs, articles, adjectives, adverbs, prepositions, conjunctions, and relative pronouns.

2. Use adjectives sparingly.

3. Use adverbs sparingly.

4. When you use a pronoun, make sure that the reader can easily tell to which noun it refers.

5. If a plural noun has a pronoun, its pronoun must also be plural; if a singular noun has a pronoun, its pronoun must also be singular.

6. If a subject is plural, its verb must also be plural; if a subject is singular, its verb must also be singular.

7. Most of your sentences should have fewer than 20 words and most of your paragraphs should be less than half a page long.

8. Usually, a period will end your sentence. However, if the last word of your sentence is in quotation marks, the period will be inside the quotation marks.

9. Use apostrophes only to indicate possession (e.g., the participant's score). Do not use apostrophes for contractions (e.g., write "it is" rather than "it's," write "they are" rather than "they're") or to indicate the plural form (e.g., write "1950s" rather than "1950's").

10. An independent clause can stand alone as a sentence. An independent clause must have a verb and must contain a complete thought.

11. If you are using a coordinating conjunction such as "or," "and," or "but" to join two independent clauses, put a comma before the conjunction.

12. If you are combining two independent clauses without a coordinating conjunction, combine them with either a semicolon or a colon.

13. Use a colon unless the words in front of the colon are an independent clause.

14. Do not overuse parentheses, hyphens, quotation marks, question marks, and dashes.

15. Often, people will use one word (e.g., "affect") when they should use another (e.g., "effect"). If you consult our "Problem Pairs" table (Table 6.3), you will be less likely to make that kind of mistake. Be especially careful not to use "since" when you mean "because" or "while" when you mean "although."

16. All paragraphs should have topic sentences.

17. Obey conventional rules of writing. For example, do not use contractions; do not split infinitives; do not start sentences with the coordinating conjunctions "and," "but," "so," or "or"; and do not end sentences with prepositions.

18. Try to use the active voice.

19. Try to use parallel structure.

20. Eliminate unnecessary words.

CHAPTER

7

Preparing the Final Draft

7.1 Presentation

Even professors who do not specifically assign points for how well papers conform to APA format tend to give higher grades to papers that adhere to it than to papers that do not. If your paper is correctly formatted, your professor will be under the impression that it was written by someone who is conscientious and competent—and will tend to evaluate the paper's content accordingly. If, on the other hand, your paper fails to meet even basic formatting requirements, your professor will be under the impression that it was written by someone who is careless and incompetent—and will tend to evaluate the paper's content accordingly. In this chapter, we show you how to turn in a paper that will make a good first impression and how to avoid the mistakes that make some students' papers "dead on arrival."

7.1.1 Paper, Margins, Spacing

Use one side of white, bond, letter-sized (8.5 × 11 in. [22 × 28 cm]) paper. Leave 1-in (2.54 cm) margins at the top, bottom, left, and right. Double-space all text.

7.1.2 Word Processing Versus Typing

If possible, use a word processor. Word-processing software will format much of your paper for you, as long as you do the following.

- Select a 12-point serif font[1] (such as Times Roman or Times New Roman).
- Select double-spacing.
- Deselect "right justify," "auto hyphenation," or anything that would automatically hyphenate words at the end of a line.
- Select the "replace straight quotes with smart quotes" option[2] so that your quotation marks and apostrophes look typeset rather than typewritten ("Jolley's examples" instead of "Jolley's examples").
- Insert one space between words and after most punctuation.[3] Do not leave any spaces after (a) hyphens or dashes and (b) periods that are part of an abbreviation (e.g., P.M.).
- Italicize where necessary (see 7.2.4).

7.2 APA Formats

APA recognizes two formats: copy and final. The first, "copy" style, is a format for authors who are submitting their work for publication. Copy style differs from the final form of the published work. Copy editors will work with typesetters to convert the submitted document into its final form. The second format, "final" style, is for authors who are producing the final form of the document themselves. Final style is similar to the format of a published article.

The focus of the *Publication Manual* is on copy style: the format used when submitting a manuscript for publication. Most professors also focus on copy style: They ask students to prepare a paper the same way an author would submit a manuscript to a journal. Therefore, our main emphasis will be on copy style. However, your professor may decide to use the style that is authorized by the American Psychological Association (2001) for final form (if so, see Appendix A). If your professor asks you to use final style (also called "final-form" style), your paper will look like a published article in a recent APA journal (e.g., *Psychological Review*) instead of looking like the sample manuscripts you can find in sections 2.11 and 3.12 of this book.

7.2.1 Running Head Versus Short Title

In articles submitted for publication, the first two to three words of the title (the "short title") should appear on the top right-hand corner of each page. Five spaces to the right of the short title is the page number. The title page is numbered "1" and is the first page of the manuscript. Thus, if your title was "The Primacy Effect in Impression Formation," the top right corner of your title page might look like this:

The Primacy Effect   1

---

[1]Serifs are the little strokes on the ends of individual letters. Research shows that serif fonts are easier to read than sans serif (without serif) fonts.

[2]You will probably find this option by going to the "Tools" menu and choosing the "AutoCorrect" tool.

[3]You can use a grammar checker program to make sure that you have left only one space after punctuation marks. Alternatively, you can find and remove unnecessary spaces by using the "find-and-replace" command: Put two spaces in the "find" box and one space in the "replace" box.

If you are using a word processor, put the page number and the short title in the "header" area (if you need help inserting material into the header, specific instructions are available at http://www.writingforpsychology.com).

On the title page, one double-spaced line below the short title, starting on the left margin is the phrase "Running head:" followed by the running head—a two- to six-word phrase, typed in all capital letters, that summarizes the title of the article. Thus, if your title was "The Primacy Effect in Impression Formation," the line below your short title might look like the following.

`Running head: DESCRIPTOR ORDER ON LIKING`

The running head has a 50-character limit—and spaces, as well as punctuation, count against that limit. In articles submitted for publication, the running head does not appear on any other page.

In published articles, on the other hand, the phrase "Running head:" followed by the running head does not appear on the title page. Instead, as you can see in Figure 7.1, the running head is the header that appears on the top of all the odd-numbered pages that follow the title page.

Another difference between copy style and final-form style is that, in final-form style, the page headers and the page numbers are not together in the top right-hand corner of each page. Instead, the headers (e.g., the running head on the odd-numbered pages following the title page, your last name on the even-numbered pages following the title page) are centered in all capital letters at the top of the page. The page number is centered at the bottom of the title page, is in the top left-hand corner of the even-numbered pages that follow the title page, and is in the top right-hand corner of the odd-numbered pages that follow the title page. (Your professor may allow you to center the page number on the bottom of each page.)

7.2.2 Paragraphs

The first line of most paragraphs should be indented five characters. To accomplish this, press the tab key once. However, there are three exceptions to this indentation rule. Specifically, do not indent the first line of (a) the Abstract, (b) the figure captions, or (c) the table notes. The first line for each of these three should begin at the left margin.

7.2.3 Headings

The *Publication Manual* provides five levels of headings. You, however, will probably not need to use more than three levels. The following examples illustrate the three levels of headings that you are most likely to use.[4]

---

[4]If you are writing a multistudy research report (you have conducted two or more studies and are writing up those studies in a single research report), you will need more headings than we describe here. To see how to format your headings for a multistudy paper, see our website.

FIGURE **7.1** Headings and Page Numbers for an Article in Final-Form Style

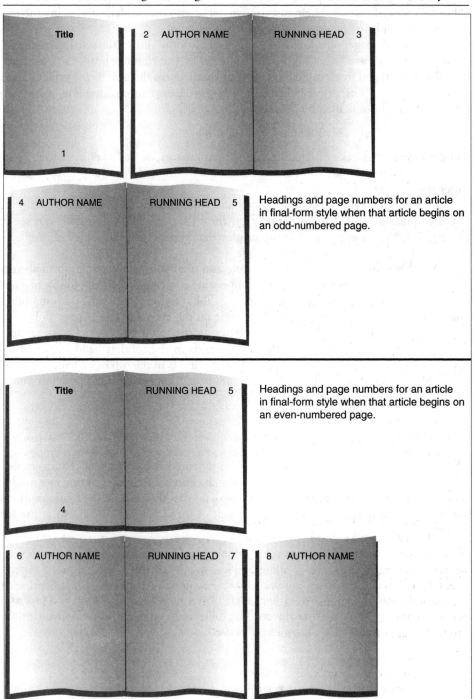

Headings and page numbers for an article in final-form style when that article begins on an odd-numbered page.

Headings and page numbers for an article in final-form style when that article begins on an even-numbered page.

For major sections of your reports, use

> A Centered and Capitalized First-Level Heading

For your subheadings under the main headings, use

> *A Flush Left, Capitalized, Italicized, Second-Level Heading*

For your subheadings that split subsections into parts, use

> *An indented, italicized, third-level paragraph heading ending with a period.* Begin your text immediately after the heading, as we have done here.

In a short term paper (fewer than 2,000 words), the first level is the only one you need. You use it to break your paper into its major sections: Abstract, main text (its heading is the term paper's title), References, and Author Note (see 2.2). In a report, you use the first level to head the major sections: Abstract, Introduction (its heading is not "Introduction" but rather the report's title), Method, Results, Discussion, References, Appendixes, and Author Note (see 3.1). Note that the numbered headings found in this book are inappropriate for APA style; we have used them to help you find the information you need as quickly as possible.

For term papers longer than 2,000 words, you may need to divide the main text into subsections. If so, use the second level. For research reports, you always use the second level to divide the Method section into subsections. For example, almost all Method sections will have Participants and Procedure subsections. In addition to dividing the Method section, you may choose to divide the Introduction, Results, and Discussion sections. For example, if you had two dependent measures, you might divide the Results section using two second level headings (e.g., "*Accuracy*" and "*Reaction Times*").

If you need to divide a second-level subsection, use the third level. For example, in a report, if you had five separate tests, all of which required detailed description, you could divide the second-level *Materials* subsection into five, third-level subsections.

7.2.4 Italics or Underlining

In your papers, italicize only the following items: second- and third-level headings, journal titles, journal volume numbers, book titles, normal (non-Greek) letters used as abbreviations for a statistical term (e.g., F, M, p, and t), names of species, words with special meanings (such as linguistic examples, words denoting procedural or experimental conditions, words serving as labels for rating scale anchors, and the first use of a technical term), and unusual foreign words. Do not italicize commonly used foreign terms such as et al., i.e., e.g., and a posteriori. To better understand how to use italics, study the examples and explanations in the following paragraph.

> Participants in the *hold* and *no hold* conditions [italicize names of experimental conditions] were asked to press the *yes* button [italicize procedural terms] when they heard words containing the *phoneme* [italicize first use of a technical term]

/a/ (such as *forgot* and *potty* [italicize linguistic examples]). After the button press, they were asked to rate the subjective strength of the phoneme [technical terms such as "phoneme" are italicized only the first time they are used] on a scale from *weak* (1) to *strong* (5) [italicize rating scale anchors such as "weak" and "strong"]. One participant complained that the task induced feelings of déjà vu [although "déjà vu" is a foreign phrase, it is not italicized because it is not unusual]. The correlation between reaction time and strength rating was $r = -.40$ [italicize r because it is an abbreviation for a statistical term].

Do not underline, italicize, boldface, or capitalize words (THUS) that you want to emphasize. To emphasize key points, employ skillful writing—not typographical tricks.

7.2.5 Abbreviations

As a general rule, do not use abbreviations in the main text of your paper. However, there are four major exceptions to this general rule. First, you should abbreviate units of measurement (see 3.6.8). Second, you can use well-accepted abbreviations such as IQ and ESP. Third, you can use an abbreviation for a term after you have properly introduced that abbreviation. To introduce an abbreviation, (a) completely write out the term, and then, (b) in parentheses, write its abbreviation in all capital letters. Fourth, you should use certain abbreviations within parentheses. For example, within parentheses, standard Latin abbreviations should be used (cf., e.g., i.e.). Furthermore, within parentheses, an ampersand (&) must be used between two authors' names (see 4.4.2). Punctuate standard abbreviations as if they were spelled-out words or phrases. Thus, you would put a comma after "e.g." (which means for example), but you would not put a comma after "cf." (which means compare). Table 7.1 is a list of the abbreviations that you can use within parentheses.

Keep the abbreviations you define free of periods. For example, "reaction time" becomes "RT," not "R.T."

If the abbreviation is singular, but you want to make it plural, simply add "s" (e.g., "RTs"). Just as adding "s" will give you the plural form of most abbreviations plural, adding apostrophe "s" will usually give you the possessive form of the abbreviation (e.g., "RT's"; for the rules of forming possessives, see 6.2.5).

If you want to avoid making some common abbreviation errors, say the spelled-out version as you write the abbreviation. For example, you will say "a reaction time" and know to write "a RT" rather than "an RT" because you would never say "an reaction time." Similarly, you will say "revolutions per minute" and know to write RPM rather than RPMs because you would not say "revolutions per minutes." To understand the main rules regarding abbreviations, study the following paragraph.

To test the hypothesis that reaction time (RT) [introduce a lesser known abbreviation by preceding it with unabbreviated term] is

T A B L E **7.1**   Abbreviations to Be Used in Parentheses

Abbreviation	Literally	Translation	Usage
&	*and per se*	and	Before the last author's name
c.	*circa*	about	Before a citation date if the date is uncertain
cf.	*confere*	compare	
e.g.	*exempli gratia*	for example	
et al.	*et alii*	and others	For secondary authors' names after first complete citation (see 4.4.3)
etc.	*et cetera*	and so forth	Rare in scientific writing; avoid
i.e.	*id est*	that is	
ibid.	*ibidem*	in the same	Rare; avoid by repeating the citation reference
n.b.	*nota bene*	note well (take careful note)	
op. cit.	*opere citato*	in the reference	Rare; avoid by repeating the citation already quoted
p.	page	page	
pp.	pages	pages	
viz.	*videlicet*	namely	
vs.	versus	versus	
–	to	to	As in "pp. 22–33"

related to IQ, [well-known abbreviation for "intelligence quotient"] 200 students were tested on the WAIS [well-known abbreviation] and their RTs [pluralize abbreviations as you would words] to light onset were determined. Mean RT was 205 ms [abbreviate standard units; see 3.6.8] (cf. [well-known abbreviation, commonly used within parentheses] Woodworth & [within parentheses, use "&" instead of "and"] Schlosberg, 1954), and the correlation with IQ was .40. It may be that RT's [indicate possession as if not abbreviated] correlation with IQ does not imply a direct relationship, but indicates a third, mediating variable. For example, [abbreviate "for example" as "e.g." only within parentheses] those with high motivation could have tried hard on the IQ test and on the RT task.

7.2.6 Numbers

When should you write out a number ("nine"), and when should you express it in digits ("9")? If the number is bigger than nine, you should almost always use digits—unless the number begins a sentence (e.g., "Twenty raters . . ."). Likewise, if the number is a whole number between zero and nine, and either a measurement or a number that is compared to any number that is 10 or greater, you should almost always use digits—unless the number begins a sentence. If, on the other hand, the number is a whole number between zero and nine, and neither a measurement nor a number that is compared to any number that is 10 or greater, you probably should write out the number. Unfortunately, however, there are many exceptions to this latter rule.[5] For example, the following whole numbers between 0 and 9 must be expressed in digits:

- Numbers in the manuscript's Abstract. Thus, in your Abstract you would have to write "3 observers" rather than "three observers."

- Numbers that relate to time, to the number of participants, or to amounts of money. Thus, in your Method section, you might write, "Participants were 6 women," "Participants were paid $6," and "Participants were retested 6 weeks later.

- Numbers that immediately precede another spelled-out number. Thus, in the Results section, you should write "3 two-way interactions" rather than "three two-way interactions."

What if you are not dealing with integers but instead are dealing with numbers between zero and one? Treat percentages as though they were integers, except that you follow them with a percent sign (e.g., 12%). If you are expressing a fraction as a decimal, take it to two decimal places. Put a zero in front of the decimal point for fractions less than 1 that are units of measurement (e.g., 0.1 cm). Never put a zero in front of the decimal point for either correlation coefficients or probability values. Provide as many decimal points as necessary for probability values. The examples and explanations in the following paragraph will help you understand these rules.

> Twenty [never use digits at the beginning of a sentence] participants completed three [number less than 10 and not a measurement] tests consisting of 15 [number greater than nine] subscales each. The mean score on the first test was 3.45 [two decimal places for a fraction] $SD = 0.45$ [zero in front of the decimal point for a fraction], but the mode was 5 [use numeral because it is based on measurements; do not use decimal point because the mode could only be a whole number] items correct. The correlation between test A and B was $r = .47$, $p < .001$ [correlation coefficients and probability values never have zeroes before the decimal point].

---

[5]Therefore, if you want to ensure that you have not written out a number below 10 that you should have expressed in digits, you need to study pages 122–128 of the *Publication Manual.*

7.2.7 Tables and Figures

In term papers, avoid using tables and figures. You should be able to communicate the salient points of experiments and theories without resorting to figures or tables. In reports, tables or figures may be appropriate; details and examples are provided in 3.6.5–3.6.7.

7.3 Conclusions

If you have followed the instructions in this chapter, your paper should look professional. To make sure that you have not overlooked any important formatting details, use the following checklists.

7.4   Format Checklists

7.4.1 General Appearance Checklist

___ I followed any specific requirements that my professor imposed. For example, if my professor said that unstapled papers would not be accepted, I stapled my paper.

___ I understood whether my professor was requiring APA copy style or APA final-form style.

___ I used white, 8.5 × 11 in. (22 × 28 cm), 20-pound, bond paper.

___ I typed my paper using 12-point type, Times Roman or Times New Roman font, easy-to-read, black print, 1-inch (2.54-cm) margins, and only one side of the page.

___ I double-spaced everything.

___ I started every paragraph by indenting five spaces with only two exceptions: I did not indent the Abstract, and I did not indent Notes at the bottom of tables.

___ I did not hyphenate words at the end of a line.

___ I did not use boldfacing or any other typographical tricks to emphasize words.

___ I italicized rather than underlined.

___ I italicized (a) letters that served as abbreviations for statistical terms (e.g., "p" as the abbreviation for probability value) and (b) second-level headings (see 7.2.3).

7.4.2 Headings and Headers Checklist

___ If I used APA manuscript (copy) style, I put the first two or three words of the title, then five spaces, and then the page number at the top, right-hand corner of every page—except for those pages containing figures.

___ I centered all my first-level headings (e.g., Abstract, Conclusion, References, etc.) in plain (not italicized, not bold-faced) font. I capitalized only the first letters of words of these headings.

___ I italicized all my second-level headings (major subheadings such as Participants, Procedure, etc.) and put them flush against the left margin (I did not indent them). I capitalized only the first letters of words of these subheadings.

7.4.3 Numbers, Tables, and Figures Checklist

___ I tried not to start a sentence with a number. If I started a sentence with a number, I spelled out that number.

___ When I wrote a number in my Abstract, I expressed it in digits.

___ When I wrote a number above nine, I expressed it in digits.

___ When I wrote a number below 10, I spelled it out unless it represented a unit of measurement (e.g., 3 cm), a fraction (e.g., 3/4), a percentage (e.g., 6%), a score (e.g., the mean was 4), a point on a scale (e.g., a 7-point scale), the number of participants (e.g., 3 participants), or was being compared to a number greater than 10.

___ I did not put a zero before the decimal point for any correlation coefficients or probability values.

___ I put a zero before the decimal point for fractions (e.g., 0.1 cm).

___ If I used tables or figures, I checked them against the checklist in 3.12.

7.4.4 Citations and References Checklist

___ I used the citation checklist (4.10.2).

___ I used the reference list checklist (4.10.4).

7.4.5 Abbreviations Checklist

___ Within parentheses, I used abbreviations such as "&" and "e.g."

___ When I used units of measurement, I abbreviated those units and did not add "s" to express their plural forms (e.g., I wrote "5 min" instead of "5 mins").

___ When I used abbreviations outside of parentheses that were not abbreviations for units of measurement, those abbreviations were usually common abbreviations or abbreviations that I had introduced earlier (see 7.2.5), were usually in all capital letters, and were usually punctuated like words (e.g., they did not contain periods, the plural form was created by adding "s," and the possessive form was created by adding "'s").

7.4.6 Title Page Checklist

___ I have a separate title page.

___ At the top right-hand corner, I have a short, two- or three-word "mini-title" of my paper. This "mini-title" is the first two or three words of my title. I also have the number "1," indicating that it is page 1. The "1" is on the same line as the mini-title, just five spaces to the right of it.

___ One double-spaced line below the short title and the page number, I have a line that starts at the left margin (about an inch from the left edge of the page), and begins with the words "Running head:" followed by a two- to six-word phrase that describes my paper's topic. (Note that the running head is *not* the same as the mini-title.)

___ My two- to six-word running head is in all-capital letters and is fewer than 51 characters and spaces long.

___ I centered the title and capitalized the first letters of each word in the title (except for words such as "and" and "of").

___ My title is short and to the point.

___ My name (first name, *middle initial*, and last name) is one double-spaced line below the title, centered, and not accompanied by the word "by."

___ My school's name is one double-spaced line below my name and centered.

___ My paper's title starts near the middle of the page.

7.5 Summary

1. If possible, use a word processor. Word-processing software will automatically format much of your paper for you.

2. Double-space your paper and leave 1-inch margins on all sides.

3. APA recognizes two formats: copy (manuscript) and final form. Be sure you know which one your professor has assigned.

4. In APA copy (manuscript) style, the first two or three words of the title (the "short title") should appear on the top right-hand corner of each page. Five

spaces to the right of the short title is the page number. On the title page, one double-spaced line below the short title, starting on the left margin is the phrase: "Running head:" followed by the running head—a two- to six-word phrase, typed in all capital letters, that summarizes the title of the article.

5. Use headings (to see how to format headings, refer to 7.2.3). For term papers longer than 2,000 words, you may need to divide the main text into subsections. If you need to divide a second-level subsection, use third-level headings.

6. If a number starts a sentence, write out the number. If the number is greater than nine, use digits to express that number.

7. Follow any special instructions that your professor gives you.

8. Type your paper using black, 12-point type, and Times Roman or Times New Roman font. Type it on to white, 20-pound, bond paper.

REFERENCES

American Psychological Association. (1974). *Publication manual of the American Psychological Association* (2nd ed.). Washington, D.C.: Author.

American Psychological Association. (1992). Ethical principles of psychologists and a code of conduct. *American Psychologist, 47,* 1597–1611.

American Psychological Association. (2001). *Publication manual of the American Psychological Association* (5th ed.). Washington, D.C.: Author.

American Psychological Association. (2002). Ethical principles of psychologists and code of conduct. *American Psychologist, 57,* 1060–1073.

Barkas, J. L. (1985). *How to write like a professional.* New York: Arco.

Clarion University of Pennsylvania. (n.d.). *Plagiarism* [Brochure]. Clarion, PA: Author.

Cohen, J. (1990). Things I have learned (so far). *American Psychologist, 45,* 1304–1312.

Cohen, J. (1994). The earth is round ($p < .05$). *American Psychologist, 49,* 997–1003.

Howard, V. A., & Barton, J. H. (1986). *Thinking on paper.* New York: William Morrow.

Keith-Spiegel, P., Wittig, A. F., Perkins, D. V., Balogh, D. W., & Whitely, B. E., Jr. (1993). *The ethics of teaching: A casebook.* Muncie, IN: Ball State University.

King, S. (2000). *On writing: A memoir of a craft.* New York: Scribner.

McDougall, W. (1914). *An introduction to social psychology* (8th ed.). London: Methuen.

O'Shea, R. P. (2002). *Writing for psychology* (4th ed.). Melbourne, Australia: Thomson.

Rosenthal, R. (1966). *Experimenter effects in behavioral research.* New York: Appleton-Century-Crofts.

Zechmeister, E. B., & Johnson, J. E. (1992). *Critical thinking: A functional approach.* Pacific Grove, CA: Brooks/Cole.

APA Copy Style Versus APA Final-Form Style

Some of you are reading this Appendix because your teacher is requiring you to use APA final-form style instead of APA copy style. Your teacher probably has excellent reasons for requiring final-form style. The bad news is that, despite the wisdom of your teacher's decision, most descriptions of APA style focus on copy style. The good news is that, although final-form style is different from copy style, final-form style gives you more freedom than if you had been required to use copy style.

Some of you are reading this Appendix even though your teacher is requiring you to use APA copy style. Your problem is that you want to use a published work as a model, but you realize that there are differences between acceptable format for published work and acceptable format for manuscript. Table A1 will help you see what you can model and what you should not. As you can see, you should not model single spacing, hyphenation at the end of lines, or the placement of both tables and figures.

TABLE **A.1**   APA Copy Versus Final-Form Style

APA Copy Style	**APA Final-Form Style**
Place tables at end of your paper.	May put a table on the same page as the corresponding text or put it on the following page.
Place figures at end of your paper.	May put the figure on the page immediately following the page where the figure was mentioned.
Place figure captions at end of your paper.	Figure captions may be typed right below the figure.
Short title appears on the top, right-hand corner of each page.	Running head is not on the title page, but is centered on the top of all the odd-numbered pages following the title page (on the pages that do not have the running head, the authors' names replace the running head).
Page numbers are five spaces to the right of the short title.	Page numbers are centered on the bottom of the title page, are on the top, left-hand corner of even-numbered pages and on the top, right-hand corner of odd-numbered pages. (Your professor may allow you to center the page numbers on the bottom of all pages.)

TABLE **A.1**   APA Copy Versus Final-Form Style—*continued*

APA Copy Style	APA Final-Form Style
Title page is restricted to short title, page number, title, author's name, and author affiliation.	Title page may contain student information such as course name, assignment name, instructor's name, date submitted, and acknowledgments.
Acknowledgments would usually be put in an author's note that appears on a separate page.	Acknowledgments are usually on the title page.
Double spacing is required.	Single spacing for tables, headings, captions, and footnotes is permitted. Some triple or even quadruple spacing is also sometimes allowed.
Right margin is ragged, and you cannot use hyphens at the end of lines.	You can have a justified right margin, and you can use hyphens to keep the right margin even.

Problem Plurals

Singular	Preferred Plural	One Brief Definition
alumna	alumnae	female graduate
alumnus	alumni	graduate
analysis	analyses	a study of
apparatus	apparatus	equipment
appendix	appendixes	supplementary material
bacterium	bacteria	germ
cannula	cannulas	tube used to administer drugs
carcinoma	carcinomas	malignant tumor
chiasm	chiasms	crossing point
continuum	continua	continuous whole
corpus	corpora	body
corpus callosum	corpora callosa	nerve fiber tract joining brain hemispheres
crisis	crises	emergency
criterion	criteria	standard
curriculum	curricula	course
curriculum vitae	curricula vitae	academic résumé
datum	data	information
degree of freedom	degrees of freedom	statistical term
die	dice	dotted cube
emphasis	emphases	importance
erratum	errata	error
focus	foci	central point
formula	formulas	equation
fovea	foveae	retinal area
ganglion	ganglia	group of nerve cells
genus	genera	group of species
hypothesis	hypotheses	conjecture
index	indexes	guide

Singular	Preferred Plural	One Brief Definition
kudos	kudos	acclaim
lacuna	lacunae	gap
locus	loci	place
manipulandum	manipulanda	stimulus object
matrix	matrices	array
medium	media	type of mass communication
millennium	millennia	1,000 years
minutia	minutiae	trivial detail
nexus	nexuses	connection, link
nucleus	nuclei	center
octopus	octopuses	eight-armed mollusk
opus	opera	work
parenthesis	parentheses	round bracket, aside
phenomenon	phenomena	occurrence, fact
phylum	phyla	taxonomic division
prospectus	prospectuses	summary
quantum	quanta	indivisible amount
radius	radii	distance from center to edge
referendum	referendums	electoral question
retina	retinas	part of eye
schema	schemas	outline, model
scotoma	scotomata	hole in visual field
sequela	sequelae	bad outcome of disease
soma	somata	body
spectrum	spectra	range
stratum	strata	layer
stimulus	stimuli	something sensed that may trigger a response
sum of squares	sums of squares	the result of calculating the difference between each score and the mean, squaring those differences, and then totaling up those squared terms
syllabus	syllabi	outline
synthesis	syntheses	combination
thalamus	thalami	brain region
thesis	theses	dissertation
vertex	vertices	apex
virus	viruses	germ

INDEX

A

a, an (indefinite articles), 169
abbreviations
  checklist, 204–205
  introducing, 200
  within parentheses, 200–201
  plural, 200
  punctuation of, 200–201
  in reference list, 130, 131
  for states, 48
  for units of measurement, 77
above (preposition), 171
abstract
  double spaced, 85
  not indented, 29, 36, 85
  numerical information in, 29, 59
  personal pronouns in, 9, 29, 58
  preparation of, 29, 58
  reading only, 102
  referencing from Internet, 137–138
  referencing journal-articles, 134
  in research reports, 58–59, 85, 96
  results in, 85
  summarizing paper, 29
  in term papers, 29, 36
  word limit for, 29, 58
academic honesty checklist, 22, 138
academic values, 3–6
acknowledgments in author
      notes, 33
active voice of verbs, 8, 168, 191, 193
ad hominem arguments, 154
adjectives
  adverbs modifying, 170
  comparatives vs. superlatives, 183
  correct usage of, 169–170
  diluting prose with too many, 188
  in prepositional phrases, 173
adverbs
  comparatives vs. superlatives, 183
  conjunctive, 172
  correct usage of, 8–9, 170
  diluting prose with too many, 188
affiliation, in author notes, 33
age
  bias in language, 10
  of participants, 89

agreement
  pronoun-noun, 19, 166–167
  subject-verb, 19, 168
almost-verbs, 168–169
alphabetical order
  citations, 39, 121
  reference list, 33, 46–47, 94, 127–128
alpha (significance) level of results, 66
although (conjunction), 172
although (transition word), 17
American Psychological Association (APA), 7–11.
    See also Publication Manual of the American
    Psychological Association copy style, 2, 35,
    84, 209–210
  "Ethical Principles of Psychologists and Code
    of Conduct," 63
  final-form (published) style, 2, 35, 84,
    196–198, 209–210
  formatting final draft
    abbreviations, 200–201
    headings, 197–199
    italics or underlining, 199–200
    numbers, 202
    overview of, 196
    paragraphs, 197
    running head vs. short title, 196–197
    tables and figures, 203
  formatting rules, 20–21
  ideals, 7–8
  journals sponsored by, 108–109
  manuscript (copy) style, 2, 35, 84,
    209–210
  personal prose, 8–9
  respectful language, 10–11
  simple language, 9–10
  Style Helper software, 20, 21, 125
American Psychological Society (APS),
    108–109
American Psychologist, 48, 136
among (preposition), 171
ampersand (&)
  in citations, 40, 87, 119
  reference list, 128–129, 133, 200
analogy, arguments by, 151
analysis of variance (ANOVA), 69
and, &, in citations, 40, 87, 119
and (conjunction), 40, 119, 171–172